BEYONCÉ

CRAZY IN LOVE

THE BEYONCÉ KNOWLES BIOGRAPHY

CRAZY IN LOVE
THE BEYONCÉ KNOWLES BIOGRAPHY

DARYL EASLEA

OMNIBUS PRESS

London / New York / Paris / Sydney / Copenhagen / Berlin / Madrid / Tokyo

Exclusive Distributors
Music Sales Limited,
14/15 Berners Street,
London, W1T 3LJ.

Music Sales Corporation,
257 Park Avenue South,
New York, NY 10010, USA.

Macmillan Distribution Services,
56 Parkwest Drive
Derrimut, Vic 3030,
Australia.

Every effort has been made to trace the copyright holders of the photographs in this book but one
or two were unreachable. We would be grateful if the photographers concerned would contact us.

Typeset by Phoenix Photosetting, Chatham, Kent
Printed in the E.U.

A catalogue record for this book is available from the British Library.

Visit Omnibus Press on the web at www.omnibuspress.com

Contents

Introduction: The Superstar Soul Of Beyoncé Knowles

"The group is serious about what they do. Nothin' comes before DC but God."

Doris Rowland, 2000

The early years of the 21st century saw tastes and the methods of delivery of popular music fracture like never before. Although still relatively in its mass-market infancy, the Internet began to enable music fans to access their favourite music directly. Napster and the concept of downloading illegally had shown that recorded music simply wasn't something that could be controlled and marketed solely from a record company office any more. This led to a great diversification in popular music. And as white indie mores were being catered for by bands like The Strokes, rap and hip-hop was completing its transition from edgy, underground phenomenon to an edgy, overground phenomenon.

The thug wars, and the ensuing shootings of the gangsta rappers 2Pac and The Notorious B.I.G. in the mid-nineties had calmed and, by the end of the 20th century, the genre received its true Elvis Presley figure in Marshall Mathers, aka Eminem. Unlike other previous white rappers, who smacked of middle-class boys flirting with the iconography, Eminem was absolutely genuine in his love of the form and had grown up on the same streets in Detroit as African-American rappers. Into the middle of this musical milieu came the newly three-piece R&B vocal group Destiny's Child: Beyoncé Knowles, Kelly Rowland and Michelle Williams. With their attitude, three-part harmonies, looks and in-your-face style, they were clearly a cut above the slew of all-girl groups that had followed in the wake of En Vogue, TLC, SWV and the Spice Girls.

Although Destiny's Child were to last only until 2005, they became a huge global entity, and finally, the biggest-selling female group of all time. Much of this success was down to their 2000 single 'Independent Women Part I'. The theme for the film *Charlie's Angels,* it caught the popular imagination on either side of the Atlantic. That Destiny's Child were young, talented, extremely photogenic and endlessly marketable helped too, of course. They became hugely successful when they already had two previous albums to sell (thus providing instantly mineable revenue streams for their company, Sony Music), *and* there was also a story: there was controversy in their recent past with disgruntled ex-members ready to tell their tale at any given point. The group also had the tunes, the personality and a lead singer with an unusual name, often reduced simply to a monomym: Beyoncé. It was soon clear that this singer, at just 18 years of age, had a prodigious talent. Few, however, would have guessed that over a decade later, as a solo artist, she would be one of the biggest figures in popular music, ever.

Over the 10 years between 2000 and 2010, Beyoncé Knowles has become a phenomenon, with mass appeal. Although part of a direct line from the classic soul divas of the sixties and seventies, her appeal seems wider and more mainstream. Her public persona is that of every woman: as happy flirting with hardcore hip-hop and R&B as playing the easy listening diva, and she remains, unusually for her position, largely untouched by scandal. It is wholly possible that she is an artist, in a very 21st century way, that actually equals the Queen Of Soul, Aretha Franklin, for sheer passion and all-encompassing talent. Her rise may not be as organic as Franklin's and nor would one ever lay claim to her being of a similar iconic historical importance, but her depth, passion and musical ability, like Franklin's, are remarkable. Beyoncé's love and understanding of music is indisputable, as is her talent and her ability to maximise opportunities and work across a variety of platforms – music, film, television, fashion and, recently, perfume.

Hers is a story of hard work and determination. Yet it seems not the naked, at-all-costs ambitions of some of her peers. It seems to be tempered by a strong Christian belief of right and wrong. She is a riddle, a conundrum. As Beyoncé biographer Janice Arenofsky says, "She remains an enigma. To fans and casual observers, she is big hearted and breathtakingly beautiful; to academics and critics alike, she is a study in contrasts – a walking, talking contradiction whose sexy disguises fail to hide a well-ingrained set of conventional values." Beyoncé's ability to select the best writing and production teams for her music has created a body of work that is as popular with children as it is with musicologists.

Some of her success is down to the iron-like influence of her father who until 2011 was also her manager. Mathew Knowles is a man who gave up his well-paid job as a medical equipment salesman to market his daughter, a far more precious commodity. His influence has seemed to be that of a benevolent dictator. Although there have been spats and disagreements between Mathew and Beyoncé, ultimately theirs seems a fairly intact father and daughter relationship.

Mathew Knowles, and his wife, Tina, who became Destiny's Child's stylist, can be seen as the embodiment of the hopes and dreams of black empowerment within the US, the so-called 'Joshua Generation'. The late 20th and early 21st centuries are a time in which the advances of the Civil Rights movement of the Sixties are finally being enjoyed. If Martin Luther King can be likened to Moses, whose struggle led to the ultimate liberation of his people and followers who benefited from his strife, African-American businessmen like Knowles and his son-in-law, Beyoncé's husband, Jay-Z, demonstrate that colour is no longer a bar to their advance. After 2000 Oprah Winfrey acted as a role model for millions of African-Americans and white audiences alike. By the end of the decade, there was an African-American president, Barack Obama, in the White House. But, as Obama said when he began running for the presidency in Selma, Alabama, in 2007, the 'Joshua Generation' still had much work to do. It was not all about material gains, it had still to focus on empowerment. Obama was clear: "I'm here because somebody marched. I'm here because y'all sacrificed for me. I stand on the shoulders of giants."

Beyoncé, who sang at Obama's inaugural ball, is emblematic of these advances. In her position as the world's most popular singer, she stands for millions of empowered women, regardless of colour, the world over. Staffordshire University's Professor Ellis Cashmore argues in his paper 'Buying Beyoncé: The Deal That Ended Racism' that through all of her considerable achievements, and by fully embracing capitalism, Beyoncé has not only broken through the colour bar, but more importantly, let white America know that she has.

That said, it is impossible to predict exactly where Beyoncé will fit in popular history in the long term. Dismissed by many as simply a pop act, there is a real strength and depth to her recordings. If it is a matter of empirical evidence, Beyoncé is one of the most successful acts of all time. Awards are certainly one barometer of her success but in the 21st century there has been an unprecedented growth in the number of awards available to rock, pop and R&B performers. There were no MOBOs, BETs, BRITs, or MTVs when Aretha Franklin or Chaka Khan were in their prime, so a purely statistical approach to her success is almost pointless. But that is not to undermine her achievement.

Beyoncé is not renowned for diva-esque behaviour. There are very few complaints about her compared with artists in a similar position. Her peers, defiantly displayed on the 2001 single and accompanying video of 'Lady Marmalade' – P!nk, Mya, Lil' Kim and Christina Aguilera – have (with Mya's exception) had a degree of notoriety attached to their careers. Britney Spears – who broke through with her debut hit 'Baby One More Time', released around the time that Destiny's Child's single 'No, No, No' was beginning to rise up the US charts, has become a veritable walking edition of the *National Enquirer*. There is little scandal to attach to Beyoncé.

For critics, there is something about Beyoncé's perceived lack of depth that has denied her the analysis reserved for similar artists. Yet she and her organisation are a paradigm for African-American business in the 21st century. She readily sponsors Tommy Hilfiger, Pepsi, L'Oréal and Armani. Her tour programmes tell you what items she will be wearing by which designer, and when. Yet in an age when all innocence is lost and the multi-dimensional, ultra-franchised deal is commonplace, there still seems to be something innocent about her. Sponsorship (and commoditisation) is the prerequisite of the entertainment industry in the 21st century, and Beyoncé's part in it appears to be conducted with a great deal of integrity.

Beyoncé's family is foremost. She has grown up in show business and, given the pitfalls and petulance of former teen-stars, she has done her utmost to remain as grounded as possible. She employs many of her relations in her entourage. Aside from her father's management until 2011, her mother, Tina, is not only her stylist, she is also her partner in her fashion line, the House of Deréon. Her personal assistant is her cousin, Angela Beyincé and her uncle, Larry Beyincé, her tour assistant. This closed circle leads to criticism, but it is what Beyoncé knows and is the circle in which she can comfortably operate. Her marriage to Jay-Z, arguably the most important African-American rap mogul of the early 21st century, has been kept as low key as possible. As Jay-Z once told *People* magazine "We don't play with our relationship." Detractors may snipe at what they identify as furtive behaviour. On the other hand, it is refreshing to find discretion and tact in a world where celebrity has become such an over-reported commodity.

Beyoncé rides the contradictions in her personality with seeming ease: in order to deal with performance, she created her alter ego, Sasha (later Sasha Fierce). Sasha was devised when she was a teenager to overcome her overall lack of confidence. Sasha is the one who struts her funky stuff, acts provocatively and performs with all the confidence of a full-tilt Madonna. On the other hand, the 'real' Beyoncé is the Christian girl who is unerringly polite, shuns the limelight and works hard to maintain her success. As Arenofsky says, "While Sasha performed, Beyoncé's inner child – the emotionally inexperienced teen relegated to a corner of her mind – claimed an adolescent's right to experiment, hang out, paint, crack her knuckles, talk on the phone and binge on fried chicken."

Beyoncé is one of the most written-about artists of the past 10 years. But when one looks, there is so very little actually said. In the era of a news story spreading across so many thousands of similar websites, the little truth in a story to start with has soon evaporated as it gets further cut and pasted down the news wires and in forums. That the press made so much of the sackings of two former Destiny's Child members in 2000, Beyoncé's supposed abortions, her visits to basketball or the beach with Jay-Z, dissing Aretha Franklin or similar, is simply because there *isn't* actually a great deal to write about. And in this Internet age, it is so much easier to fan the flames of a fabricated story than report the slightly less-headline grabbing truth about a woman who has grown up in public and is a phenomenally hard-working role model. And on top of that, she helped write and record three of the pop classics of the 21st century: 'Independent Women Part I', 'Crazy In Love' and 'Single Ladies (Put A Ring On It)'.

Beyoncé Knowles is a 21st-century superstar. She has a great deal in common with the soul divas of the sixties and seventies. She has grown up in public. Her love of experimenting musically and mixing up genres is apparent. Her crossover into Hollywood films has moved from the tentative to the accomplished. And there is still so very much time ahead of her. *Crazy In Love: The Beyoncé Knowles Biography*, provides another view of this very modern superstar.

CHAPTER 1

Imagine . . .

"He showed me pictures of Martin Luther King. I paid attention. I wanted to make him proud of me."

Beyoncé Knowles, 2002

Beyoncé's upbringing is a tale of a new American South, a South very different from the one experienced by her parents just 30 years earlier. Beyoncé has only had to work hard to further her career, whereas her parents, father Mathew especially, had to work hard against Southern racism, segregation and colour bars.

Mathew Knowles will loom large in any biography of Beyoncé. A true product of the American South, he saw at first hand segregation and the hatred from whites in a changing, troubled America. In his youth, the country was a cauldron of uncertainty and change, yet outwardly, it was almost impossible to notice. The world image of the country was one of a happy, smiling, white suburbia. In 1945, America had stood victorious. It had successfully fought a war on two fronts and, by ending its period of isolationism, took its place as a hegemonic superpower on the world stage.

Less than five years later, the United States had seen the advance of communism in Eastern Europe and China and the Soviets develop their own atomic weaponry, and faced very real concerns regarding internal security. Wisconsin's Senator Joseph McCarthy had sprung up to exploit the prevailing mood of fear and uncertainty with the House Un-American Activities Committee.

Yet in black inner cities, concerns were still more primal – concerns about basic rights and, often, where the next meal was coming from, were paramount. For African-Americans, there had been little change; despite their central role in America's campaign in the Second World War, they were still marginalised and segregated, living in once prosperous areas that had become, simply put, ghettos.

Mathew Knowles, born on January 9, 1951, in Gadsden, Alabama, 65 miles north of Birmingham, was determined to better himself. His father ran a scrap metal business and was a truck driver, while his mother was a maid for a white family who also made quilts for a living. She was a smart woman who had attended Lincoln Normal School in Marion, Alabama at the same time as the young Coretta Scott, who would later marry Martin Luther King.

Alabama was arguably the most racist of all the Southern states, and had seen the re-emergence of the Ku Klux Klan against the progress of the Civil Rights movement, the bus boycotts and the rise of Alabaman preacher Dr Martin Luther King. Although it was a period of tumult and his family was poor, Mathew's education was encouraged, and he became one of the first African-American children to go to Litchfield Junior High in Marion, a direct result of the integration resulting from the US Supreme Court's landmark 1954 ruling, *Brown v Board of Education*. Because feelings were running so high on the matter, the young Mathew Knowles had to have state troopers escort him to school. It was while he was at school in July 1964 that the Civil Rights Act was passed, which outlawed discrimination based on colour. However, a statute is one thing: it would be a long time before attitudes in the South changed along with the law.

It was via a basketball scholarship that he earned his place at university. Again, Mathew was one of the first African-Americans at the University of Tennessee in Chattanooga. Knowles turned 18 in 1969, and could not help but be politicised. He marched on demonstrations and participated in sit-ins. The assassinations of Martin Luther King and Robert Kennedy in April and June 1968 and the escalation of the war in Vietnam all played a vivid part in his youth.

While playing basketball at Tennessee, he met and befriended Ronnie Lawson, who invited him to play for his team, the Fisk University Bulldogs. In a year that saw the moon landing, the Woodstock Music & Art Fair and the Black Panther movement at its height, Knowles was influenced by the radicalism of youth but also understood that one of the most powerful political statements would be to study and work hard in order to advance himself.

In the early seventies, Knowles transferred to Fisk University in Nashville, Tennessee, one of America's leading black universities. It was while at Fisk that he began to think about the possibility of developing musical acts in conjunction with the local radio station, and applying some of the business techniques he was learning to music. This was the era of Motown at its peak, as Berry Gordy began to diversify his record label into film, and successful black artists proved that they could easily match white success. Stevie Wonder, Marvin Gaye, Sly Stone and Curtis Mayfield all took control of their careers and their business. However flawed The Beatles' Apple dream of 1968 – where they made a very public attempt to run their own organisation – may ultimately have been, it created an appetite for young people to think about the business side of music as an attractive career option.

Knowles graduated with degrees in economics and management in 1974. He has always maintained strong links with his alma mater, and, in 2011, he was appointed to the university's board of trustees. Smart, urbane and capable, Knowles found that sales was a perfect area to showcase both his management and economics skills. After a period in various sales roles, including life insurance and telephone sales, he got a job with Pickering International Medical Supplies, selling medical equipment. By the end of the seventies, he was working for the Xerox Corporation. Based in Rochester, New York, Xerox was the photographic reproduction company which had leapt to world prominence with the introduction of the Xerox 914, the world's first plain paper photocopier in 1959. Its fortunes were further bolstered by the introduction of the laser printer in 1977. Knowles joined Xerox as a salesman for its medical imaging division, and became very successful in the role, earning by the late eighties, according to several reports, a six-figure salary.

His future wife, Célestine Ann 'Tina' Beyincé, was born in Galveston, Texas, on January 4, 1954, the daughter of Lumiz (sometimes spelled Lumis) Beyincé and Agnéz Deréon. Agnéz grew up in Delcambre, Louisiana, and came from mixed parentage – Jewish American, Choctaw Native Indian, African-American and Louisiana Creole. To improve their life, the couple moved to Galveston. Agnéz was a seamstress, while Lumiz was a longshoreman who worked the port in Galveston. He was of Chinese, Indonesian, French and Spanish descent.

"My parents were both Creole from Louisiana," Tina Knowles told *Luxury Las Vegas*. "My mother was the youngest of 15 kids. From an early age she was always looking at fashion magazines and could knock off anything she saw. She would create patterns out of newspapers and make the most beautiful dresses and evening clothes. Growing up, we were so poor I wondered how my parents could afford the tuition to send us to Catholic school. It wasn't until I was an adult that I found out my mom had bartered her services. She made the altar clothes, the nuns' habits, and school uniforms while my dad drove the nuns around in exchange for us going to private school. I was glad to find that out because as a kid I was resentful, wondering why they did all that stuff for them."

Although a talented student, Tina made her name at junior high by singing in the school's Motown/girl group influenced act, The Beltones (sometimes referred to as The Veltones). It was while in the group that Tina began to design their costumes, while her mother would realise Tina's designs. Her love of design, and Creole styles and fashions, would remain with Tina forever. Agnéz taught Tina how to make dresses from remnants of fabric and save considerable amounts of money. "Everything I did prepared me for what I ended up doing with Destiny's Child, which was really a blessing," she was later to say. Although Galveston was not as incendiary as Alabama, Tina was deeply affected by the changes in American society through the later sixties and seventies. She studied hard and on leaving school, although possessing a flair for hairdressing, got herself a job in a bank.

Although her political activism was not as strong as her future husband's, a record that strongly influenced Tina's late teens was Marvin Gaye's 1971 masterpiece, *What's Going On.* "It is one of my favorite albums of all time because in the songs he talks about social changes, the Vietnam War, and the environment being torn apart," Tina said in 2010. "He talks about God and spirituality. It's a masterpiece. For the first time, young people started becoming more aware of things that were going on in the world and how they could make a difference rather than just being concerned with looking good and partying. It was a time of sit-ins and racial change." There was a deep sense that although ostensibly things were improving, in reality, often, they were not. "Things were desegregated but they really weren't," Tina continued. "It was such a conscious record. I spent so many hours listening to it. It was like a coming-of-age for me. I still listen to it. There's one song that's so honest where he talks about being in so much pain from the drugs. The Vietnam War affected so many people who came back shell-shocked. Their lives were a mess and people didn't want to talk about it. We still don't like to talk about it." Marvin Gaye telegraphed the concerns of a section of America. Tina, then 17, was the record's core audience. It profoundly affected her.

By the late seventies, Mathew and Tina and their respective families had relocated to the affluent city of Houston, Texas. Houston was founded in 1836 by Augustus and John Allen. Situated on the banks of the Buffalo Bayou waterway, its success was based on the discovery of oil there in the early 20th century. It was this black gold that created a surge in the city's population. Houston's place in the world's consciousness was further cemented in the sixties when space travel focused eyes on the Manned Spacecraft Center (later the Johnson Space Center), the home of NASA's mission control. The Apollo programme made Houston synonymous with that strange, progressive, expensive interlude in world history.

With its significant Mexican population, unification with African-Americans was not straightforward in the Civil Rights struggle against white supremacy in Houston in the sixties. Houston is the fourth largest city in the United States, a city that celebrated hard-working and prosperous residents. It was here that Mathew Knowles and Célestine Beyincé met at a party in the late seventies. Mathew had just begun working for Xerox and Tina was employed by a local bank; they met and had a pleasant evening together, but realised that they hadn't swapped numbers. When they met coincidentally several times during the next day, they thought that possibly fate was intervening. Their relationship started in earnest after a meal at a local restaurant. They were married in 1979. By Christmas 1980, Tina was pregnant with their first child.

Beyoncé Giselle Knowles was born at the Park Plaza Hospital, Houston, on September 4, 1981, the first child of Mathew and Tina's union. Beyoncé was named after a derivation of her mother's family name, Beyincé. Tina was the youngest of seven children and realised that there was only one male child in the family. "I said, oh God, we'll run out of Beyincés," she told *Rolling Stone* in 2004. Beyoncé's grandfather Lumiz was not overjoyed at the prospect of his granddaughter having a surname for her Christian name. "My family was not happy," Tina said. "My dad said, 'She's gonna be really mad at you because that's a last name.' And I'm like, 'It's not a last name to anybody but you guys.'" Already Beyoncé had a talking point, a name that had to be spelled out and repeated. It would also see her ridiculed at school.

After Beyoncé was born in 1981, Tina set up a hair salon – Headliners – on Montrose Avenue. It became one of the swankiest, most upmarket and well-to-do salons for upwardly mobile African-Americans in Houston. With its success, and Mathew's progress at Xerox, the family moved to a comfortable six-bedroomed house in a racially mixed affluent section of the Third Ward in Houston. The area was later to be enshrined in hip-hop as 'the Trey'. In 1986, the family was completed when Tina gave birth to a baby girl, Beyoncé's sister, Solange Piaget Knowles.

The Knowles household was full of music and singing. "My parents used to sing to me all the time," Beyoncé wrote in Destiny's Child's autobiography, *Soul Survivors*. "My dad tells me that as a baby I would go crazy whenever I heard music." Mathew and Tina were huge music fans and their teenage years and early twenties had been full of the latest

African-American pop, whether it was the string-heavy flourishes of Kenny Gamble and Leon Huff's Philadelphia International Records, the urbane political revolt of Marvin Gaye and Gene Page or Barry White's love symphonies. Many of these records were steeped in black history. They evoked an era of the big orchestras favoured by Duke Ellington or William 'Count' Basie from several decades previously, which demonstrated an elegance and sophistication not synonymous with rock 'n' roll. By the early eighties, the sound of singers such as session man-turned-love man Luther Vandross, the superstar pop of Michael Jackson and the naughty-but-nice contradictory funk 'n' roll of Prince filled the Knowles household.

Beyoncé's parents recalled her excitement when she sang and danced her way around the house. Beyoncé attended St Mary's Elementary School, where she took an active interest in dance, ballet and jazz. It was in her first grade that Beyoncé rushed home to her mother to sing the song that she learned. "I was sitting at the kitchen table, and I stood up to sing it for her just like my teacher had taught me," she recalled. "I'll never forget that feeling. I loved performing for my mom – it was a rush."

It was in dance lessons at St Mary's at the age of seven that Beyoncé was encouraged to perform. Her teacher, Sister Darlette Johnson, persuaded Beyoncé that she had singing as well as dancing ability. "Miss Darlette had a unique gift," Beyoncé wrote. "She could get anybody to dance. Aside from basic moves, she taught me self-esteem, confidence, a positive attitude, and, most importantly, discipline." Johnson recognised there was something special and unique about Beyoncé, and gently coerced her to perform in the school talent show. "I was terrified and I didn't wanna do it and she's like, 'C'mon baby, get out there,'" Beyoncé said in 2004. "I remember walking out and I was scared but when the music started I don't know what happened. I just . . . *changed.*"

Beyoncé could find an outlet that put a front on the shy, hard-working but unremarkable student that she was. It was here that Beyoncé first thought of her alter ego, later to become known as Sasha. "I don't have a split personality, but I'm really very country and would rather have no shoes on and have my hair in a bun and no make-up," Beyoncé said. "And when I perform, this confidence and this sexiness and this whatever it is that I'm completely not just happens. And you feel it and you just start wildin' and doin' stuff that don't even make sense, like the spirit takes over. That magic, that's what I love. If you see me on TV I'm not a humble, shy person, but it's a transformation into that. It's a job. In real life I'm not like that."

It was Johnson who alerted Mathew and Tina to just how good their young daughter was and the potential that lay within her. She began to enter a welter of dance contests and beauty pageants, and gained further confidence during the two years she spent in the choir at her local church, St John's United Methodist Church.

Beyoncé entered her first major talent competition at the age of seven singing John Lennon's dour and idealistic 1971 ballad, 'Imagine'. Although her parents had not heard her rehearse, Mathew Knowles sat Beyoncé down and had an intense conversation with her. "He knew I was too young to fully understand the song," Beyoncé was to say, "but he wanted me to know what the lyrics meant. So he wrote them down and explained them to me." Knowles sealed the deal by showing his daughter a picture of Martin Luther King. Considering this slightly grandiose pep talk to a seven year old, it is little surprise that young Beyoncé was triumphant.

"She was a sweet but really shy kid," Tina Knowles later said to *Ebony* magazine. "She'd come into a room and just want to be invisible. But when she got onstage and sang The Beatles' [sic] 'Imagine', we couldn't believe it was the same kid. Her confidence came out. She'd get a standing ovation." It was the beginning of the road to stardom.

"From that moment on," Beyoncé recalled," I decided all the world would be a stage – tables, chairs, the kitchen countertop. I made my own stages. That's how I expressed myself. I only felt comfortable when I was singing or dancing."

Her parents entered her into a variety of talent competitions, which were a cross between talent shows and beauty contests. "She must have done 30 of those competitions," Mathew Knowles told *Ebony* magazine in 2001. "And she carried first place in every last one of them." It was difficult for Beyoncé; as she grew up she wanted to be nothing but a tomboy. "Then I lost some of my baby fat and felt more comfortable with my body," Beyoncé was later to write. "That's also when it became fashionable to have shapely legs."

In 1988, Beyoncé was mentioned in the *Houston Chronicle* on being nominated for the prestigious Houston arts award, The Sammy. In 1990, she went to the Cynthia Ann Parker Elementary School at 10626 Atwell, Houston. It was Houston's original Music Magnet School, with a mission statement to 'develop knowledge and character of one child at a time'. Its focus on music meant that while undertaking her education, Beyoncé sang in the choir and received vocal coaching for one hour a day amid her other lessons. She then moved on to Houston's High School for the Performing and Visual Arts, and finally to the Elsik High School in Alief, the south-western suburb of Houston.

By the time she met LaTavia Roberson in 1990 at the age of nine, Beyoncé was a seasoned performer. Her bedroom was overflowing with trophies; uncomfortable with performing, she would overcompensate at the talent show by forgetting what she was supposed to do and, as a result, "became a huge ham. I don't know what came over me, but once I got my turn, I'd just strut my stuff and even finish by blowing a kiss to the crowd."

Roberson and Knowles met at The People's Workshop for the Visual and Performing Arts, which had grown out of an informal arrangement of musicians at Texas Southern University. After it was extended to non-students in the late seventies, it became a big annual event that took place in Houston. It was here that Beyoncé was spotted by local entrepreneur Andretta Tillman, who asked her to audition for a girl group that she was putting together.

Roberson, a dancer, was a native of Houston and was two months younger than Beyoncé. The girls would form impromptu vocal groups with friends and put on shows. One such was at a local community centre: "It had a little stage," Beyoncé told *Rolling Stone* in 2001, "and before the performance, we were trying to figure out the name of our group. It was about 15 little kids in the audience, who didn't know what was going on." Tillman had big ideas for this pool of talent she was overseeing.

Chapter 2

Tyme For The Girls

"Beyoncé particularly always had that thing about, 'I want to do it right.'
She wanted to work on it, like her singing and her voice lessons and her
dancing."

Vernell Johnson, 2001

With the success of the five-piece male boy band New Kids On The Block, single-sex teen-oriented groups had once again become all the rage. From California, the four-piece En Vogue – Terry Ellis, Cindy Ellis, Maxine Jones and Dawn Robinson – had just achieved chart success with 'Hold On'. A much more sophisticated proposition than NKOTB, they evoked the haughty glamour of The Supremes and Martha & The Vandellas. With an eye on what was happening in the US pop charts, the new pre-teen band Girl's Tyme, featuring Beyoncé Knowles, would be Houston's answer. After all, all these boys were making it big, why shouldn't it be time for the girls?

An all-singing all-dancing group of pre-teens, Girl's Tyme was put together by entrepreneur Andretta Tillman. Auditions for the group were held in 1990. The line-up was to fluctuate around availability of stage-struck 10 year olds, but a core was established of Tamar Davis, Beyoncé, LaTavia Roberson and Nikki and Nina Taylor.

Mathew and Tina Knowles established a boot camp approach for Beyoncé's participation in the group. They would rehearse frequently in Tinas' hair salon; "We made them cut off the blow dryers," Beyoncé was to recall. "It's like, 'We're about to perform! Everything has to shut off!' Everything stopped, but then after a couple of times, they weren't paying any attention to us at all." When not rehearsing in the salon, they would practise in backyards, bedrooms and open spaces. In fact, absolutely anywhere they could find.

"They were about nine or ten," family friend Vernell Jackson told *Rolling Stone* in 2001. "They would do their little routines, and Mathew would ask us to critique: 'Well, what do you think? What needs to be worked on?' And they would start all over again. Beyoncé particularly always had that thing about, 'I want to do it right.' She wanted to work on it, like her singing and her voice lessons and her dancing. She always wanted to be maybe like Janet Jackson or Michael Jackson – those type of people."

It was around this time that Beyoncé had a vocal epiphany: she heard Mariah Carey. Although never overly popular with the critics, New York born Carey became a megastar at the age of 20 with her debut single, 'Vision Of Love', and self-titled album released in 1990. Her powerful, ornate, mannered vocal style has widely been credited with reintroducing melisma into popular music. The style, which originates in sacred music, is best described as singing a single syllable while moving through several notes in succession. Done correctly, this is a powerful, emotional approach, which evokes the greatest moments of Aretha Franklin. Done badly, it is one of the most over-the-top, unnecessary vocal practices of all time. Within days of hearing 'Vision Of Love', which topped the US charts for four weeks in August 1990, Beyoncé was practising her own melismatic vocal runs. Although she would be greatly influenced by many other artists, hearing Mariah Carey was to shape her style and approach to singing.

Kelly Rowland moved from Atlanta, Georgia, to Houston in 1990. Born in February, 1981, the nine-year-old thought that the city was going to be all about "cowboys and horses". Within a matter of weeks, through

LaTavia Roberson, whom she'd met at Briargrove Elementary School, she auditioned for Girl's Tyme and was delighted to be accepted, given that there were so many girls already in the band.

Rowland was the product of a broken home, after her mother, Doris, relocated to Houston to work as a nanny after leaving her husband, Christopher Lovett. Doris realised that Kelly craved some stability, and as Girl's Tyme began to dominate so much of her life, she jumped at the offer from Mathew for her to move into the Knowles' household. "At Beyoncé's house, there was always financial security, and that was something that I never had as a little girl growing up in Atlanta," Rowland recalled. "Aunt Tina's hair salon did good business, and I was grateful that I didn't have to move all around any more." Moreover, Kelly hit it off with Beyoncé right from the start. Sharing a room was like having a slumber party every night. The girls shared their passion for Mickey Mouse and both liked similar things musically: groups such as Guy, Jodeci and SWV. But the group that grabbed them the most was the vocal quartet En Vogue.

It has been written and rumoured that Rowland was actually adopted by the Knowles family. Tina rebutted these claims in her 2001 interview with *Ebony* magazine: "We never officially adopted her. We never asked for custody. All those rumours are so crazy. I've never had legal guardianship. Kelly's mother was a certified live-in nanny, and she moved from place to place. Her mother used to leave her job and bring Kelly across town for rehearsals every day. Her mom was in a job transition, so Kelly came to live with us . . . Kelly's mom had a key to our house and to our car. Most weekends she stayed with us. She has been a part of Kelly's life every day. And even now not a day passes that her mom doesn't call her. Let some people talk, [they are saying] her mom sold her to us . . . I've always had a houseful of kids. My nieces and nephews, friends of my girls." There was also reported a darker unsubstantiated rumour that Rowland's errant father was Mathew Knowles himself, underlined for detractors by Rowland's nickname for him: Dad. "I always know where Mathew is," Kelly wrote in 2002. "He looks after me as if I were his own. But it was only two years ago I started calling him Dad. I'm not even sure why. All of a sudden, I just felt like calling him Dad. One day I just said, 'Dad can I go to the mall? And he was like, I love that name. I like you calling me Dad.' And that was one of the most beautiful days of my life." Rowland, who has been frequently questioned on the matter, said once and for all in *VIBE Vixen* in summer 2006 ". . . it's a lie from the pit of hell".

Although his career at Xerox was going from strength to strength, Mathew Knowles became involved in Girl's Tyme as part-time co-manager with Andretta Tillman. He knew that the only way to get the group absolutely ready was to get them performing at every opportunity. The troupe, now with Rowland in their number, became regulars on the Houston circuit at shows such as Black Expo, Miss Black Houston Metroplex Pageant, and People's Workshop Sammy Davis, Jr. Awards at the prestigious Wortham Center, the home of Houston Ballet and Houston Grand Opera.

The group were also impressed with the new pastor at their local church, St John's United Methodist Church in Houston. Rudy Rasmus was a gospel music loving, generous, spirited man who encouraged the girls and prayed for their progression. When he joined the church in 1992, the congregation of St John's averaged around nine people. Soon, membership would be in its thousands. Rasmus could see the potential within Girl's Tyme to be unlocked.

"These girls have always had the desire to do this thing," he told *Rolling Stone*. "And when we met 'em as children, you could see that: 'We're gonna do it.' And Mathew is a very determined guy, so I had few doubts that he was gonna ultimately do it. And I've seen the sacrifices that he and Tina have made to see this happen. And that's one thing I really admire about them – they're taking no prisoners as it relates to someone messing with their kids. I mean, just because the kids are making money doesn't mean you just release them to the wolves, who are circling."

Rasmus' progressive preaching struck a deep chord with Beyoncé, and it is a relationship that continues to blossom to this day. She started going to the church when she was 11 years old; soon, she was baptised. "Whenever I need him to pray for us," Beyoncé said in 2002, "[Rasmus] is always here. And I know a lot of times when we go overseas, he'll ask the whole church to pray for Destiny's Child. It's amazing to have that kind of extended family."

There was a great deal of initial reaction to Girl's Tyme. Local producer Alonzo Jackson began to work with them. The *Houston Chronicle* tipped them, saying they presented a mixture of rap and vocal, loosely based on the then all-conquering pioneering girl group En Vogue. The group appeared in a feature, 'GIRLS TYME: OK guys, step aside. Six Houston preteens figure it's their turn for success in the music business,' on August 18, 1992.

Staff writer Cheryl Laird spent some time with the group and wrote a big piece. Ashley Davis acted as their spokesperson and said with all the optimism of a 12 year old: "We hope to be the number one girls group and send positive messages and bring people to see what we're talking about and make this world a better place." It was rumoured that Prince was interested in signing them. Although that wasn't substantiated, it was clear that there was some interest from the diminutive Minneapolitan, as Ashley Davis, later known as Tamar Davis, sang with Prince later in her career.

Veteran producer Arne Frager, who had then recently worked with Mariah Carey, was interested. He became aware of the group and brought them to The Record Plant Studios in Sausalito. He felt that nationwide exposure would benefit them. At Sausalito, the group, then a collection of 11 and 12 year olds, recorded some demos under the guidance of the experienced Frager.

The first time the wider public saw Beyoncé was in 1993, when Girl's Tyme appeared on the television show *Star Search*, filmed in Orlando, Florida. Created by legendary Hollywood TV producer Alfred 'Al' Masini (the man responsible for *Lifestyles Of The Rich And Famous*) and hosted by US TV stalwart Ed McMahon, the show ran from 1983 to 1995. Recorded at the Earl Carroll Theatre on Sunset Boulevard, LA, before *American Idol* and *The X Factor* emerged, it was the golden opportunity that all young singers and dancers aspired to win. When one looks at the roll call of its contestants, it reads like a *Who's Who* of the superstars of the nineties and noughties.

The group was soon to join other future megastars, such as Justin Timberlake and Britney Spears, by *not* advancing in the *Star Search* competition. Appearing after reigning champions, Detroit rock band Skeleton Crew, had played, old-school presenter McMahon announced: "Your challengers are a young group from Houston, welcome Beyoncé, LaTavia, Nina, Nikki, Kelly and Ashley (calling Tamar by her first Christian name), the hip-hop rapping Girl's Tyme." Singing the song 'All Over My Baby' (written by Alonzo Johnson and Tony Moore), the girls gave a spirited performance, with the group all bouncing around in quilted Day-Glo tops, long shorts and Kicker boots. LaTavia took the opening rap, Beyoncé took the main vocal performance, while the other five street-danced furiously in the background.

The show worked simply. Votes were cast for the two acts in the vocal group category – the champions or the challengers. Skeleton Crew got a perfect line of fours, the maximum score for the competition, while Girl's Tyme was awarded threes. The group, buoyed by the invincibility of early youth, cannot believe there is any other route for them but victory. They all visibly crumple when they realise they are to lose.

Producer Masini was sanguine about the matter and informed Mathew that the groups who lost were the ones more likely to go ahead and enjoy success. "For those who lose, something happens," he said, utilising his years of experience. "They go back and rededicate themselves, reorganise and some of them go on to make it. For some reason, those who win, don't go on."

Words of wisdom were not what the inconsolable group wanted to hear. "That was my first time I lost something that I really wanted to win," Beyoncé was to say. "We thought our lives were over." Kelly Rowland: "We ran backstage and burst into tears. I've never cried so much in my life. Imagine a bunch of 11 and 12 year olds crying like they were about to die." It was because of this that Beyoncé believes her father actually stepped in to manage the group, because he couldn't bear to hear the girls crying so much. A trip after the recording to nearby Disneyland partially assuaged their feelings of anguish, but they were all stirred up again when the show was aired on national television the following week.

For weeks, the girls would torture themselves by watching VCR recordings of their failure over and over again; painstakingly dissecting their blunders until, one day, Mathew Knowles forbade them to watch any longer. "My parents sat us down for a talk," Beyoncé was to say. "'Y'all can't let this get you down,' my mom said. Then my dad chimed in, 'So you lost on *Star Search*. That's just one TV show. Do y'all still want to be performers? Is that what you really want more than anything? Because if the answer is yes, are you just going to give up?" It was all about moving on. The appearance did, however, galvanise Beyoncé. She was now absolutely sure that this was what she wanted to do, above all else. And now, her father gave up his job so that he could concentrate, with Tillman, on getting the group ready for the big time.

"Him leaving his corporate job was very scary for me," Tina told *Rolling Stone* in 2004. Moving out of her comfort zone was somewhat uneasy for her. "I don't know many people who would give up a job making the kind of money he made. I thought he had gone a little nuts. I was like, 'What are we going to do?' I had a large salon and it was generating good money, but we were accustomed to two incomes. All of a sudden, we have to totally alter our lifestyle. But he's just like that about whatever he does. He's just really passionate."

It was Mathew's professionalism and unwavering determination that spurred Girl's Tyme on. The group, in his eyes, were going to go places. Mathew had a definite role model in Joe Jackson, the controversial patriarch of the Jackson family, whose single-minded determination brought The Jackson 5 into being. Mathew could be just like Joe.

The group ultimately found its feet as its line-up stabilised: Beyoncé, Kelly and LaTavia stayed together and were joined by fourth member LeToya Luckett. Born in March, 1981, Luckett had been an active member of the choir at Brentwood Baptist Church in Houston and wanted to emulate her heroes Janet Jackson and Whitney Houston. Beyoncé knew her from school. The new foursome, after losing Davis and the Taylor sisters, regrouped quickly. "The vibe between the four of us was wonderful, and when we'd have our interviews and we would say we were sisters, it was true," Roberson said.

Beyoncé introduced a new code into the group, a pact to improve themselves. As she later wrote, it was like this: "Rule one: start working out. Rule two: rehearse every day. Rule three: get some new songs. Rule four: learn how to sing *a cappella* . . . Rule five: no matter what, keep up the good work. Rule six: quite watching *Star Search* – really, what kind of TV show puts small children against adults who are twice their age?" It was now all about determination and dedication.

The group played countless shows supporting acts passing through Houston, and they became involved with vocal coach David Brewer, who gave Kelly, Beyoncé and LeToya vocal lessons. He stated in 2000 that he'd had greater influence over the girls than Mathew Knowles, developing their vocals.

Girl's Tyme began to gather plaudits as time passed. Beyoncé's parents' commitments to her and the group led to strains within their marriage, and in 1994, after 14 years of marriage, Tina and Mathew temporarily separated. "I had to remember that my dad was not just my manager, he was also my mother's husband," Beyoncé was to say. "Father, manager and husband are three very different roles, and each one comes with its own set of expectations. I was too young to realise what was going on then." It was a landmark in what was ultimately to prove a stormy marriage. Tina, Beyoncé, Kelly and Solange moved into a small house in Houston.

By the time the girls were 14, Mathew' perseverance was beginning to pay off: the craft they were learning through endless practice brought them to the attention of not one, but two record companies. Columbia was very interested, as was Elektra.

The group performed an audition for Columbia at the Jewish Community Center in Houston. It was watched by Teresa LaBarbera Whites, who would later become the group's A&R person at Columbia. The girls stayed up late and went swimming the night before and sounded sinus-heavy at their audition. Mathew lambasted them for their unprofessionalism and made them perform again, but they were not signed by Columbia.

Thankfully, they had been spotted by Daryl Simmons of Silent Partner Productions at Houston's Black Expo and he mentioned them to US industry legend Sylvia Rhone. Rhone had signed En Vogue during her tenure as Senior Vice President at Atlantic Records and had moved to Elektra in 1994 at the invitation of mogul Doug Morris, to oversee a merger with Sire and East West Records, and bring her policy of innovation to the label. Naturally sensing Beyoncé was the greatest talent, Rhone enlisted Simmons to ensure that her vocals would be featured prominently in any recordings made by the group.

Tina Knowles took time away from her Houston hair salon to become the girls' stylist and personal assistant. While still at Xerox, Mathew had set up his production company, Music World Entertainment (MWE), in the early nineties. This would be the way he could really use his education. He was a salesman, after all, and he could sell the wonderful music that his daughter and her friends were now producing. His business model was clear: Motown. "That's where I developed my concept, from Berry Gordy," Knowles told *Ebony* magazine in 2001. "He doesn't get the credit he deserves. He had everything in-house. He had his choreographers, stylists, producers and writers. He taught his artists etiquette. He had real artist development. And his artists were glamorous. That's really what the music world is all about."

In 1995, now aged 14, Girl's Tyme was signed to Elektra by Rhone (who, ironically, would go on to run Motown). The group was clearly thrilled to be spotted by the woman behind En Vogue. They relocated to Atlanta to record with L.A. Reid and Babyface sideman Simmons. Roberson's mother acted as chaperone, and the other girls' parents would come out and visit. A tutor would be on hand to ensure that the group studied during this period. They had, as Beyoncé was to say, "a little cash and a lot of freedom".

But it simply wasn't working out. After eight months, without any warning, the girls were dropped, for being too young and underdeveloped. "The label put us on the shelf," Beyoncé said. "They still had us signed but they would never put any money behind us or do anything else for our career . . . getting dropped was quite a shock, but being a signed act was a whole lot of fun while it lasted." When the final severance came, it was via letter. Although the group had an inkling it was going to happen, seeing it in print had a terrible finality.

Again, like *Star Search* before it, the rejection was too much to bear. Only this time, they had it on a piece of paper, to which they could frequently refer. "I hope whoever worked at Elektra Records and made the decision to let us go watched the 2000 Grammy Awards," Kelly Rowland wrote in 2002.

DC1 in all its short-lived glory. L-R: LaToya Luckett, Beyoncé Knowles, Kelly Rowland, LaTavia Roberson. (CORBIS)

The writing was indeed on the wall, DC2 holding an award won by DC1, 2000. (CORBIS)

The short-lived 2000 line up: Kelly Rowland, Farrah Franklin, Michelle Williams and Beyoncé Knowles. (PAM FRANCIS/TIME LIFE PICTURES/GETTY IMAGES)

One big happy family: Destiny's Child and Matthew Knowles pose for a portrait October 30, 2000 in Houston, TX. (PAM FRANCIS/GETTY IMAGES)

Another night out, another award: backstage at the 43rd Grammys, Staples Center, Los Angeles, February. 21, 2001.
(SCOTT GRIES/IMAGEDIRECT)

Hello England. Performing at London Arena, June 11, 2002.
(RUNE HELLESTAD/CORBIS)

Performing for US President-elect George W. Bush at the MCI Centre during the pre-inaugural event "Celebrating America's Youth" in Washington, DC, January 19, 2001.
(MIKE NELSON/AFP/GETTY IMAGES)

Beyoncé and Kelly at The Joint inside the Hard Rock Hotel & Casino July 2, 2000, Las Vegas. (ETHAN MILLER/GETTY IMAGES)

Beyoncé's first solo live show at the illustriously titled *Ford Presents Beyoncé Knowles, Friends & Family, Live From Ford's 100th Anniversary Celebration in Dearborn, Michigan*, June 14, 2003. (NEVILLE ELDER/CORBIS SYGMA)

Yeah Baby!: Mike Myers and Beyoncé pose at the post-premiere party of *Austin Power In Goldmember* at the Universal Amphitheatre in Los Angeles, July 22, 2002. (REUTERS/CORBIS)

Beyoncé and Matthew arrive at the 46th annual Grammy Awards show, February 8, 2004. (FRED PROUSER/REUTERS/CORBIS)

With the five Grammy awards she won that night. Among them were Best Contemporary R&B Album for *Dangerously In Love* and Best R&B Song for 'Crazy In Love'. (MIKE BLAKE/REUTERS/CORBIS)

Onstage at the 2003 MTV Europe Music Awards at Ocean Terminal on November 6, 2003 in Edinburgh. (FRANK MICELOTTA/GETTY IMAGES)

Fulfilled . . . and lovin' it in Australia. Destiny's Child at the Rod Laver Arena, Melbourne, April 2005. (MARTIN PHILBEY/CORBIS)

Baby, I'm A Star. Duetting with Prince at 46th annual Grammy Awards. Prince was effusive in his praise for Beyoncé, and it was, of course, reciprocated. (GARY HERSHORN/REUTERS/CORBIS)

Beyoncé performing at Usher's live Showtime concert, *One Night, One Star, Usher Live* in San Juan, Puerto Rico, March 5, 2005. (FRANK MICELOTTA/GETTY IMAGES)

In one of their final acts as a group, Destiny's Child accepted a star on the Walk of Fame on a rainy March Tuesday in Hollywood. (MARIO ANZUONI/REUTERS/CORBIS)

Bonnie and Clyde 06: Beyoncé and Jay-Z performing 'Déjà Vu' at the 2006 BET Awards at the Shrine Auditorium in Los Angeles. (MARIO ANZUONI/REUTERS/CORBIS)

Stop browbeating her, can't you see she's sexy?" Beyoncé as Xania on the set of *The Pink Panther*. (ETIENNE GEORGE/CORBIS)

Chapter 3

"So Get Your Act Together 'Cause You're Running Out Of Time": Columbia and Destiny's Child

"If someone tells us to get up there and do something that we don't want to do, we're not going to do that."

Beyoncé, 1998

"When we were signed, we were prepared."

Beyoncé, 1998

With the ultimate rejection by Elektra Records fresh in their minds, the group knew that if they were to be successful, it was time to take it to another level. And with that, they knew that they needed to change their name, to step away from Girl's Tyme, which, by now, they saw as synonymous with failure. They grappled with different ideas: Somethin' Fresh, Borderline, Cliché, of which Beyoncé was to comment, "We just liked the word 'cliché' because it sounded kind of ... fresh!" It came down to a decision between The Dolls and Destiny. Destiny was a name that wouldn't go away. Tina Knowles found it in her Bible in the Book of Isaiah, in which destiny is a common theme, at the page where she had used a picture of the girls as a bookmark. To show the name had relevance for the future, Mathew added 'Child'.

The group continued to play gigs in the Houston area, and received words of encouragement from visiting artists whom they supported, such as The O'Jays and SWV, whom the nascent Destiny's Child regarded as big sisters. With his mini-Motown production company and his eager charges, Mathew Knowles was instrumental in getting the group a deal with major label Columbia Records.

Mathew took the girls for another showcase at Columbia, again in New York, in front of Teresa LaBarbera Whites, who was still very interested in signing them. Whites and fellow A&R creative Kim Burse were key in getting the group signed. The audition was simple – the girls had to sing *a cappella* for them in a conference room at Sony's headquarters on Madison Avenue. "There were a bunch of men and women of all different races sitting so close," Beyoncé recalled. "We could put our arms out and touch them if we wanted to. It was that small and informal. It felt too intimate – being that close and having to make eye contact was very scary."

The group came face-to-face with record company inscrutability as they performed, without microphones, a version of Bill Withers' 'Ain't No Sunshine', alongside one of their own vocal workouts, 'Are You Ready'. Amid all the strategic nodding and over-emphasised toe tapping, nobody gave anything away. The group returned to Houston with another sinking feeling; another feeling that a false dawn had again broken. Whites discussed them with executives at Sony, and looked at the old audition tapes that they had of the group, including a poorly shot demo of a song called 'Open Wide' that had become a staple of their live act.

Destiny's Child heard nothing for several weeks. Each day seemed to get longer as the dawning realisation of rejection reared its head. The decision arrived by mail. Mathew and Tina – now reconciled – thought it amusing to trick Kelly and Beyoncé. They put the acceptance letter from Columbia in an envelope from the local diner that the girls went to on a regular basis after attending St John's on a Sunday. When the girls read the real contents of the Luby's envelope, they went wild with joy, with Kelly remembering it still as the happiest day of her life.

And if you're going to be signed, you may as well be signed to Columbia. It was not any old imprint. The company had an illustrious history – it is the world's oldest and arguably most successful record label. Founded in Maryland in 1887, the label began producing 7" and 10" discs, and by the time of the First World War, it already had offices in Paris and London. Destiny's Child were to be in illustrious company – Columbia had been home to many legendary jazz, blues and easy listening artists, such as Duke Ellington and Frank Sinatra, before artists such as Bob Dylan and Bruce Springsteen continued its success throughout the sixties and seventies. However, it was Michael Jackson's ascent to the apex of pop in the eighties that demonstrated just how capable the label was of creating and sustaining multi-platinum talent. In 1987, the conglomerate had been controversially taken over by the Japanese-based Sony Music Entertainment corporation. Acts such as Mariah Carey, Celine Dion and Michael Bolton prolonged the label's success.

As the group signed to Columbia, although Andretta Tillman was still very much on the scene as co-manager, Mathew wanted all the girls in the group to sign his management contract with Music World Entertainment simultaneously. Roberson and Luckett and their parents had reservations about signing with him, but, ultimately, they signed. Knowles was clear that he needed to marshal the group and be their outright manager. "The way you manage a 10 year old is different from the way you manage a 20 year old," he said in 2001. "A 12-year–old kid is not going to tell me that she is going to do something that is detrimental and I just say 'OK.' I remember when I had Columbia Records come in to see them audition when they were 12. The day before, I told the girls not to get in the swimming pool, that they would get congested. They didn't listen to me. In the middle of the audition, I stopped and told them: 'This is exactly what I was talking about. You guys decided to go swimming, and now you are not sounding good.' That's one of the reasons the label signed them. They liked knowing that the girls had guidance."

Teresa LaBarbera Whites assigned former *Black Beat* editor and senior Columbia publicist Yvette Noel-Schure to the group. This Grenada-born PR was one of the best and shrewdest in the business and had helped to make Beyoncé's idol, Mariah Carey, an international phenomenon.

From signing with Columbia in early 1996, the girls got to work crafting an album. Tragedy struck however, when Andretta Tillman, their co-manager and founder, died of lupus in 1997. The mother of two teenage boys, she passed away tragically young. Although there was time for reflection, the group knew they had to continue to ensure that all Tillman's initial hard work would come to fruition. Destiny's Child's first three albums all contain songs dedicated to her.

Destiny's Child made their recording debut with the track 'Killing Time' on the *Men In Black* soundtrack in July 1997. The Will Smith-Tommy Lee Jones vehicle, based on a comic strip about a secret agency that keeps check on the aliens on earth, was hugely successful. It chimed with *The X-Files* conspiracy theory-craze that was so prevalent during President Clinton-era America. The accompanying soundtrack album was immensely popular as well, reaching the top of the *Billboard* charts for a week at the end of July 1997. The album was produced by the pool of producers that were working with Destiny's Child – Jermaine Dupri, and Poke & Tone – and it contained a snappy selection of up-to-the-moment R&B flavoured grooves, topped off by Will Smith's humungous Patrice Rushen-sampling summer hit 'Men In Black'.

'Killing Time' proved a beautiful debut for Destiny's Child. Produced and co-written by D'Wayne Wiggins, it is a sophisticated, mature song, with metronomic percussion, acoustic guitar and a beautifully understated string arrangement by Benjamin Wright. Wright was the sort of person you could easily get if you were working with a label the size of Columbia. One of the most sought-after string arrangers in the business, he oversaw many Temptations, Quincy Jones and Commodores records, as well as Michael Jackson's *Off The Wall*, one of Beyoncé's all-time favourites. 'Killing Time' initially sounds just like another slow jam until its innate sophistication takes you by surprise, showcasing Beyoncé's deep and sensual voice perfectly. Although it could be said it is somewhat naïve, it was an appropriate introduction to the group.

After all the struggles encountered in their young, middle-class lives, Destiny's Child were signed to one of the world's biggest record companies, had appeared on a platinum soundtrack album and had people working with them who had worked on Michael Jackson's *Off The Wall*. It was to bode extremely well for their debut album.

Released in February 1998, Destiny's Child's self-titled debut album can now be viewed as a work of sophisticated juvenilia. Overseen by 16 producers, *Destiny's Child* sounds exactly like what it was: a work by committee. Recorded throughout 1997, the release was trailed by the single 'No, No, No' in November 1997.

The song came in two parts – the original, and initial, A-side was the sweet, swing-beat ballad produced by Rob Fusari and Vincent Herbert. Whites at Columbia felt that the group needed something more significant as their debut single release. As the album was readying to print, 'No, No, No' was recut with Wyclef Jean. The group was in the Sony office in New York when Wyclef walked past. He was then ubiquitous, as the ensemble in which he'd made his name, The Fugees (Wyclef, Pras Michel and Lauryn Hill), had become the go-to act. Jean, a garrulous singer/producer of Haitian origin, seemed to be rapping or using his production skills on virtually every record in 1997. Star-struck, but keen to introduce themselves, the group performed an *a cappella* for him.

Impressed, he asked the group to sing on his 'We Trying To Stay Alive' remix. Of course, according to guest star etiquette, he had to return the favour. Wyclef was instrumental in forging the group's soon-to-be-trademark staccato style of singing. "We were in the studio one night with Wyclef, all really tired," Beyoncé said in 2000. "I sang melody to the fast music track for a joke and Wyclef said, 'That's hot! Do it like that.'" Although Beyoncé was initially reluctant, she tried. It gave the group a defining sound that they were soon to use to their advantage. Kelly told it slightly differently; Beyoncé was simply responding to Wyclef's call telling her to hurry up. "There was never a dull moment in the studio working with Wyclef," Rowland said in 1998. He sped up the original and created a slice of unusual R&B, based around a sample from The Love Unlimited Orchestra's 'Strange Games And Things'.

It was accompanied by a video that set out the group's stall perfectly. They were pictured initially sitting on the stoop of a brownstone singing to Wyclef's acoustic guitar, before he stops the song and suggests that all the girls need to do is "drop a phat beat for the clubs and they'll lose their mind". Suddenly the girls are seen gyrating in silhouette while Wyclef intones that this version is the remix. In three minutes the group appeared street smart, sexy and up-to-the-moment. There are frequent cuts between the group on the dance floor and in their casual clothes by the brownstone. Wyclef makes the, at the time, bold claim in his rap that Destiny's Child "went from a dream to the young Supremes". The single began its climb up the R&B charts and topped the listings on March 21 for a solitary week. It reached the US Top 40, and also, due to the overriding popularity of Wyclef Jean, made the Top Five in the UK in early 1998. By 1999, 'No, No, No' had turned double platinum. It was an auspicious start.

The rest of the album, although not as strong as the single, showed a great deal of promise. *Destiny's Child* was produced mainly by D'Wayne Wiggins, the mainstay from the recently defunct rap ensemble Tony! Toni! Toné! Wiggins had signed Destiny's Child to his production company, Grassroots Entertainment, in 1996 around the time of the Elektra deal. Wiggins then, in conjunction with Mathew Knowles and Sony, sought out the best producers to work with the group.

The album opens with a blues electric guitar solo, sounding like something that could be heard on a Texan verandah. 'Second Nature' is a slow jam that sensually builds, based on 'Make Me Say It Again Girl', an Isley Brothers sample from their 1975 *The Heat Is On* album. It located the group fully in the old school, a very knowing introduction to their debut record.

'No, No, No Part 2' comes next – in its remixed form, turning the beat inside out. It's a strident piece of late nineties R&B, unlike the smooth late night soul of 'No, No, No Part 1', which appears as the sixth track. "People loved it when we dropped the single, 'No, No, No'," Kelly

Rowland said. "They liked how Beyoncé and the rest of us sang fast. The beat was hot and the song did well. I loved that sound, which was a happy accident."

'With Me', which became the second single from the album, appears twice also, with and without a rap from Master P, who, at that time, was arguably the hottest rapper in the world. Produced by and featuring Jermaine Dupri, it is based around a deeply annoying nine-note piano figure that owes something to Randy Newman's 'Simon Smith And The Amazing Dancing Bear', which was sampled from P's 'Freak Hoes'. Again, it came with a video that showed the group as sassy – an appropriate balance between celebrating their youth, yet not appearing childish. Dupri, in his rapper guise JD, replaced Master P on the single version. He looks through a View-Master-type machine at various slides of the girls, who seem to be underwater, an illusion underlined when Beyoncé appears as a mermaid. It was good, but not good enough as a follow-up. Beyoncé felt they should have stayed with the Master P version. "I'm sure people thought, 'What happened?' So the second single didn't do as well as the first one."

'Tell Me' is an impassioned ballad that continues the split between the uptempo and the soporific, sophisticated late-night love songs on the album. 'Bridges', which features elements of Al Green's 'Simply Beautiful', was a lovely mid-tempo groove. Produced by Wiggins, it has a hip-hop influenced beat, with trumpets played by LA session legend and future member of Santana, Bill Ortiz. 'Show Me The Way', produced by Carl Washington, could have fallen off a 1983 Evelyn King album. Loosely based on Keni Burke's 'Risin' To The Top', it is intelligent jazz-funk.

Wyclef Jean and his Fugee cohort Pras Michel turn up again on 'Illusion'. It was a perfect example of the magpie production style that was so prevalent in the late nineties. Based on the UK eighties act Imagination's hit 'Just An Illusion', it has elements of many other melodies, creating an infectious, if superficial melee. 'Birthday', written and produced by Wiggins, is another sultry jam, based around 'Happy Birthday'.

Where the album is at is probably best illustrated by the version of The Commodores' Lionel Richie-written 1979 country-soul standard 'Sail

On'. Sincerely delivered, it is clear that Destiny's Child is determined to cover all bases, pleasing the grown-ups as well as their core audience. It's good, but it's all a bit like little children trying on their parents' shoes. One of the album's most tender moment comes on 'My Time Has Come (Dedicated To Andretta Tillman)', where the girls sing to their recently passed manager with astonishing emotion. There are no producers or remixers to back this up – it is just pure and simple sentiment, heartfelt and expertly delivered.

Wyclef Jean also provided some further inspiration for the group that was to shape their future appearance. They went to Cancún, Mexico, to record with him and shoot the video. The outfits that Columbia dispatched got waylaid somewhere along the journey and Tina Knowles realised she had to create something for the group to wear. "I went to the army surplus store and got real camouflage outfits and converted them into sexy costumes," Knowles recalls. "Wyclef Jean asked, 'Who styled you?' and Beyoncé said, 'My mom.' He said, 'She needs to style you all the time.' That's how it started. Destiny's Child started the whole camouflage craze during their *Survivor* album. As things progressed I did what my mom taught me. I bought beautiful fabrics and made outfits rather than buying cheaper clothes." From that point on, Tina was fully on the team as the group's principal stylist.

Destiny's Child supported Boyz II Men on their 2008 summer tour in the United States, which further increased their profile. Although it was a slow starter commercially, *Destiny's Child* became a prolonged seller due to the group's increasing popularity. The boot camp training that Mathew Knowles had instilled in them came to fruition with their capable handling of the variety of daft questions that were thrown their way in a myriad of television interviews. The four girls came across as equal personalities with LaTavia full of street smarts, Kelly sweet and generous, LeToya a trifle ditzy and Beyoncé coolly in control. Endless questions about upbringing, families and sex appeal were dealt with politely and fully. However, no one could deny their absolute belief in themselves, God, family and friendship. And also, possibly conveniently forgetting their Girl's Tyme origins, they revelled in the fact that no record or management company had manufactured them. Beyoncé summed it up perfectly when talking to Rachel Stuart, the Jamaican-Canadian model host of BET's *Planet Groove* in early 1998; "When we were signed, we were prepared." There was little doubt in that fact.

Destiny's Child was a good, if not great, start for the group. It reached number 67 on the *Billboard* Hot 100, and made it to number 14 on the *Billboard* R&B chart. It also reached number 45 in the UK charts. The album came, as would all future Destiny's Child recordings, with a long list of individual thank yous from each member of the group, as well as collective group thank yous. Andretta Tillman – to whom the album was dedicated above all others – was singled out in each girl's list – from Kelly saying to "the late, great Andretta Tillman, your spirit lives on, I love you", to LaTavia's "you live within me", to LeToya's "Ms Ann luv and miss you very much", to Beyoncé, who dedicates the album to her and says that she is "her guardian angel". Tillman would have been pleased by the relative speed of the group's success, and by the way in which Mathew Knowles kept masterminding more and more work for them, to ensure their name got as far around the world as possible.

Destiny's Child went on to sell in excess of three million copies and was certified gold. "The first record was successful but not hugely successful," Beyoncé said when promoting *B'Day*, eight years later. "It was a neo-soul record and we were 15 years old. It was way too mature for us." It certainly helped Destiny's Child to make a name for themselves, which was cemented when the group were asked personally by Whitney Houston to play her 35th birthday party in August 1998.

"She invited us to her 35th birthday! We were so excited!" Beyoncé told Q magazine in November 2000. "We scrambled up all our money, got us some outfits. We were the only group that came dressed as a group. Everybody was sayin', 'Y'all are like The Supremes.'" Y'all are like The Supremes: this became the lazy comparison made by journalists talking about Destiny's Child during 1998.

Now that the group was really making it, Beyoncé had little time for a social life. Her boyfriend, an unassuming local Houston dweller called Lyndell Locke, kept a low profile, and it was unlikely that the two ever actually slept together. The relationship was played down as, frankly,

Beyoncé had little time for love. "I watched Destiny's Child grow, I knew all the girls and I saw them progress," Locke told online celebrity site Celeb wohoo. "I was there when they got their first deal, when they rehearsed. I was a close member to the family even though some people didn't approve of me being there. The DC Empire looking back now was very cleverly orchestrated and every member of the team was under a microscope. Whether that was on a personal or working relationship. Anyone close to those girls, especially Beyoncé at that influential time in her life, was a threat. It was all about focus, focus, focus. Apparently, boys don't equal focus, which I kind of understand."

"Lyndell and I went out from when I was 12 to 18, about six years. I went to his prom," Beyoncé was to write in *Soul Survivors*. "I would have rather gone to my own, because I didn't know anybody at Lyndell's school. I had to be home early that night, because I was in the tenth grade and he was a senior. After I left school to start recording, dating got kind of hard. We didn't see each other all that much."

Although the group were excited by their success, already underlying tensions seemed to be growing between Roberson and Luckett and Rowland and Knowles. All was not well. When the group were due to go on their European tour, LaTavia was laid low with a fever. Mathew suggested that dancer Janelle went in her place.

Chapter 4

The Writing's On The Wall

"Why would we ask a guy to pay our bills? Only if he runs them up!"
Beyoncé Knowles, 1999

"When it came time to work on our second album," Kelly Rowland wrote in *Soul Survivors*, "we sat down together and wrote down all the things we didn't like about the last album and all the things we did like." Their debut had been a good, if unremarkable, start for the group, but they knew that they could better it. The only real hint of their commercial potential and future direction was Wyclef Jean's later added remix of 'No, No, No'. The group had continued its punishing regime of rehearsing and recording, and had supported K-Ci and JoJo, as well as Boyz II Men around the US.

Working closely with Teresa LaBarbera Whites at Columbia, it was suggested that Destiny's Child consult producer Kevin Briggs, known by his production name of She'kspere. Briggs wrote with his then girlfriend, Kandi Burruss, who sang in the group Xscape. He had made his name producing Xscape and was just about to break big with the record he had produced and written for TLC, 'No Scrubs'.

She'kspere flew down to Texas with Burruss to meet Destiny's Child. "I didn't know much about them," he was later to say. "But I was trying to do whatever it takes to establish my credibility as a producer and a songwriter. I went to Texas and at first it was a little uncomfortable, because they weren't expecting to see Kandi." The group were expecting Briggs alone, and were a little in awe of Burruss, the Atlanta-born 23 year old who, as Kandi Girl, was one of their girl group peers.

The producer and his partner were told that they could produce one track for the Destiny's Child album. When they met the girls and Mathew, they initially presented the track 'Bug A Boo'. The girls were not over enamoured until Burruss started to discuss melody ideas with them. Soon, the pair were contributing five songs to the album – songs that would guide the group in their new direction.

Although She'kspere and Burruss would be just two of the 16 producers that would ultimately work on the album, their contributions would help define Destiny's Child's sound. It was She'kspere that would introduce the otherworldly, skittering quadruple-time beats into the album and encourage the strange, stuttering vocal phrasing that so marked this era of the group.

"With *The Writing's On The Wall*, we did the whole album in about three weeks," Beyoncé recalled. "Sometimes we did two songs a day. Some songs might take two days, but we're very, very quick in the studio." With production and post-production between October 1998 and April 1999, Destiny's Child's second album, *The Writing's On The Wall*, was released on July 27, 1999. It took its name from the Book of Daniel in the Old Testament of the Bible, where supernatural writing foretold the demise of the Babylonian empire.

Again, working with their plethora of producers, Destiny's Child created a considerable, if stylistically fractured, improvement on their debut. Ten of the songs were co-writes with the girls and their production and writing teams.

Importantly, it was a step forward. Lyrically it marked a huge advance, moving away from direct love songs, to more mannered, staged dramas that centred on the condition of relationships, female empowerment and, often, the duplicity of men. For a group that were forged in a hair salon, Beyoncé picked up on the tics and mannerisms of the customers, their grievances and complaints, talking about men, relationships and financial hardships.

The Writing's On The Wall starts with 'Intro (The Writing's On The Wall)', a Mafia-style skit, where Destiny's Child are brought in front of 'the Don'. A Spanish guitar plays, evoking 'Speak Softly Love', the love theme from Francis Ford Coppola's 1972 Oscar-winning film, *The Godfather*. The four families ('LaTavia Menser', 'Beyoncé Corleone', 'Kelly Steraki' and 'LeToya Barzini') are brought together to discuss their objective: Destiny's Child's commandments of relationships. Conflating their personal code with the most sacred of texts was a bold move; but strong morals course through the album. Although we hear later 'thou shall get your party on', we also learn that 'thou shall cherish life' and 'if thou can wait, then thou can stay'.

The She'kspere produced 'So Good' started off their new 'anti-hater' manifesto, flaunting their success to an old lover/band member. The term 'hater' was ever-present in the urban lexicon of the late 20th century, and meant a person who could not applaud another's success. Although the protesting and repetition of the title make overall for a slight piece of work, it introduced this new ornate, almost baroque sound – with every instrument played by She'kspere and speeded-up loops of acoustic guitars underpinning the group's vocal work.

It was the next track, 'Bills, Bills, Bills', that brought Destiny's Child fully into the mainstream. With every instrument again played by She'kspere, the track was recorded in Houston, and mixed at Los Angeles' legendary Larrabee Sound Studio to give it further gloss. It was similar in many respects to TLC's 'No Scrubs', with a wronged lover challenging her boyfriend over unaccounted for charges that appear on credit card and cell phone bills. With Beyoncé on lead vocals and Kelly singing the bridge, and all four providing backing vocals, it was a powerful song. The idea for the song came to Briggs while he was paying for groceries on his second visit to Houston to see the girls, as he overheard someone asking to pay their "bills, bills, bills". Burruss started to add a melody, thinking about a man she'd dated who would routinely use her phone without asking.

Burruss discussed the lyric with Destiny's Child. "She'kspere kept humming the melody to the chorus," Beyoncé recalled. "It was so catchy. We loved it. We knew it was a hit but we weren't sure of what the song was talking about." Many saw the record, which was released as a single on June 15, 1999, as a tale that portrayed the group as young ladies in thrall to their men, who would use their bank accounts to bail out the ladies' frivolity. The girls were quick to state that this was not the case. "Why would we ask a guy to pay our bills?" Beyoncé continued. "Only if he runs them up! We wrote the verses about him taking advantage of us even though nobody paid attention to that part. People took it the wrong way." However, a misunderstanding can sometimes be extremely good for business. The record entered the US chart on June 22 and began its ascent to the number one spot, where it remained for a solitary week, in between Jennifer Lopez's 'If You Had My Love' and Will Smith's 'Wild Wild West'. It would spend a total of 20 weeks on the *Billboard* Hot 100. It spent nine weeks atop the *Billboard* R&B chart, the longest-running chart topper of that year. In the UK, the record entered the chart at the end of July, and rose to number six, one place lower than their previous UK best, 'No, No, No', in March 1998.

Its video cemented its appeal, shot in a fake hair salon – a lovely in-joke reference to Tina Knowles' Headliners in Houston. The girls are portrayed as hairdressers, listening and gossiping with their clients, interspersed with dance routines and Beyoncé singing to camera. Rowland's bridges show the extravagant-at-the-girl's-expense men sitting in mock-up living rooms staring at paperwork. It was stylised, mannered and, most of all, modern. Tina Knowles had styled the group in silver outfits that gave them a touch of the strange and the space age.

'Confessions' was produced by and featured Missy 'Misdemeanor' Elliott. It is gorgeous, seventies-influenced soul, although Elliott more or less phones in her contribution, with her spoken vocal introducing verses, mirroring choruses and her rather perfunctory rap three-quarters in. However, to have Elliott – arguably the coolest African-American musical personality at that moment – on their record was hugely significant. Here was a group that could roll with the best of them. Although arguably Columbia's cheque book was a significant factor in their appearances, the outside artists who were to work with the group still had high quality thresholds. And when Elliott heard them, she was extremely impressed. She admired Beyoncé's working methods: "She's very into her craft," Elliott said in 2006. "That's what I like about her, she takes that very seriously. It's not just about getting in there and doing a record, it's got to be right."

Introduced with 'thou shall not bug', 'Bug A Boo' is one of the album's signature tunes, and the track that commenced the relationship between the girls and She'kspere. It builds on the sass of 'No, No, No' and captures the group at their early, strident best. It was released as the album's second single in October 1999. It faired better in the UK than in the US, where it peaked at number nine, compared with its US position of number 33, which was something of a surprise after the success of 'Bills, Bills, Bills'. An infectious and propulsive groove, it is a play for female independence away from the ballers and playas who would bug them and cramp their style.

Its supporting video is also tremendous fun. Directed by Darren Grant (who'd helmed the 'No, No, No', 'With Me' and 'Bills, Bills, Bills' promos), it shows the girls walking down a crowded street (a favoured device of nineties video directors, featured in both Massive Attack's 'Unfinished Sympathy' and The Verve's 'Bittersweet Symphony'). The girls look at themselves on closed-circuit TVs; the walk/don't walk street signs flick on and off in rhythm. As they walk, they are hounded by four men in a soft top, clearly the 'buggers' of the narrative. To get away, in pure comic book fashion, the girls escape through an open door. The door leads to a men's locker room. The girls snigger and look aghast as they see a variety of athletes in varying states of undress, including US basketball superstar Kobe Bryant. Looking to escape, they find a clothes rail with four cheerleader costumes on it, and have the idea of putting them on. Suddenly, the action moves to night, at a football game where they are dancing in front of the UCLA Bruin Marching Band, led by none other than Wyclef Jean dressed in a UCLA drum major uniform. It ends back on the street, and despite the girls looking initially displeased as they see the soft top again, they smile and drive off in it. Men are needed in their life, but on their own terms. They have had their peace and freedom for a period, now it's time to get with them again.

'Temptation' is a fine slow jam, with an intense chorus vocal, based on the children's verse 'This Old Man (Knick-knack, Paddy-whack)'.

Again, it is mature subject matter for the group. Written with D'Wayne Wiggins and Carl Wheeler, it puts forward the simple moral dilemma of having to reject the advances of a young man at a club while their man is at home. Of course, with Destiny's Child, there is little dilemma; they will remain strong and go home.

'Now That She's Gone' is a stop-start groove produced by Donnie 'D-Major' Boynton and Ken 'K-Fam' Fambro. Recorded in Houston, it sounds like something directly from the Angie Bofill or Regina Belle songbook, with a beautiful vocal arrangement by one of the track's co-writers, LaTrelle Simmons. 'Where'd You Go' – produced by Platinum Status and Chris Stokes – was a co-write with all four group members and speeds things up slightly, but this, like much of the middle of this somewhat lengthy album, sags slightly and it sounds pedestrian compared with the rest of the material.

The She'kspere produced 'Hey Ladies' is another call for females to take a stand against unfaithful men. Written again following production and writing sessions with Briggs and Burruss, it calls for strong female empowerment. Why indeed should they 'keep holdin' on' while their man is running around with a 'tenderoni', street slang for a younger female companion? What makes for the song's drama is the dilemma the girls face as they gather the strength to depart, but their personal well-being is far more important than staying with an unfaithful lover. She'kspere's production, using a fantastic break and rewind two minutes in, compliments the girl's harmonies perfectly.

With the next commandment of 'thou shall move on to the next', a reference to the album's other significant guest artists, 'If You Leave' continues the late night, slow-jam feel of the middle section of the album. It features vocal group Next – R.L. Huggar, Raphael Brown, Terry Brown – who had enjoyed hits with 'Wifey' and 'Too Close'. Their vocal, very much in the new jack swing style of the era adds a sweetness, especially when they support Beyoncé's vocal when she reappears toward the end of the second verse. Produced by Chad 'Dr Guess' Elliot and Oshea Hunter, it is once more a tale centred around a dilemma – whether a couple should leave their respective partners and start a relationship. Again, it speaks to an audience which faced this common situation – Next are so impressed with the girls that they have even, in the song, 'told their dad, you're the finest girl I never had'.

Destiny's Child were feted in the US and started to rack up success. Introduced with the commandment 'thou shall get your party on', 'Jumpin', Jumpin'' was the track that made white rock journalists become interested when it was selected as the album's fourth and final single in July 2000. It was also Beyoncé's first significant writing and production credit. With its vocal interlude by Byron Rittenhouse, 'Jumpin', Jumpin'', was co-written and produced by Beyoncé with Chad Elliot. It showed the group observing nightclub shenanigans, urging ladies to leave their fellows at home, as the club is full of ballers – i.e. men who had made their money, the name taken from ball players.

It was interesting to read how Destiny's Child was perceived in the UK media. As critic Garry Mulholland wrote in his acclaimed book, *This Is Uncool: The 500 Greatest Singles Since Punk and Disco*, 'Jumpin', Jumpin'' was a "crusade to convince all happily married women to have as much adulterous sex as possible". Over its "juddering, propulsive rhythm", the girls showed their ability to make the repeated cry of 'ballers!' "sound somehow ladylike, even religious. And then you smile demurely, thank God and deny everything in interviews."

It is an astounding piece of late 20th century R&B, with the group following the nagging synthesiser riff. The girls are fed up with their men who are out hangin' with their homies; they want to party. Not that they are actually going to be adulterous: they just want fun. The video that accompanied the single captures a marvellous cartoon-like caricature of the US club scene at the turn of the millennium.

However, it was 'Say My Name', produced by Rodney 'Darkchild' Jerkins, that was the album's centrepiece. Released as a single in February 2000, it became the group's second US number 1, remaining at the top of the chart for three weeks in March. "Rodney was a lot of fun to work with," Kelly Rowland recalled. The group chatted with Jerkins, his writing partner LaShawn Daniels and his brother, Fred Jerkins III, in the studio to get ideas: "It was like men and women getting together and talking about relationships," Beyoncé recalled. "We had our debates. When you get women and men in a room and you're saying what men do and what women do, it's just fun. We laughed and we ate and we sang and we acted crazy and a great song came out of it." Fred Jerkins remembered that this was the way they worked and it worked well: "When we're working with an artist . . . we sit down and vibe with them and try to figure out where they're at in their life, what's going on in their relationships, so we can cater for them."

This meeting of minds led to a track that would define the group. Their vocals were recorded at Pacifique Studios in North Hollywood by LaShawn Daniels, and Jerkins prepared a mix. Initially unhappy with the track, Jerkins took it away and remixed it. The girls first heard the new mix while shooting the cover for the album, and all agreed they preferred the remix. The track compliments the work of She'kspere perfectly and acts as a superb sister record to 'Bills, Bills, Bills'. It also has a fastidious production, with Beyoncé's vocal delivered in a similar, mannered way. Again, the girls are exposing a lover's mischief, who is clearly running with someone else. He has stopped calling his partner by her name, instead using generic names for sweethearts. It is a perfectly paranoid record, with Jerkins' orchestrations sounding like dramatic detective music.

The rest of the album, although good, nestles in the shadow of the two classic singles that precede it. 'She Can't Love You' is a return to more traditional balladry, the final She'kspere production on the album, while 'Stay' was produced by Daryl Simmons from Silent Partner, the production company that had briefly guided the girls career while they were signed to Elektra. Shorn of any production trickery, it is a sweet, unadorned yet touching ballad that highlights the blend of voices perfectly. 'Sweet Sixteen' features LaTavia on lead vocals on the first verse, her deep, dark voice adding much to this tale of a headstrong teenager.

The album's final tracks returns the group's writing to the backyards of Houston. With a simple introduction, "This is for you Miss Ann, who's with the heavenly father who made the real commandments," the song 'Outro (Amazing Grace . . . Dedicated To Andretta Tillman)' is a straightforward tribute to the Girl's Tyme founder and Roberson and Luckett's previous manager, Tillman. Recorded at Digital Services, Houston, and produced solely by Beyoncé, the group perform an *a cappella* version of the English Christian hymn, written by John Newton. Placing it at the end of the album demonstrates that no matter how many machines and effects are used throughout the main body of *The Writing's On The Wall*, it is still all about the talent and the harmonies of the vocal quartet at the album's core.

The group had started working with vocal coach Kim Wood Sandusky around the time of the album, and she understood fully the need for the group to rest their voices as much as use them. Based in Nashville, Wood Sandusky built on the work that David Brewer had done with them and prepared their vocals for ever more demanding live work.

The Writing's On The Wall became the album that truly broke Destiny's Child, with strong and strident tunes such as 'Bills, Bills, Bills', 'Bug A Boo' and 'Say My Name'. It was also their last 'ghetto' album. Their values coursed through it; this was strong music that placed emphasis on empowered women, who still had a definite place for a partner in their life, but most definitely on their own terms. The overall message of *The Writing's On The Wall* was 'thou shall not hate'.

The album received mixed reviews. Rob Brunner reviewed it in *Entertainment Weekly*, alongside R&B group Blaque's self-titled debut album. Brunner spoke about who would be who if the golden age of Motown was still upon them.

"*Wall* gets bogged down by too much banal balladry ('Stay', 'Sweet Sixteen'), proving Destiny's Child to be capable of sounding exactly like any other group of snooze-inducing slow jammers. But more often they recognise the difference between extremes of pitch and extremes of passion, a distinction lost on many R&B balladeers. Destiny's Child have learned a thing or two from The Supremes, singers who knew how to use a well-placed pause or a quietly sung harmony to maximum effect. No, they haven't managed to reach that lofty level on *Wall*, but if you're casting *Motown '99*, the album's worth a listen. It's best stuff is close enough to the spirit of The Supremes to at least win them a callback."

However, the album's success depended little on what critics said. After entering the US album charts at number six on its first week of release, *The Writing's On The Wall* went on to become one of the biggest-selling R&B albums of all time.

In 1999, the group embarked on their first proper coast-to-coast tour, supporting TLC, then at the very top of their game with the success of their *FanMail* album and its attendant single smashes 'Unpretty' and 'No Scrubs'. Destiny's Child received positive reviews and their stagecraft was developing well.

The Writing's On The Wall simply kept selling. In May 2000, it was still being mined for singles, and as 'Say My Name' reached the top spot in the States, the album surged back up the charts, reaching number five, one position higher than its original success the preceding year. A variety of formats were put out across the world. Added to the end of the album was the non-album single 'Get On The Bus', which was taken from the motion picture soundtrack *Why Do Fools Fall In Love*.

In summer that same year in the UK a special two-disc edition was brought out to capitalise on the success of 'Independent Women Part I', meaning the group were promoting a record that was nearly two years old, the sleeve of which prominently featured the faces of the original four-piece group. The album peaked at number 10 in the UK and spent a remarkable 87 weeks on the chart. In total, it sold over 16 million copies worldwide.

Three days before 'Say My Name' reached number one in the United States, on March 15, 2000, LeToya Luckett and LaTavia Roberson filed a civil lawsuit against Mathew Knowles. *The Writing's On The Wall* would prove a chillingly prescient title.

Chapter 5

Destabilisation And Independence

Beyoncé: "Each one of us is a part of each one of us. We really do love each other, we couldn't go solo."
LaTavia: "A group that prays together, stays together."

Canadian television, 1998

"We knew everything had happened for a reason. God had his hand on our group, and it was going to work out just fine – like it had already been written on the wall."

Beyoncé, 2002

In February 2000, Destiny's Child underwent what Beyoncé was later to refer to as 'the change'. As the group was about to film the promotional video for 'Say My Name', Luckett and Roberson fired Mathew Knowles as their manager. The two wanted outside representation, as they felt they had been increasingly sidelined by Knowles. They believed his role was compromised by being Beyoncé's father and having Kelly living under his roof.

As they were the duo initially closest to former manager Andretta

Tillman, and they had harboured doubts about signing with Music World Entertainment, there had always been some tension amid the friendship of the four girls. Given also that they were still all so young and were just starting to see some of their first proper royalties come through, Roberson and Luckett felt that Beyoncé was getting the lion's share of the profits. She was driving around in a Jaguar, while Roberson's mother, who had been the group's on-the-ground chaperone for their countless television performances and support tours, was still driving a battered old car. They had no issue with Beyoncé or Kelly, and could appreciate their tightness with and support for Mathew, but they felt increasingly excluded.

Strain had been growing for some time between the four of them, and as the group started earning good money, the issues were only exacerbated. "Once Destiny's Child started to get successful," Beyoncé noted in *Soul Survivors*, "that's when we found out who our friends really were. Our whole world changed, and that makes friendship more complicated, especially with females. I hate to say this, but women are too competitive – they let it make them crazy. A lot of the time when we were younger, that competitive instinct – jealousy and envy – got so out of control that it was scary. It can sometimes make some people do crazy things." Roberson and Luckett wanted a voice within the group. It was alleged that they had been hanging with Columbia hit makers and Jermaine Dupri prodigies Jagged Edge and were starting to depart from the wholesome lifestyle required to be in Destiny's Child.

"We tried everything. Counselling with our church, our youth pastor. Rotating rooms," Beyoncé told Q magazine. "But it was two and two. Our vision of the group was different from theirs." Roberson and Luckett wanted Destiny's Child to be raunchier and less Christian. Whatever the reasons for the alienation and separation, the way Roberson and Luckett discovered they had been replaced was pretty stunning. "At the time of the split, we had a lot of promotional appearances to do because we were just starting to make a name for ourselves," Beyoncé said. "We were also scheduled to shoot the 'Say My Name' video in two weeks. So not only did we need to find someone who looked similar to LaTavia and LeToya – we didn't want the drama to overshadow what people thought about our music. We just didn't want the press making a big deal out of the split. So much for that!" After protracted negotiations, the two had a shock when they saw the brand new video for 'Say My Name'. In it, they were replaced by Monica's backing vocalist Michelle Williams (born Tenitra Michelle Williams, July 23, 1980, in Rockford, Illinois) and Farrah Franklin, who'd danced with Destiny's Child in the hair salon in the 'Bills, Bills, Bills' video.

Roberson and Luckett realised they had simply been removed. The two looked at each other in awe. "Wow, seven years down the drain, just like that," Luckett said. And one of the girls, Michelle, looked a bit like LeToya; and Farrah looked just like LaTavia. And it was a great video too. The similarities of the replacements to the originals meant many had no idea that they were watching two new group members, who were mouthing the words that the other girls had sung.

Roberson and Luckett filed a lawsuit against Mathew, Beyoncé and Kelly, suggesting that they had been forced out of the group, and that their careers had been ruined as a result. It was one thing having a suit filed against Mathew, but to bring their teenage friends into it seemed to underline the scale of their feelings. Allegations made included that Mathew had denied them money and had acted abusively towards them.

It became the hot topic of conversation, and one that destabilised Beyoncé. Spotting who the new members were in the 'Say My Name' video became something of a youth obsession as the promo was shown nationwide, while the record made its ascent to the top of the US charts. Despite their differences, LaTavia had been Beyoncé's first friend in the group. "Up until that point, we were squeaky-clean nice girls who grew up in Texas," Beyoncé wrote in *Soul Survivors*. "We had all been together for years – lifelong friends since childhood. We couldn't get on the covers of any magazines. I guess the media felt our story was too boring. Then two members were gone, and soon all eyes were on us." Beyoncé told *JET* magazine on May 29, 2000, that the girls had left owing to creative differences. She knew that the US public had become accustomed to seeing the group, and that she would now be asked at every interview about her former friends' departure. Their again seemed to be similarities to The Supremes, with members being replaced as the group progressed.

"It was a stressful time for Kelly and I," Beyoncé said. "We were very depressed and hurt." Although Knowles and Rowland maintained a dignified silence, the sniping in the press began to take its toll. By November 2000, Rowland was ready to let off steam. "They were very negative and jealous. Am I right? I don't sound mean, do I? I'm just tellin' the truth. They weren't able to do leads by themselves. We went to voice lessons because we wanted strong vocals. They wouldn't do that. They'd just show up when it was time to make money."

The departure of LeToya Luckett and LaTavia Roberson heralded probably the most controversial sequence of Beyoncé's career. When Destiny's Child first crossed over to the UK, all press stories seemed to be solely about the machinations within the group. The fact that Beyoncé's father was their manager and that he had fired Luckett and Roberson because they did not want to be managed by him made the stories even spicier. The publicity generated made Destiny's Child all the hotter.

To give the story further impact, there was also the brief sojourn of Farrah Franklin with the group. She was with Destiny's Child for a grand total of five months; long enough to be heard on their forthcoming single, 'Independent Women Part I', but that was about it. Franklin was asked to join the group in 2000, after playing her bit part in the 'Bills, Bills, Bills' promo. Born in Des Moines, Iowa, in 1981, she had been in a fledgling vocal group called Jane Doe, which ultimately came to nothing.

In the end, Franklin simply could not take the punishing schedule that the group believed in, and was frequently withdrawn and monosyllabic at press conferences. As the group were due to depart for Australia, Franklin, who'd had issues with her bandmates from the get-go, left on the eve of the prestigious MTV awards. "That was such a huge thing for us," Beyoncé said. "It took us nine years to get on MTV. We'd worked so hard to get to that point. Whatever your problems, can't you hold off until you get back to the hotel? It showed how she'd only been in this for five months. That's what happens when you give somebody that kind of success in two weeks and they don't have to work for it."

Franklin went off muttering about disharmony within the group, which strengthened Beyoncé's resolve even further: "Destiny's Child is going to be fine," she told MTV defiantly. "We've done three or four shows already without Farrah and they've been phenomenal."

The group departed for their Australian tour on July 17 without Franklin. With a video shoot beckoning for their forthcoming promo, it was here that the decision was taken to continue as a three-piece. "That's when we officially agreed not to bother looking for a replacement," Beyoncé wrote in *Soul Survivors*. "Kelly said, 'Hey, the *Charlie's Angels* movie is gonna be coming out soon. There were only three women in *Charlie's Angels!*' Michelle said it was a weird coincidence. And I said, 'It's perfect! Ladies, we can do this.' We knew everything had happened for a reason. God had his hand on our group, and it was going to work out just fine – like it had already been written on the wall."

"She just couldn't handle the stress and the work that comes with this," Michelle Williams told *Rolling Stone*. Williams seemed to field most of the questions about Franklin, with many writers smacking their lips believing she'd be next to leave the soap opera that the group was becoming in the popular imagination. "I don't know if she thought that it was going be all fun and games, but it's not." As the pair had roomed together, Williams knew how unhappy Franklin had been over not having a say in the band, having to dye her hair and having to meet their punishing schedule. "I kind of always knew that Farrah would leave the group," Williams was to say. "Farrah could not let her concerns go – like amount of time on camera. She'd say things like 'How come they show Beyoncé more?' And I'd say 'She's the lead singer. So why, when Beyoncé is singing lead, would they want to show us in the background doing nothing?'"

The press was ready and willing to listen to the words of another disgruntled member of Destiny's Child. "I felt like I was losing my identity and I was not being treated as you would personally want someone treating your daughter," Franklin said to the E! show *The Boulevard Of Broken Dreams*. "I just couldn't handle the situation any more, I had to leave." Beyoncé wrote two years later that, "It seemed like Farrah didn't really want to be in a group. I think she wanted to be on her own."

The matter was not assisted by comments Beyoncé made on national television such as, "all of the bad seeds are now out of Destiny's Child. We've had changes and we've finally found the recipe that is perfect."

"That's right," Rowland agreed, making a praying gesture.

"As long as it was Beyoncé and Kelly doing the singing, the belief of all of us was that it wouldn't make a major difference, and sure enough it didn't," Mathew Knowles said in 2001.

What it did do was make the group seem more interesting than they actually were: "Destiny's Child was always very talented, but I think the thing we were lacking was controversy," Beyoncé told *Newsweek*. "I think in order for your group to be successful your story has to be interesting. Our story was very squeaky clean, so I thank God for the controversy. I'm happy because it helps me sell records."

Aside from all the high drama, 2000 was a year of exceptionally hard work, change and consolidation for Destiny's Child. It was the year that was to cement Beyoncé as a superstar. The group toured throughout the year, with their first major worldwide headlining 59-date tour commencing on July 1, with gigs each month until their final show at San José State University on December 31. The scale of their success is typified by their UK shows of that year. They played a showcase in March at the Shepherd's Bush Empire, the historic 2,000-seat venue in West London that started life as a music hall and spent considerable time as the BBC Television Theatre. By November of the same year they were headlining the 15,000-capacity O_2 Arena.

The scale of Destiny's Child's success was due to one song. It was the inclusion of 'Independent Women Part I' as the lead single on the soundtrack to *Charlie's Angels* that changed everything. One night in April 2000, Beyoncé was furious with her boyfriend, Lyndell Locke, wary of the criticism that had been levelled at her with the single 'Bills, Bills, Bills' and shell-shocked by the departure of Roberson and Luckett and reactions to it, and she went into the studio by herself. She wrote what was to become 'Independent Women Part I'. Mathew Knowles and Sony, the parent company of Columbia, heard the track and immediately identified it as the single for the film *Charlie's Angels*, a reimagining of the legendary seventies TV series.

Beyoncé told MTV: "When the label heard it, they were like, 'The song is hot. It has to be on the soundtrack.' Of course, we were like, 'That would be wonderful.' So we changed it up and put a little *Charlie's Angels* flavour in it, and there it was. It was a great experience for us."

With additional writing by Cory Rooney, Jean Claude Olivier and Samuel Barnes, the track – a strident call for female empowerment – was finished by producers Rooney, Dorine Catan and Poke & Tone (Olivier and Barnes). It was recorded at Lobo Recording Studios in New York, with Beyoncé singing the verses and Kelly singing the bridge. Beyoncé produced all the vocals on the track. Initial sessions included Farrah Franklin on vocals as well. As sessions progressed and she became alienated from the group, it is said her contribution was removed.

The original version of the song became 'Independent Women Part II', the single's B-side. It was a jerky dance track in the style of 'Jumpin', Jumpin''. Choosing the slowed down version as the A-side was a masterstroke.

Released in September 2000, with its stuttering beats and announcing the three actresses playing Charlie's Angels (Drew Barrymore, Lucy Liu and Cameron Diaz – "Lucy Liu, with my girl Drew, Cameron D and Destiny, Charlie's Angels, come on") in the record's introduction, it was an irresistible hit, and climbed to number one on both sides of the Atlantic. It refocused the group and introduced them to a worldwide market far beyond the US urban hardcore who had so admired their work to date.

By placing themselves alongside the actresses and the film in the introduction, they were making a huge claim for their own importance, something that the public were to lap up. The sleeve, the first to depict the group as a threesome, also marked out new territory for them. Gone were the floating fabrics or nightclub wear of previous releases; here were Kelly, Beyoncé and – making her sleeve debut – Michelle, dressed in leather, with Beyoncé's cleavage in full view. The girls adopted fight poses.

That 'Independent Women Part I' came from one of the year's highest-grossing films was another bonus. Drew Barrymore (who was to co-produce) had long wanted to re-create the series that made superstars of

Farrah Fawcett, Kate Jackson and Jacqueline Smith. Directed by former video director McG, it was a high-powered romp with its tongue firmly in its cheek. It was described by *Halliwell's Film Guide* as a "light-hearted, hyper-kinetic version of the 70s series. Though its insistence on 'female empowerment' amounts to no more than its stars' ability to do high kicks on wires and look good in skin-tight clothing." Made for a budget of $75 million, the film made over $264 million at the box office. The image of Destiny's Child mirroring the three strident leads in the film helped to cement the group as a trio in the popular consciousness.

The video supporting the single was directed by Francis Lawrence. Filmed in Los Angeles at the end of August 2000, it intercut footage from *Charlie's Angels* and featured Destiny's Child sitting at the top of a boardroom table. They are effectively put through a Charlie's Angels style boot camp in the footage. Much motorbike riding and standing in flames marked them out as strong, independent role models. It sealed the image of Destiny's Child that was to be so all-conquering in the early days of the 21st century. Here was something harder, more powerful, more mature than had been seen previously.

'Independent Women Part I' reached the US top spot in November 2000 and stayed there for 11 consecutive weeks, through to February 2001. The single's success was extended due to the huge box office of the film and the fact that radio simply seemed to adore it, and Sony had prolonged its life by issuing a maxi-single version in time for the Christmas market including a new track, '8 Days Of Christmas'.

In the UK, it went to number one for a week in November 2000 in a very strong chart. There was certainly a willingness, an arms-open readiness to embrace the group in the UK. For the previous few years, The Spice Girls' call for 'girl power' had made that group a global phenomenon. By 2000, they released their final album, *Forever*, and their final single, 'Holler'/'Let Love Lead The Way'. Produced, ironically, by Rodney Jerkins (who had written and produced 'Say My Name'), the single made it to number one (for a week, also), but more as a tribute to The Spice Girls' memory as opposed to any real love for the colourless tunes that they were now releasing. By spicing up their act and aligning themselves with a stellar movie Destiny's Child, on the other hand, effectively became the new Spice Girls in the hearts of those early teens whose ears had been opened to music by the UK five-piece. 'Independent Women Part I' was certified gold in the UK with 250,000 sales in January 2001.

It was clear, worldwide, that things were not going to be the same again for Destiny's Child. By the end of 2000, Roberson and Luckett had dropped their lawsuits against Beyoncé and Rowland. "LeToya and LaTavia have amicably resolved their differences with Beyoncé and Kelly," Randy Bowman, who represented Luckett and Roberson, said at the outset of 2001. Although the suit still stood against Mathew, all parties agreed to stop sniping in the press.

CHAPTER 6

Survivors

"It is difficult to ascertain whether Destiny's Child are genuinely sweet, God-fearing girls, or simply incredibly slick media machines."
Evening Standard, London, 2001

If 2000 had been a breakthrough year for the group, 2001 saw them go stratospheric. Everything hinged around the release of their album *Survivor*. It was a key release, as it was the first full-length album with the group as a three-piece. European markets especially had been selling huge amounts of the repackaged double disc version of *The Writing's On the Wall* in the wake of 'Independent Women Part I' and they were now loudly demanding some fresh product.

In April 2001, Destiny's Child had a bit of unfinished business to attend to, a farewell of sorts to the performances they had given in school halls and gymnasiums for the past decade. The students of Millard North High School in Omaha, Nebraska, had won a radio contest by scraping together 1.6 million pennies to benefit underprivileged children. The prize was a visit from Destiny's Child, booked before 'Independent Women Part I' had taken them into the stratosphere.

Rolling Stone, there to cover the group at the height of this wave of fame, reported:"When the group hit the stage, however, the kids slowly lowered their YOU RULE signs. As the three members of Destiny's Child pranced onstage," writer Jancee Dunn said, "with their tiny gold-lamé hot pants and gyrating backup dancers and glossy make-up and long, long legs clad in gold stiletto boots – it was as if they had just debarked from George Clinton's Mothership. The three impossibly tall glamazons smoothly ran through their hits: 'Independent Women Part I', 'No, No, No', 'Jumpin', Jumpin''. 'How y'all doing over here?' hollered a radiant Beyoncé, her golden hair in a ponytail. Fine, except for the kids who have the wall-eyed look of the Today's Catch section of the supermarket, clearly on funkiness overload." Destiny's Child had honed their act into an all-guns blazing spectacle. The show was an extravaganza, whether they were playing Madison Square Garden or a school hall.

The group knew that whatever they came back with, it had to be something special that would ride high on their current popularity and notoriety, and follow up the ever-growing success of *The Writing's On The Wall*. "The album has sold almost five million records," Beyoncé told MTV. "Everybody is just loving the second album. We would have never known that it would be so successful when we first recorded it. So we're kind of nervous, to be honest with you, because we have to top that. It's possible, because we've grown and we've learned. Definitely the reason why the second album was so good is because we grew and learned tremendously between the first album and the second. We've grown and learned and things have changed . . . so the album will be just as hot." Fortunately for them, it was.

Released on May 1, 2001, *Survivor* will be the album that everyone will recall when thinking about Destiny's Child in years to come. It was polished, balanced and full of hits. Its packaging, styled by Tina Knowles, was like that of 'Independent Women Part I', showing the group now as women rather than the girls of the previous sleeves. It folded out to a poster of the trio looking triumphal standing on rocks on a desert island, a reference to the album's title track.

And 'Survivor' was written to be talked about: Beyoncé, bruised and reeling from the treatment she had received in the press about the personnel shifts within the group, heard a DJ likening the experience of being in Destiny's Child to the then-recent reality TV phenomenon, *Survivor,* on which contestants would get voted off an island weekly until there was a solitary winner. It gave her an idea, a message to all the haters. It was the first song written for the album, and no record better summed up the group's new direction, building on the goodwill and interest generated by 'Independent Women Part I'. "'Survivor' is a message to everybody," Beyoncé said in 2001. "Right from the record label who dropped us when we were young [Elektra Records] to the people who made fun of us for having big dreams when we were in the fifth grade and to the group members who let us down." It was a powerful set of vocals. Beyoncé took the lead, with Kelly singing the middle eight. It also introduced Michelle's strong, gospel-influenced solo vocal towards the end. It ends with an *a cappella* of the chorus to again emphasise, amid all the studio trickery, the power of the three girls' voices. If 'Independent Women Part I' had been a record made in a state of transition, this showed what the new Destiny's Child would be.

Written by Beyoncé, with some input from Mathew and with producer Anthony Dent from State Of Mind Muzic, it was the tale of Destiny's Child, or 'DC3' as they had taken to calling themselves. "The lyrics to the single 'Survivor' are Destiny's Child's story, because we've been through a lot," Beyoncé told *Rolling Stone* in 2001. "We went through our drama with the members, and everybody was like, 'Oh, well, no more Destiny's Child!' Well, we sold even more records after all of the changes. Any complications we've had in our ten-year period of time have made us closer and tighter and better."

Strong, focused, getting back off the ropes – it was a message to all modern women. "When I wrote 'Survivor' I heard some really deep stuff from people that were in rehab and people that lost family members or their homes," Beyoncé was to say about the song's impact. "Every city on our tour, we'd invite kids from the Make A Wish Foundation. We'd sing to them, and the eye contact makes you feel like you did something more than just dancing and whatever. When you write a song like that that connects to people, that's the hugest compliment."

The lyrics could easily be interpreted as highly inflammatory. In the supposed tale of a wronged lover moving on from her boyfriend, there seemed to be little ambiguity in the suggestions that instead of being 'nothing' without them, they sold 'nine million', or in lines like, 'I'm not going to hate you in a magazine' or 'diss you on the Internet' or 'compromise my Christianity'. It seemed to be a flagrant thumbing of the nose to LaTavia and LeToya.

'Survivor' was released as a single ahead of the album in March 2001, and demonstrated that their quality control was unimpeachable. With a video directed by Darren Grant, it depicted the girls being shipwrecked and then surviving on a desert island. First seen emerging from the sea in rags and then dancing on the sand, the girls perform a dance routine before heading into the jungle, where they head to a waterfall with hunting spears. It all culminates in a spectacular dance routine in what looks to be a Mayan temple, where the girls don their camouflage outfits. All the time, a man in the distance is watching them. Subtle it may not have been, but its cartoon-like tendencies translated well around the world. With TLC resting and The Spice Girls disbanded, Destiny's Child had become the biggest girl group in the world.

'Survivor' entered the UK charts at number one in April 2001. In the US, it stalled at number two, behind Janet Jackson's huge success, 'All For You', which spent seven weeks atop the chart. The song would, in true Destiny's Child style, come with controversy. Aside from the lines that would later enrage ex-members, in 2003, a $200 million lawsuit was filed against Mathew Knowles by Miami producer Terrence Robinson, aka 'T-Rob', who alleged he had given a song, 'Glorious', to Mathew and Beyoncé in 2000 before he had copyrighted it that bore striking similarities to 'Survivor'. T-Rob told the world that "right now I would be one of the biggest, most sought-after producers" if he had been credited on the record alongside the Knowleses and Anthony Dent. It wasn't the first rumour that the song was not original. "Three people have said they have either written or did the music or the lyrics were against them," Mathew Knowles told the BBC. "So somebody has got to be lying." Beyoncé's lawyer, Tom Fulkerson, issued a counter-writ, suing Robinson for libel. The matter was settled out of court.

Aside from the title track, and the addition to the album of the almost-a-year-old 'Independent Women Part I', the track which caused most interest was 'Bootylicious', which celebrated the fuller figure. Based around a guitar sample from Stevie Nicks' record 'Edge Of Seventeen', it was a fulsome, sensual paean to the pneumatic posterior. "I want to be healthy and I want to feel good about myself, but my whole life doesn't revolve around dieting," Beyoncé said in 2003. "That's crazy. I think everyone should accept who they are and know that they're like that for a reason, and know that everyone's not supposed to be the same. It's beautiful that everyone's different." It was this positivity and openness that made her a role model for millions of women. In an industry that either demanded women to be ultra-sexual, stick-thin beauties or sizeable mamas with big voices on the chorus, here was a superstar being completely comfortable in her skin.

The track came together from a writing session with producers Rob Fusari and Falonte Moore – who had recently worked with Will Smith on his *Willennium* album. They had a groove together and Fusari suggested using the guitar line from 'Eye Of The Tiger' by Survivor. He didn't have the record at home, so instead used the Stevie Nicks track as a temporary measure. The track remained with them for six months, before Fusari sent it over to Beyoncé for the song selection for the forthcoming album.

Beyoncé was flying to London when she came up with the lyrics to the song. "I was delirious from the long flight," she told writer Fred Bronson. "It was a song of empowerment for people who didn't look like everyone in the magazine. They had a little meat on the bones, a little jelly . . . if someone tells you you need to lose weight or you don't look a certain way, you tell them you're too bootylicious for them."

Fusari – who later went on to mastermind Lady Gaga's initial career – heard various different accounts of the song's inception over the years, but phoned Mathew Knowles after he had heard Beyoncé tell Barbara Walters a different tale about how she arrived at the idea for the track. "He explained to me, in a nice way," Fusari told *Billboard*, "'People don't want to hear about Rob Fusari, producer from Livingston, NJ. No offence, but that's not what sells records. What sells records is people believing that the artist is everything.' And I'm like, 'Yeah, I know, Mathew. I understand the game. But come on, I'm trying too. I'm a squirrel trying to get a nut, too.'"

The record was a neat update of the R&B/rock interface, driven by the nagging guitar part, and its title struck a chord: in 2006, 'Bootylicious' was accepted as a new word into the revered *Oxford English Dictionary*, meaning shapely, voluptuous, especially with reference to the buttocks. Beyoncé was not thrilled at the prospect of this being her lasting contribution to English literature: "I wrote the song," Beyoncé told *TV Hits*, "but I wish there was another word I could have come up with if I was going to have a word in the dictionary." Friend and contemporary Missy Elliott was blown away when she heard the track: "It was like wow, their talking about ass! They've got asses too. It was the first record that felt naughty for Destiny's Child."

'Bootylicious' had a freewheeling video that was part-romp, part-fashion parade. It featured lots of cameos from plus size women gyrating, as well as Stevie Nicks, who was seen re-creating the guitar part that gave the single its bite. The single was released in May 2001, entered the charts on June 9 and reached the US top spot on August 4. In the UK, it reached number two.

The record also made considerable waves in a version that was very popular on the 'mash-up' or 'bastard pop' scene, which took the vocal track from one record and added it to another record's instrumental, often pseudonymously by producers, as this was highly illegal. UK producer Freelance Hellraiser did a version called 'Smells Like Booty', which combined Kelly, Beyoncé and Michelle's vocals with the grunge propulsion of Nirvana's 'Smells Like Teen Spirit', while DJ Frenchbloke combined The Dead Kennedys' 'California Über Alles' with 'Jumpin', Jumpin''. These tracks found their way to market on underground releases such as *The Best Bootlegs In The World Ever. . .* It is sometimes easy to forget that for a considerable while in the early noughties, Destiny's Child were seen as extremely hip.

Dedicated to "all of you who made it through bad relationships, health issues, discrimination, being abused, death of a loved one, loss of a friend, not being popular, low self-esteem, growing up poor, physical limitations, finances, job loss, pain and suffering, drugs and alcohol, sadness, loneliness . . . and survived," *Survivor* was Destiny's Child most cohesive release to date. Using fewer producers with their own signature sound, it sounded like the girls' album.

'Nasty Girl' – which referenced Baltimora's 'Tarzan Boy' and contained elements of the theme from the cartoon show *Peabody's Improbable History* – continued the street sounds of the earlier albums. Produced by Beyoncé and Anthony Dent, it was released as a single in Europe and Australia, where it made the Top 10. While 'Fancy' may be perfunctory, the listener senses the new blend of the group on 'Apple Pie À La Mode', a superb piece of lurching, minor R&B, which recalls Michael Jackson's 'Wanna Be Startin' Somethin'', delivered at a slower pace. Beyoncé's wordplay was getting wittier, and it was clear that producers Fusari and Moore understood Destiny's groove musically.

'Sexy Daddy' takes it further – this is the first song that you truly feel DC1 or 2 could not have delivered. It was produced and written by Beyoncé and Dame – Damon Elliott, the son of Dionne Warwick – who would later go on to write and produce 'Get The Party Started' by P!nk. It has dancehall bhangra and Spanish influences over distinctly Teutonic beats. Yet it is the girls' vocal that truly surprises. It is obvious to see the coaching influence of Kim Woods Sandusky. They sing mostly in unison, in between strange solo vocals, before morphing into a soulful Andrews Sisters. Beyoncé's lyrics are almost nursery rhyme in their quality, restating the need to have fun with her sexy daddy, her sweetie pie. It could be said that this song, more than any other from the Destiny's Child era, struck the template for her risk taking and sense of adventure in her later solo career.

Other highlights included 'Happy Face', another Fusari-Moore co-write. This light rock/R&B shows how the group had broadened its sound for the mainstream market. Although it applied the universal rock cliché that 'everything would be all right', it did so with some élan, and was an autobiographical moment for Beyoncé through all of the recent troubles. ("Woke up and realized/This world's not/So bad after all"). It was one thing being a teenager with a raft of issues, and another having to deal with negativity in the press over the group. Beyoncé biographer Janice Arenofsky suggested that it was another example of Beyoncé "writing and recording songs that were cathartic – a therapy-like activity she used to unburden herself of negative emotions and energy".

The ambiguous intensity abates with 'Dance With Me', which displays a relentless positivity over a sun-kissed dancehall groove. There was also an opportunity for a solo showcase by Beyoncé, 'My Heart Still Beats', which set out her diva credentials. On 'Dangerously In Love', Beyoncé talks about the future in 'his' eyes, and it is a 21st century example of the classic spiritual/secular love song. She is dangerously in love with her man/and or God. "Created in this world to love"; over such a delicate, meandering groove, it demonstrates quite how remarkable Beyoncé's voice was becoming.

The fourth and final single from the album, released in November 2001, was 'Emotion', the Barry and Robin Gibb-penned 1978 hit for Australian singer Samantha Sang. Given the riches elsewhere on *Survivor*, it was slightly strange to go with such an obvious cover. That said, obvious covers are easily identifiable, and The Bee Gees have something of a track record for creating big hits. Produced by Mark J Feist, it was a slow-tempo, downbeat acoustic version of the song, and followed the pattern of many of the songs of the album, with Kelly singing the first verse, Beyoncé the second and Michelle the third. It reached number 10 in the US, prolonging the album's sales life, and number two in the UK. It became a radio anthem in the wake of the 9/11 attacks. It was also accompanied by a split-screen video directed by Francis Lawrence, which featured all three girls in separate states of emotional turmoil, before uniting together at the end.

The two final songs on the album highlighted the condition of this new Destiny's Child. The 'Gospel Medley' of 'You've Been So Good'/'Now Behold The Lamb'/'Jesus Loves Me'/ 'Total Praise' was the group's third and final dedication to Andretta Tillman. Beautifully arranged and perfectly sung, it put gospel music more powerful than on spiritual albums into millions of world households. It would be the last time the group would refer to 'Miss Ann' on their album sleeves. Critics could argue it was on there just to show Roberson and Luckett that Beyoncé and Kelly cared as much about her too, and they were clearly making this point.

If the 'Gospel Medley' was all about the past, then 'Outro (DC-3) Thank You' was about the future. Over techno-style glitches, the three members speak to each other of their love and belief in Destiny's Child, and give thanks and praise to God, but especially to Michelle for joining the group. There was no past now for the group, there was only the future.

Destiny's Child's blend of sexual and spiritual on *Survivor* made reviewers sit and up and listen – it was here that their buffed up, not-exactly-the-girl-next-door shtick debuted, a mass of provocative poses and pouts, of innuendo and strident statements, blended with a straight-ahead appreciation of Jesus and incorporation of family values. It was as attractive as it was incongruous. One thing was certain – they had the tunes. Pop historian Simon Warner summed the album up thus in a thoughtful review on popmatters.com: "Black and beautiful, these three glamazons, these simmering sirens of Jesus, may prove to have more than just staying power." The reviews in the music papers for the album were mixed, but generally positive. *NME* said, "*Survivor* is brimful of staccato Timbaland skew-beats and a heroic disregard for the 'all-important' milkman whistleability factor. It is, quite frankly, nuts." *Spin* magazine suggested, "*Survivor* is relentlessly inventive in its recombinations." *Rolling Stone* said, "The only real weakness on *Survivor* is the self-righteous tone creeping into the songs." *New York Magazine* took a slightly less positive tone: "All fifteen tracks are one-dimensional disses and dismissals of scantily clad women, vengeful boyfriends, and the group's assorted doubters." Simon Reynolds wrote in *Uncut* that, "As a self-portrait, though, *Survivor* is incoherent, cutting from the coquetry of 'Bootylicious' ("I don't think you're ready for this jelly") to the prudish 'Nasty Girl', which reprimands a scantily-clad tramp for flaunting her flesh. And even when the bump'n'grind is rhythmically in full effect – the almost-great 'Sexy Daddy' – the raunch is sabotaged by tame, lame lines like "Sweetie pie/I think it's your lucky night." It was of little consequence what reviewers thought – ultimately, the album went on to sell over 12 million copies worldwide.

Although *Survivor* did not sell as many as *The Writing's On The Wall* – which was promoted over a longer period of time – Destiny's Child went stratospheric. The album rocketed to the top of the US charts, selling 663,000 copies in its first week, the highest week-one sales figures in Columbia Records' history. They also became the first female group to reach number one with an all-new album of material and the first to top the charts for 24 years, since a Diana Ross and The Supremes hits collection reached pole position. In the UK, the album topped the chart and made Destiny's Child the most successful US girl group, with two number one singles from the same album. To underline the album's success, Destiny's Child spent most of 2001 on tour, and their live shows became ever more spectacular.

The album worked because the group's sources and references were remarkable and substantial. They had grown significantly through their first two albums, and their experience was building. Beyoncé was gracious and almost regal at this stage. Brushing aside any bad press or ill will resulting from the split, the group was clearly refocused, with her at the dead centre. The Vincent Skeltis photograph of Destiny's Child as The Supremes in February 2001's *Vibe* magazine shows perfectly the shift in power. Rowland looks convincing and serene as Mary Wilson, while Williams conveys the clumsy innocence of Flo Ballard perfectly. But in the middle, with her hand above her head as Diana Ross, was Beyoncé. With her mouth opened in a broad smile, her gown was simpler, more straightforward than the others, yet her earrings stole the show – a three-drop-pearl affair, they screamed superstar. Throughout the next decade Beyoncé would frequently be compared with Ross, something that culminated in Beyoncé playing Deena Jones in *Dreamgirls*.

Mathew Knowles and Music World Entertainment came increasingly under the spotlight – people were curious to see and read about the mother and father team that controlled the group. In a revealing article for *Ebony* magazine, 'The Untold Story of How Tina & Mathew Knowles Created The Destiny's Child Gold Mine', the couple laid to rest many of the myths surrounding them, such as them forbidding Beyoncé to have boyfriends, that they were living off their daughter's money and that they were adoptive parents to Kelly. It concludes with Mathew making the prescient statement, "Five years from now, I'd like for them to have happiness and financial freedom. I can see them in movies and doing separate solo projects."

CHAPTER 7

Carmen And The Independence Of Beyoncé

"We desperately need a rest from the public and the world. And during that break we are going to work on solo projects, then we will come back and do more Destiny's Child records."

Beyoncé, 2002

As Beyoncé had proved the photogenic centrepoint for Destiny's Child, it was only a matter of time before her looks and talent were co-opted into movies. And within a matter of years, she had two significant roles under her belt. The transition from singer to actress is not always the easiest or most commercially viable. Although Diana Ross started her movie career spectacularly with *Lady Sings The Blues*, *Mahogany* was a significant misstep. Whitney Houston created a huge stir in the blockbusting *The Bodyguard* in 1992, but was less graciously received by the time of *The Preacher's Wife* in 1996. Mindful of that, Beyoncé began her movie career in a low-key manner.

MTV approached Beyoncé to play the lead role in *Carmen: A Hip Hopera* in 2000. They had seen her act in the Destiny's Child videos and felt she would be perfect to play the title role of the siren Carmen in a new version of Bizet's opera. The network wanted to update the forties Broadway musical and the fifties Dorothy Dandridge/Harry Belafonte film *Carmen Jones*, scored by Oscar Hammerstein II, that had recast the opera with African-Americans. The new version was an 88-minute made-for-television film that was premiered on May 8, 2001, coincidentally the week of release of *Survivor*.

The character of Carmen was a complete opposite to Beyoncé. The God-fearing 19-year-old was not, as Beyoncé wrote, "a devious and shady lady". As Carmen, she had to be an evil, seductive actress whose love for policeman Derek Hill (Mekhi Phifer) gets her into all sorts of trouble, especially when she falls for rapper Blaze (Casey Lee) in the New York ghetto. She fights, she seduces. On seeing the initial script, Beyoncé asked for the role to be sweetened slightly and so more was made of her unintentionally causing trouble, rather than the devious nature of the original character in Bizet's work. What really concerned her was the seduction scene. "I knew that in order for me to seduce a guy, I would have to do something that was, well, seductive. At the same time I had to maintain my image and not do anything I wouldn't want kids to see." Image again. Beyoncé knew she was too recent a star and currently too much the media's sweetheart, to jeopardise anything. "I was not about to participate in an R-rated love scene, and yet, if I wanted to be an actress, a real actress, I had to play this part. I had to realise that I wasn't playing Beyoncé; I was playing Carmen. She is not a Disney character! This movie was a lot sexier than Snow White!"

Beyoncé learned a great deal during the three-month shoot of *Carmen*. She understood the principles of acting, and, although always used to playing in a team, here she was only one small part of it, as opposed to being the star. It tested her comfort zone fully for the first time, especially the fact that she was living in LA, and for the first time in over a decade was not with Kelly and didn't have her family in the same house. "I had to talk to directors, learn how to communicate my concerns, and speak up for myself," she recalled. "Essentially I grew up a lot, as both a woman and a businesswoman." Away from the other girls, the experience forced her to interact better in social situations, without the safety blanket of Destiny's Child. Beyoncé in interviews was no longer asked about the group, or if so in passing, but more about her personal life and her current situation. As she commented, "My downtime during *Carmen* forced me to learn how to talk to people, let my guard down, and be myself – all of that stuff that most girls probably learn how to do when they're 13." It had a great effect on her; "Besides Kelly and Michelle, I'm not around people our age for more than 45 minutes," she told *Rolling Stone*. "So I was around people my age for a month and a half, and I made friends. So it was way more than a movie for me."

Carmen: A Hip Hopera was broadcast to mixed reviews. There was, of course, a great novelty in seeing hip-hop stars such as Mos Def, Da Brat, Jermaine Dupri, Wyclef Jean and Rah Digga alongside Blaxploitation icons such as Fred Williamson re-creating the world famous opera. That said, it lacked finesse and struggled to get over its basic conceit. It did, however, demonstrate that Beyoncé had great potential as an actor. Although tentative at times, she came across exactly as she did in her videos.

Destiny's Child had become superstars, and were asked to join many superstar bills. They had played the VH1 tribute concert for Diana Ross in April 2000. On January 20, 2001, they played a concert for new Texan-born US Republican President George W. Bush's inauguration at the Lincoln Memorial Theater in Washington, alongside Clint Black, Van Morrison and ZZ Top. During their US tour, on September 7, 2001, Destiny's Child completed their move into the establishment by performing 'Bootylicious' at Michael Jackson's 30th Anniversary Special at Madison Square Garden in New York. They played in the company of Marlon Brando, Elizabeth Taylor, a reunited Jacksons, Britney Spears, Ray Charles and Liza Minnelli. They mimicked Jackson's dance routines during their performance and joined the all-star cast for the closing rendition of 'We Are The World'.

Destiny's Child's US tour was halted due to 9/11. As the event continues its journey from world-shattering event to a line in history books, one must stop, pause and reflect on the enormity, the scale, the complete and utter shock of the moment. "All I could think about was how I just wanted to go home," Beyoncé wrote. By a twist of fate, her father was in New York, her mother in Houston and her sister Solange in Seattle, while Beyoncé and the girls were in Los Angeles, preparing for the Latin Grammys, which were swiftly cancelled. The group had been in New York just days earlier for the Jackson tribute concert. Beyoncé rode out the experience by praying through the answerphone to her mother.

The group played benefit concerts in New York City and Washington, DC. The Concert For New York City, staged at Madison Square Garden on Saturday 20 October, 2001, showed the company Destiny's Child was now keeping. More than 6,000 of the 20,000 capacity was made up of firefighters, police officers and rescue workers who were onsite as the World Trade Center was targeted by al-Qaeda. The concert was "a special way to remember the 343 firefighters who were lost". Destiny's Child played alongside artists of the calibre of David Bowie, Bon Jovi, Jay-Z, Billy Joel, Eric Clapton, Mick Jagger and Keith Richards, The Who, James Taylor, Elton John and Paul McCartney. Although extremely nervous, the trio performed their latest release, 'Emotion', and a gospel medley that Beyoncé had arranged especially for the show. The stripped-down, raw, emotional appearance showed that the group were not simply a manufactured studio confection. In Washington, DC the following night, the group performed, at the advice of Mathew Knowles, 'Survivor', which had an extra-special resonance with the American people. "It was the best crowd response and energy for that song because it was so real and so many people felt it," Beyoncé reflected. Because of the flight bans and the general paranoia that resulted in the weeks and months after the attacks, the group cancelled their European tour. It was shifted into the next year.

Kelly surveyed the audience during the performance of 'Emotion' and looked to her bandmates for comfort. "We felt how they were feeling. They were crying and holding up pictures and big pieces of paper that said 'I Miss You'. It made us really emotional. I thought, 'Oh my gosh, I'm so thankful that I'm still breathing.'"

There was also other family business to attend to that year. Solange Knowles, Beyoncé's kid sister who, five years younger than her, had watched the group grow up, and had deputised at times because of various illnesses and absences, got her chance to record, and Kelly, Michelle and Beyoncé supported her. With the group, she recorded the theme song for *The Proud Family*, the animated series that was a big hit on the Disney Channel. She was also to sing with Destiny's Child on 'Little Drummer Boy' for their forthcoming Christmas album, which the group had been recording throughout summer 2001. It contained seven traditional Christmas songs and four new specially written pieces. Working with 12 different producers, they crafted *8 Days Of Christmas*, which sat somewhere between the usual festive fare and uptown R&B.

Released in October 2001, the album reached number 34 in the US charts and was certified gold. Kelly took lead vocals on a version of 'Do You Hear What I Hear', while Michelle sang 'O' Holy Night' and Beyoncé sang 'Silent Night'. The album's lead track, '8 Days Of Christmas', was written by Beyoncé and Errol 'Poppi' McCalla, Jr., who had worked with the group on the track 'Emotions'. Opening with the sound of 'Jingle Bells', the song updated the festive standard, 'The 12 Days Of Christmas'. Gone were drummers drumming and leaping lords, instead replaced with a list of the material gains that modern women could expect, from the generosity of a beau. The 'baby' gives a candlelit dinner, a Mercedes, a voucher for CDs, diamond rings, a poem and a back and foot rub. It was this track, written in 1999, that hatched the idea for the whole album. The song had first appeared on the 2-CD UK reissue of *The Writing's On The Wall*.

The group ended 2001 with an appearance on *Oprah*, promoting the album. Dressed in white, they performed '8 Days Of Christmas'. It had been a remarkable year. The group had won *Billboard* Artists of the Year, and they had also announced that they were going to take some time to embark on solo projects. There was a Japanese and European leg of the tour to complete, which ran from May to June 2002. After that, it would be time to strike out on their own.

On February 7, 2002, Destiny's Child joined a select band of performers by appearing on the still-groundbreaking television show *Sesame Street*. Although a long time had passed since acts like Stevie Wonder would appear on the show and Luther Vandross and Nile Rodgers were in its touring band, it still had a potency for promoting education and racial tolerance to a pre-school audience. On Episode 3984 in Season 33, the girls appeared singing 'A New Way To Walk' with Grover, Elmo and Zoe.

Also released during this period was *This Is The Remix*, a 12-track confection of remixes from the first four years of the group's career. Released on March 8, 2002, it featured Da Brat, Missy Elliott, Wyclef Jean and The Neptunes and underlined what splendid company Destiny's Child kept. And how shrewd Teresa LaBarbera Whites' A&R policy had been. As the tracks had often been strewn across the various formats of CD singles and 12"s that accompanied their single releases, *This Is The Remix* was a neat encapsulation of the urban side of the group. Dedicated by the group to "all the producers and remixers that helped make this CD bangin'", it opened with the extended version of Wyclef Jean's 'No, No, No (Part 2)', which had first highlighted their music's remix potential back in 1998. Most successful was The Neptunes' (Pharrell Williams and Chad Hugo) reconstruction of 'Emotion' as a beat-heavy funk. The extended mix of 'Jumpin', Jumpin'' with Lil' Bow Wow emphasised quite how aggressive the synthesised pulses were during this era of the group, before opening out into lush disco-house. The girls revoiced quite a few of the tracks, and the album also contained the *Charlie's Angels* soundtrack-only track, 'Dot', in its E-Poppi mix. The song, a minor work, is a chronicle of Beyoncé's feelings regarding the stress she suffered during the departure of Roberson and Luckett.

This Is The Remix also pointed to the future. The bonus track, 'Heard A Word', was a Michelle Williams solo track, from her then-forthcoming solo album, *Heart To Yours*. It seemed strange not to hear Beyoncé on a Destiny's Child number. Its position on the album was a clear expression of thanks for the support and encouragement Michelle had provided to Kelly and Beyoncé during the two years she had been in the group.

With its striking cover image of the three girls applying their make-up to get out on the town, *This Is The Remix* was an upbeat, defiant end to the superstar phase of Destiny's Child. It was a stopgap that meant that the group had released three albums in the space of a year. *Slant Magazine* said about the release: "Any new Destiny's Child material? No. Scam to get your money? Yes. Good fun? Of course." Showing how strong their fan base was, the album reached number 29 in the US charts, selling over 100,000 copies. It reached number 25 in the UK.

The release of *This Is The Remix* also reignited the dispute between Destiny's Child and its ex-members. In particular, the track 'Survivor' had stoked Luckett and Roberson's ire. It was suggested that it was a carefully calculated swipe by Beyoncé that certainly gained maximum publicity for Destiny's Child. Luckett and Roberson issued a new lawsuit in February 2002. They had been assuaged by getting to keep their publishing share of the songs written for Destiny's Child, but their old group was now seemingly ridiculing them. Those tricky lines in 'Survivor' such as, 'I'm not gonna hate you in a magazine', seen as a direct reference to their split, were released again on the *Remix* album. It therefore breached the terms of the previous settlement agreement that prevented either party from making 'any public comment of a disparaging nature concerning one another'.

The matter was further inflamed when the song won a Grammy for Best R&B performance by a duo or group. The lyric that seemed to cause the most hurt to Luckett and Roberson was quoted in the lawsuit filed in a Houston federal court: 'You thought I wouldn't sell without you/sold nine million.' Tom Fulkerson, Destiny's Child's lawyer, was dismissive. "It's unfortunate," he said in Houston, "that the plaintiffs have nothing better to do with their time than to dream up new lawsuits to file."

It could be argued that the out-of-court settlement – so amicably agreed upon – was another part of the process to garner maximum publicity. The wake of the court case left Beyoncé vulnerable, and only several years later did she talk about the depression that she was heading into. She was also aware she was fair game and stories appeared frequently in gossip magazines, including those claiming she'd had at least two abortions with Lyndell Locke, and that she was an insufferable diva. "I had my days where I cried, where I was like, 'Why are they doing this?' But eventually people started seeing who I really am," Beyoncé said in 2003. "If you say all these things about someone, you have to have some facts to back them up and no one could ever tell a story. No one could ever say that I was mean or unfair, so eventually it went away. Once you get a certain level of success then there has to be some kind of scandal for people to talk about and if there's not one, they'll create one."

The old saying of 'where there's a hit, there's a writ' seemed to ring true throughout the early 21st century for the group and their manager. It was reported that Mathew Knowles suddenly found himself being sued in June 2002 by the two sons of Andretta Tillman, Armon and Chris. They alleged that he had appropriated $32 million of Destiny's Child's earnings that should have gone to Tillman's family from the group's early success. Beyoncé was reportedly deeply embarrassed by the allegations, which did not reflect well on her or her mother. It is not reported how the case was settled

At the height of this first flush of fame, it became apparent that Beyoncé was not at all well. It later transpired that she was suffering from depression. According to reports, in between engagements, she would take to her room and refuse to eat. She decided not to discuss the matter with the world's press, as she was concerned about what impression it would create. Nineteen-year-old freshly minted superstars are supposed to be the happiest people in the world.

In 2002, the group published their book, *Soul Survivors: The Official Autobiography Of Destiny's Child*. Written with James Patrick Herman, it detailed the girls' career from birth to their hiatus. Although light and, like all authorised books, easy to swallow, it was a heartfelt reading of their tale from the three main protagonists. It made you realise that no matter how swaggering and sensual they were portrayed in their promo clips, these were still little girls who had done nothing since their childhood other than practise for the stardom they were now enjoying. Beyoncé underlined their need to take a breather in its pages. "Destiny's Child is more than a full-time job, it's a twenty-four seven lifestyle, and it can be exhausting. We have been out and about for nearly three years non-stop. We desperately need a rest from the public and the world. And during that break we are going to work on solo projects, then we will come back and do more Destiny's Child records." And at this point, Destiny's Child were no more.

CHAPTER 8

"Yes Sir, I'm Cut From A Different Cloth": *Goldmember, Crazy In Love* And The Entrance Of Jay-Z

"I just don't talk about it. I see a lot of the actresses that have had successful relationships and I see that a lot of people don't talk about it. I just wanna protect my private life."

Beyoncé, 2004

As she prepared to embark upon her solo career, Beyoncé told *Vibe* magazine in 2002 that "if nothing happens with our solo records, there's still Destiny's Child. And if something happens with our solo records, there's Destiny's Child." However, Beyoncé's first major move in her new Destiny's Child-sabbatical solo career was in film as opposed to music. Her choice of *Austin Powers In Goldmember* meant that she wasn't going to appear in any old film – she had aligned herself with one of the most successful comedy franchises of all time.

By the turn of the 21st century, the Austin Powers series had become very big business indeed. Canadian comic actor Mike Myers had created the first film, *Austin Powers: International Man Of Mystery*, in 1997, as a spoof not only of James Bond but, more importantly, all of the copycat films that followed in the wake of the Bond films in the sixties. Myers has in his sights all of the huge, Technicolor examples of tongue-in-cheek excess with secret agents such as Matt Helm and Derek Flint. With his intimate knowledge of British humour (Myers' parents are both from Liverpool and he holds a dual passport), he could exploit every British seaside postcard joke and use risqué terms unknown to Americans – most notably the word 'shag', the UK slang for intercourse, which in the US has no sexual connotations, and is merely a bird, a type of carpet pile or a dance.

Austin Powers: International Man Of Mystery and its 1999 follow-up, *Austin Powers: The Spy Who Shagged Me*, were both huge successes at the box office. Everyone loved the silliness of the enterprise, and the central gag was a good one – Agent Powers and his nemesis, Dr Evil (also played by Myers), have both been cryogenically frozen in the sixties and are defrosted to continue their battles in the modern day. Elizabeth Hurley played Powers' female sidekick, Mrs Kensington, in the first film, a direct pastiche of Diana Rigg's role as Emma Peel in the sixties TV series *The Avengers*.

While the first film had grossed $67 million worldwide, the second, which featured Heather Graham playing Powers' love interest, Felicity Shagwell, took $312 million. It was clear that with business like this, a third film would go into production. Myers, looking for more rich seams to mine, brought Powers into the seventies, which provided an opportunity to satirise the Blaxploitation film genre.

The film, which was to become known as *Austin Powers In Goldmember*, began casting in 2002. Beyoncé went along with her mother, Tina, and met Jay Roach, the director, Mike Myers and producer Toby Emmerich, to audition for the role of Foxxy Cleopatra, a composite of seventies Blaxploitation film heroines Foxy Brown and Cleopatra Jones, and Powers' principal female interest in the film. "I was not my usual calm self for the *Austin Powers 3* audition," Beyoncé wrote. "The environment didn't help at all – the office was stuffy and the lights were too bright. It was uptight and intense. It hardly helped to make me feel shagadelic.

My heart was beating fast, my mouth was dry, my palms were clammy – I had to wipe my hands on my pants before I shook hands with Mike Myers." Myers, however, was charm itself, putting Knowles at ease with his repertoire of impressions and joke telling.

When asked by Emmerich how she felt about doing a comedy, she replied, "I love comedy, but I don't know if I'm all that funny." Although she was concerned that she could well have failed the audition, Myers, Roach and Emmerich thought she was funny enough, and she got the part. It was also a shrewd move as she was one of the most recognisable faces in the world at that juncture and could easily raise the film's profile among the teen audience.

The film is a good bit of fluff. There are many high jinks from Myers, including knowingly sending up his own franchise, with stars queuing up to perform cameos. In the opening sequence, Tom Cruise plays Austin Powers, Gwyneth Paltrow his love interest and Kevin Spacey is Dr Evil. Myers, as Powers, is watching a dramatisation of himself in a movie theatre. It is a film within a film, one of myriad in-jokes that rattles through the script. Stephen Spielberg directs this film within the film, and music legend Quincy Jones provides the score. Britney Spears, Ozzy Osbourne and John Travolta take cameo roles as well. Michael Caine appears as Powers' father, Nigel. It was clear that the series had reached a certain level of pulling power, now that celebrities of such magnitude all wanted to be in on the joke. However, the series formula is stretched as far as possible, with jokes about Preparation H, and all the groovy swinging is, by now, a tad lame.

Dutch millionaire Johan Van Der Smut, also known as Goldmember (a chance for Myers to overplay a Dutchman), has the key to a global tractor beam that will melt the polar ice caps, and the only way to stop him is to go back to 1975 and halt his evil work. He is hiding in his roller disco, Studio 69, in New York.

Thirty minutes in, Beyoncé appears singing in a vocal trio at the club, an affectionate homage to Studio 54, the club that so influenced Beyoncé's parents' generation. With her sister, Solange, and singer Devin, she sings 'Hey Goldmember.' The trio appear more Three Degrees than The Supremes. The song is a well written and produced pastiche of KC

& The Sunshine Band's '(That's The Way) I Like It'. Accompanied by much general excess in the roller disco, it was a memorable introduction to Beyoncé in her first Hollywood blockbuster.

Not the most demanding of roles, Foxxy is one of Austin's old paramours and also an FBI agent. When she learns she will be moving into the future to defuse the rather tenuous grand plan of Goldmember, she screams, "The future better get ready for me, I'm Foxxy Cleopatra and I'm a whole lot of woman." The basic problem throughout the film is that she isn't really. She appears tentative, and rather too young to be playing Powers' foil, a part defined perfectly by the winking ripeness of Elizabeth Hurley as Mrs Kensington. She grimaces a lot during the character Fat Bastard's (played with relish again by Myers) farting scene. There's also a little broad comedy at Beyoncé's expense: Dr Evil and Mini Me (Verne Troyer) deliver an amusing Jay-Z parody during the film, performing their version of his hit 'Hard Knock Life (Ghetto Anthem)'.

Austin Powers In Goldmember stands or falls on where you stand on smutty humour, such as when Powers praises Cleopatra's translation skills: "You're a cunning linguist, I'm a master debater." Whereas Hurley or Graham would be in on the joke, it actually seems distasteful that Myers is reciting such dubious material to a girl in her early twenties. Jokes are wrung out without subtlety. Fundamentally, the part for Beyoncé is simply a succession of hats and bra tops. There is a marvellous scene where she sends up Ursula Andress' role as Honey Ryder in the first James Bond film, *Dr. No*, when Beyoncé shakes out her Afro as she emerges from a wetsuit.

Austin Powers In Goldmember made up for slightly threadbare material with a series of dazzling set pieces and a parade of past-their-prime gags. The film received a mixed reception. *The Sun* called it "an absolute treasure trove of laughs". *The Observer* suggested it was "an aimless, scatological pastiche". *Halliwell's Film Guide* describes it as an "amiable spy spoof, though most of the jokes are of a rude and rudimentary kind", and concludes "in the end, though, its childish glee wears you down", But, no matter what critics felt, *Austin Powers In Goldmember* was huge. The film grossed $71.5 million in its opening weekend in July 2002. It was a tentative start in Hollywood for Beyoncé but, overall, a good one.

Her delay in issuing new material meant that by the time she released her first non-soundtrack single in 2003, there was enormous anticipation. Her first solo single was featured over the film's closing credits. 'Work It Out' was enjoyed – much loved even – but it was somehow dismissed simply as a film project offshoot. Produced by The Neptunes, at that point possibly the hottest production team on the planet, it was grinding, futuristic funk. Although it topped the US Hot Dance Club chart, it failed to make the mainstream US charts. In the UK, however, the song reached number seven. It was widely loved in the UK press: *NME* said, "'Work It Out' is an absolutely faultless take on classic JBs & Lyn Anderson super-heavy funk"; and also "it's Beyoncé yowling, testifying and wigging out in only slightly studied retro fashion that's most striking. Uh! Good God! She's gonna do her thing!" Directed by Matthew Rolston, the video that supported 'Work It Out' was a fantastic re-creation of seventies dirty US, with Beyoncé in a studio surrounded by a 10-piece band containing a variety of funk freaks. She gets the opportunity to work through some soul moves and most notably apes Tina Turner. It is rawer, more mature and less staged than her previous video work with Destiny's Child.

Thanks to the film, Beyoncé was everywhere. Celebrity sponsorships and endorsements started to roll in. After previous endorsements from Houston-based Pro-Line hair products and then New York's Candie's Shoes, at the end of 2002, Beyoncé's finances received another major boost. She was chosen as the face of Pepsi, replacing the troubled Britney Spears. She appeared in a series of commercials, culminating in the brand's *Gladiator* homage which saw Spears, Beyoncé and P!nk perform Queen's 'We Will Rock You' in a Roman amphitheatre.

Shawn Carey Carter, known worldwide by his persona Jay-Z, first met Beyoncé at The Concert For New York City in October 2001. Within 18 months they would be recording together and would begin a relationship. It was ironic that only Michelle Williams noted the group's meeting him in Destiny's Child's autobiography, *Soul Survivors*. By 2002, he was one of the most successful US rap stars ever. 'Jay-Hova', to give him another of his monikers, came to embody the ultimate rags-to-riches rap dream, advancing from poverty to power, through his rhymes combining incredible dedication and conviction.

Peter Shapiro, writing in *The Rough Guide To Hip-Hop*, suggests that "replacing Biggie, Nas and Christopher Walken as the King Of New York, Shawn Carter's status is such that both the streets and the charts call him Jay-Hova . . . his relaxed flow and attention to hip-hop punctilios make Jay-Z the most influential, if not the best, MC around." More than simply a rapper, he was the founder, with Damon Dash and Kareem 'Biggs' Burke, of Roc-A-Fella Records and the owner of clothing line Rocawear. His business acumen was later to propel him to the position of president of no less a label than Island Def Jam in 2004, where he worked at the heart of the Universal organisation, the largest record company in the world, for five years. He has a net worth of over $450 million and has won 13 Grammy Awards.

Born in the Bedford-Stuyvesant area of Brooklyn, New York, in December 1969, Jay-Z has been described as many things, but the *Village Voice's* outline of him as a "hustler poet" is one of the very best. His recordings are complex and sincere. From his 1996 debut *Reasonable Doubt* onwards, his work has been thoughtful, and although he initially ran with artists such as The Notorious B.I.G (his second album, *In My Lifetime*, was dedicated to the then-recently killed B.I.G.), he soon transcended his East Side gangsta origins.

Carter was anxious not to replay himself, and consequently created new sounds, ever more inventive, with each subsequent release. "The easy and safe thing to do would be to re-create the last album," he said in 1999. "I don't want to have a safe career. Sometimes you're not gonna agree with the stuff that I do, but I'm gonna take the challenges, I'm gonna bring people new and exciting stuff so that I can grow as an artist. And then hip-hop can grow."

And growth is what Jay-Z has always been about. Although it was his friend Eminem who successfully became the Elvis Presley of rap, Jay-Z became its key entrepreneur, less flash than his old producer Sean 'P. Diddy' Combs. He was also a controversial figure, as different to Beyoncé as was humanly possible – an adolescent crack cocaine dealer; he sang choruses like "Jay-Z and Biggie Smalls make you shit your drawers".

He feuded, old-school style, with other rappers such as Nas; and, more seriously in 1999, he stabbed a rival, Lance 'Un' Rivera, in a New York nightclub. Although he initially denied the incident, he was later charged and given three years' probation. He has also released some incredible music, including his 2000 high-water mark, *The Blueprint*, some of which was produced by his protégé Kanye West.

Despite coming from very different backgrounds, Beyoncé and Jay-Z got on very well during the making of their first duet together, '03 Bonnie & Clyde', a track produced again by West for Jay-Z's 2002 album, *The Blueprint 2: The Gift & The Curse*. It had a video (that featured Lance Reddick, who went on to play Cedric Daniels in the HBO drama *The Wire*), which showed them behind the wheel of a car heading towards Mexico. Jay-Z makes clear his intent: "You ready B? Let's go and get 'em." The only time this couple doesn't talk is "during *Sex And The City*". All they need is each other. It is fascinating to see how Beyoncé has accentuated her African-Americanism in the video. Whereas Destiny's Child emphasised her light colourings, here her baseball cap and crop top relocate Beyoncé right in the heart of the ghetto.

Two and a half minutes in, the song offers Beyoncé one of the best vocal opportunities of her career when she breaks into Prince's 'If I Was Your Girlfriend', from his groundbreaking 1987 album *Sign O' The Times*. The video is a classic tale of police evasion, and provides an iconic reading of a mythological American tale.

What Jay-Z and Beyoncé shared in common was an appreciation of business and hard work. The pair soon started a relationship. As news leaked out, it was irresistible for the media: Jay-Z, the ultimate mogul who had grown up on the wrong side teaming up with Beyoncé Knowles, the God-fearing girl from down South. Although the duo would remain discreet and fairly cagey about their relationship, they would provide a sweet and enduring love story throughout the noughties and theirs has become one of the most significant and talked about relationships in popular culture.

Beyoncé was quizzed about the relationship by *Glamour* magazine in 2003. She retorted sweetly: "I've learned that it's better if I don't talk about my personal life relationships. I once said that I needed a boyfriend and it was everywhere that I was lonely and desperate. People just take things and twist them up . . . We honestly did bond and glide together. I was really lucky to have him help me. All in all, he's just a great person and he always has so many great ideas."

When Beyoncé appeared in the DVD of the tour documenting Jay-Z's retirement from live performance in 2003, *Fade To Black*, her screen time was brief, but it is clear to see that Jay-Z was smitten. Beyoncé continued her reticence to discuss the relationship when speaking with *Rolling Stone* in 2004: "I don't say I'm single," she said. "I don't deny anyone. I just don't talk about it. People are like 'Why does she say that they're just friends?' I don't say that. I just don't talk about it. I see a lot of the actresses that have had successful relationships and I see that a lot of people don't talk about it. I just wanna protect my private life."

Beyoncé was photographed again for *Vibe* magazine by British photographer Kayt Jones in October 2002 for the article 'The Metamorphosis', written by *Vibe* editor, Mimi Valdes. It took as its basis Maya Angelou's autobiography, *I Know Why The Caged Bird Sings*. Known as "America's most visible black female autobiographer", Angelou's 1969 book laid bare the racism and struggles she faced. It didn't matter if a majority of the magazine's readers or Beyoncé's listeners were entirely unaware of the reference, it made for a wonderful photograph; but Beyoncé knew the reference and what it meant not only to her parents, but the parents of her fan base. This new solo star was an artist with depth and understanding. Her Afro was in full, unruly effect, and her look was one of sexuality, provocation and command. Since Beyoncé is standing in front of a screen, however, there is an implicit suggestion that this is simply another moment in the dressing-up box.

Beyoncé's newfound blackness coursed through her next single. However, while 'Work It Out' was an exercise in homage, her next release would define Beyoncé as a solo artist and demonstrate to the world that she no longer needed her group. 'Crazy In Love' was a bold, audacious calling card of a single. Whereas 'Work It Out' saw her toying with the funk of her *Goldmember* screen persona, Foxxy Cleopatra, with 'Crazy In Love', everything changed. This was a new, confident, grown-up woman.

The idea for 'Crazy in Love' came from producer Rich Harrison. It was a strident, adult record that united the old school with the new school. Beyoncé rushed into Sony Music Studios in New York one day to find Harrison tinkering on a new song he'd written, but he simply couldn't find a suitable lyric to go with it. Flustered, Beyoncé is alleged to have caught sight of herself in the glass of the studio and said that she was looking 'crazy right now'. That gave Harrison an idea, and the central lyric motif was born. Realising that the song needed a killer horn riff, he reached back into his record collection and found the 1970 Chi-Lites hit 'Are You My Woman (Tell Me So)', with its enormous brass section figure. Beyoncé was initially unsure of its retro sound, as she had just been there with her last single. She had fully embraced old-school soul with 'Work It Out', and although it had been a Top 10 hit in Britain, it had hardly made a mark in the US charts. But there was something about this new song; she knew it could work. Her new beau, Jay-Z, dropped by the studio late on and got involved in the production, making up his rap more or less on the spot, and allegedly not writing it down. His Master of Ceremonies role added drama to the proceedings.

Released on May 18, 2003, 'Crazy In Love' operated something of a scorched earth policy. It was like there had never been a Destiny's Child, any other singles, no films, nothing to this point. This was bold, screaming immediate soul. It is hard to explain now just how exciting it was when you first heard this record. Beyoncé explained 'Crazy In Love' to *Glamour* magazine in 2003: "The song talks about how, when you're falling in love, you do things that are out of character and you don't really care because you're just open. The song came from me actually looking crazy one day in the studio." Its chugging, raving 100bpm swagger and infectious chorus made it the record of that summer.

However, it was the video that really took the song around the world. Directed by English-born filmmaker Jake Nava, it captured completely the feel of this new Beyoncé. She said to MTV that she wanted the video to celebrate "the evolution of a woman. It is about a girl who is at the point of a relationship. She realises that she is in love, she is doing stuff she would not normally do but she does not care. It does not matter she is just crazy in love." Shot on a deserted road similar to LA's storm drains system, famous for their appearance in *Grease*, Beyoncé appears in the middle of the road, about to be run over by a Cadillac hurtling towards her as Jay-Z delivers his opening rap from the back seat. The car stops as Beyoncé asks her audience 'if they are ready'. The immovable object has halted the irresistible force.

And then Beyoncé marches towards the camera in her vest top and tight denim hot pants and red high heels. Shorn of the intricate outfits that marked out Destiny's Child's finest moments, here was Beyoncé, raw, *au naturel*. She walks up to a platform and performs what can only be described as an overtly sexual dance, with an electricity warning sign clearly visible.

She is then lifted above the streets to a rooftop for the chorus, to perform on a podium with straightened hair. Night falls and her dancers (including future Pussycat Doll Carmit Bachar) gather round her. Beyoncé is now in street attire with a baseball cap on. Together they perform the defining action of the video – what has become known as the 'booty bounce'. Each of the dancers and Beyoncé raise their arms above their heads and vigorously shake their behinds in time to the tracks irritatingly catchy 'uh-oh-uh-oh-uh-oh-oh-no-no' refrain. In the second chorus, she insouciantly blows a bubblegum bubble, intercut with footage of her looking sultry, ready to ensnare her prey.

Jay-Z reappears; his baseball hat silhouetted against the night, looking every inch the menacing street figure of urban mythology. He flames his Zippo lighter and hurls it to the ground, finding a line of petrol, which leads to a car, soon a raging inferno. Beyoncé is quite literally playing with fire, again capturing the zeitgeist of the moment, as many were wondering what a God-fearing girl was doing with a bad boy like Jay-Z. She appears draped in fur and dances around him. She kicks open a fire hydrant to cool the situation down, dancing in silhouette, getting drenched under the showering fountain of liquid. The video ends with her and her dancers performing a final routine in front of a huge fan, as if to dry out. Beyoncé's hands run up and down her body, and there is frequent finger biting. The final shot is of her looking away from the camera seductively chewing her thumb. The video is symbolism a go-go.

It is remarkable, then, that in some respects the video still manages to seem wholesome. No brazen sexual activity has happened, no swearing, no nudity. It's true we've seen arson, and lots of shaking behinds, but it manages to capture the essence of Beyoncé. She's all grown up now, but there is still a decent core to the performer.

It was both a fantastic record and a memorable video. The record picked up two Grammys the following year: Best R&B Song and Best Rap/Vocal Collaboration. At the BET Awards, it won Best Collaboration and Best Female R&B Artist, and to show how cool the record was, it was the *NME* Single Of The Year in the UK, an award previously won by Bob Marley & The Wailers, Sex Pistols and Joy Division.

Jake Nava's video scooped three awards from MTV – Best R&B Video, Best Female Video and Best Choreography. The song topped the charts in the UK (where in early 2004, Beyoncé performed it at the BRIT awards), US and Ireland, and was a Top Five hit in New Zealand, Norway, Denmark, Holland, Hungary, Switzerland, Australia, Belgium, Italy and Canada. As her first 'proper' solo single, 'Crazy In Love' was the best selection possible. It is a release apart. It joined 'Independent Women Part I' as Beyoncé's second all-time classic track.

'Crazy In Love' captured the zeitgeist perfectly. It had the appropriate mix of sex and sass, an innovative video, an easy-to-copy dance, and, most of all, was tremendous fun. It was grown up enough to bring in an older audience, but daft enough not to lose the Destiny's Child fans who were growing older with their idol. *NME* was to vote it the Best Song Of The Decade in 2009, and it has been covered by artists as diverse as Snow Patrol, Hue & Cry, Antony and the Johnsons and The Puppini Sisters. Could Beyoncé emulate this success over a full-length album on her own?

CHAPTER 9

Dangerously In Love

"I know that folks love me as a pop star. Now I want them to understand me as an artist."

Beyoncé, 2003

Beyoncé's debut solo album, *Dangerously In Love,* flirted with her new grown-up persona: hanging with Jay-Z, strident in her sexuality, an independent adult. Unlike the haste with which Destiny's Child's albums were assembled (usually, towards the end of the group's career, in about two weeks), Beyoncé spent time and care putting her first album together. Although flawed, it is the sound of a 21-year-old growing up, and ruminating on the subject of love. "Love is something that never goes out of style," Beyoncé told MTV. "It's something everybody experiences, and if they are not in love, people usually *want* to feel that. So if you hear the album, it's very romantic."

Recorded in Houston, New York, Florida, Miami, Atlanta and Stone Mountain, Georgia, and made by over 60 people, *Dangerously In Love's* title was a clear reference to her being with a rougher crowd. Forty-three tracks were recorded for the album, resulting in the final 15 track selection. As time passes, it is an album that, although a little gauche at times, is a very confident calling card. Before she started recording,

Beyoncé had to decide who to work with. She had meetings – 30 minute interviews – for two days solid with key producers from the East and the West Coast to decide who would produce the album.

Dangerously In Love is a finely balanced concoction that references most of her influences. There is material for the hip-hop community, the girl-group lovers and, importantly for crossing over, the older crowd. Beyoncé was clear about this in her interviews supporting the album: "I want them to hear all of the musical influences from hip-hop to rock to jazz, there's even a Shuggie Otis sample," she told New Zealand culture magazine *Thread*. "I want them to really hear the talent. I know that folks love me as a pop star. Now I want them to understand me as an artist." It had a new sound, and a cohesion lacking from Destiny's Child releases. It is a sensual album that explores the condition of the heart. On *Dangerously In Love*, Beyoncé is a 'Naughty Girl', who wants to 'Be With You,' her 'Baby Boy', a 'Hip Hop Star', who leaves her 'Speechless'.

The most significant problem of *Dangerously In Love* was how to follow the strength of its opener, the now worldwide hit, 'Crazy In Love'. Although it created such a positive overture for the rest of the album, it also found some of the lesser material wanting in its wake. UK publication *NME* definitely thought so: "B sounds genuinely, hip-grindingly fruity and, consequently, the whole thing *reeks* of The Nasty. Sadly, ['Crazy in Love' is] so good, a deep shadow is cast that the rest of the album never manages to escape."

Overseen by Dr Dre/Christina Aguilera producer Scott Storch, 'Naughty Girl' contained elements of Donna Summer's 'Love To Love You Baby', a classic sultry piece of bedroom soul. Storch brought his hip-hop dancehall and reggaeton experience to the production and crafted an Arabic-influenced piece of R&B. It was chosen as the album's third single in March 2004, and reached number three in the US, and number 10 in the UK. Its video was a fruity homage to Cyd Charisse and Fred Astaire's dancing in the 1953 film *The Band Wagon*, with Beyoncé dancing at a club while being watched by singer Usher, who joins her for a routine midway through the performance. It culminates in Beyoncé frolicking onstage in an oversized glass of champagne, with bubbles becoming bath suds as Usher liberally covers her legs with the foam. She ends on top of a piano while confetti showers her. 'Crazy In Love' director Jake Nava captures Beyoncé's new naughty-but-nice approach.

Featuring Jamaican dancehall superstar Sean Paul, 'Baby Boy' was a Bollywood-influenced groove. It details Beyoncé's fantasies and talks about a world where music is the sun and the dance floor is the sea. It likens this world, full of tunes and love, to her paradise. In keeping with the rest of the album, it conveys the shock and surprise of deep-felt passion; after years singing about it, the listener feels as if she is truly experiencing it. Produced again by Storch, it is grinding, modern, at times atonal and incredibly infectious. When released as a single in August 2003, it gave Beyoncé her second solo US number one and remained at the top of the chart for nine weeks, a week longer than 'Crazy In Love' had been there. It was only kept off the UK top spot by The Black Eyed Peas' all-conquering 'Where Is The Love?'. Its video, directed again by Nava, found Beyoncé writhing lustily in various scenarios. It was another clear marker between the visual stridency of Destiny's Child's promos and the overt sexuality of the solo Beyoncé. In the instrumental break, Beyoncé's athleticism runs riot as she somersaults and gyrates on the sand.

Not forgetting her urban roots, Big Boi and Sleepy Brown join her on 'Hip Hop Star'. It's a strange, almost-out-of-place track. All a little weird, it contains the line, "Take off that tank top and pull off them drawers/the girls all pause, got them dripping down they sugar walls," suggestively intoned by Brown. Lisa Verrico of *The Times* said that the track was "the highlight by a mile ... Rock guitars, heavy bass and a truly odd rhythm combine behind Beyoncé tripping out lines like Björk – you'd never guess it was her – a bumpy rap by Outkast's Big Boi and some chirpy couplets from Sleepy Brown." It was another welcome sign that she was very much ready to experiment. Although the record doesn't get this strange again, the fact that she was willing to place it on the album showed her fearlessness.

Beyoncé's playing to the older crowd is nowhere more obvious than on the track 'Be With You', a marvellous confection that unites Shuggie Otis' 'Strawberry Letter 23' and Bootsy Collins' 'I'd Rather Be With You'. The sultry suggestion of the lyrics shows Beyoncé's authority over the material. It relocates the seventies bubbling sleaze of the originals to a clean, crisp modern jazz-funk. This sultry groove continues on 'Me, Myself And I', which was chosen as the album's third single in October 2003. It is a sensual, slow groove, co-written by Beyoncé, Robert Waller and its producer Scott Storch. After the invention of the album's first two singles, this was much more along conventional lines. Beyoncé said that the song was one of her favourites on the album, as it showed the strength that can be gained from a break-up. "It's kind of like a celebration of the break-up . . . ," she told MTV. "I like to look at it when something like that happens that the guy kind of taught you a lesson and now you know yourself and now you know better than those excuses." Swedish director Johan Renck oversaw its promo. Renck had enjoyed hit singles under the name Stakka Bo, before directing for artists such as Kylie Minogue and New Order. After the glitter and writhing of the previous promos, 'Me, Myself And I' featured Beyoncé leaving a relationship in reverse. The video begins with her walking backwards through a door, through sobbing baths, heartache and ultimately the break-up. It is intercut with her singing, with straight, sober hair, on a chaise lounge.

'Yes' was written and produced with Focus, another direct link with the old school. He is the son of CHIC's co-founder, bassist and writer, Bernard Edwards, who passed away in 1996. The record owes something to The Isley Brothers' 'Sensuality', all sensuous grooves, lazily tinkling piano, and Beyoncé's expressive vocal. However, the song still suggests some propriety; Beyoncé is being bugged by a suitor, who refuses to believe her as she declines, presumably, the sexual act. The idea came to the singer as she was contemplating the demands of superstardom. "I can sign a million autographs and the first time I have to say, 'Sorry, I'm gonna miss my plane,' it's like I never signed the other million," she continued. "That happens all the time with all different situations of life. That's why I thought it was such a good concept."

'Signs', written by Beyoncé with Craig Brockman and Nisan Stewart, was another bit of mid-seventies tosh updated, a sweet slow jam about birth signs being played out like an astrological quiet storm. Any reference to the woman-conquering showboating of The Floaters' massive 1976 hit 'Float On' is dismissed with this sensual groove, abetted

Performing 'Déjà Vu' on *MTV's Total Request Live*, July 12, 2006 in New York City. *The Village Voice* called the song "a luxuriant wide-screen love-crazy squelch-funk jam". (EVAN AGOSTINI/GETTY IMAGES)

Beyoncé and Jennifer Hudson perform Best Original Song nominee 'Love You I Do' from *Dreamgirls* at the 79th Academy Awards ceremony, Kodak Theatre, Los Angeles, February 2007. (MICHAEL CAULFIELD/WIREIMAGE)

The Dreams made real. Jennifer Hudson, Anika Noni Rose and Beyoncé arrive at the premiere of *Dreamgirls* in New York City. (LUCAS JACKSON/REUTERS/CORBIS)

Wearing Armani (not Deréon), Beyoncé holds Grammy for Best Contemporary R&B Album for *B'Day* in the press room at the 49th annual Grammy Awards in Los Angeles. (MIKE BLAKE/REUTERS/CORBIS)

Another year, another award: accepting the International Award of Excellence at the 2007 American Music Awards in Los Angeles. (MIKE BLAKE/REUTERS/CORBIS)

A family affair. Tina, Solange and Beyoncé, 2007. (MIKE BLAKE/REUTERS/CORBIS)

Performing at the 50th annual Grammy Awards, Los Angeles, February 2008. (MIKE BLAKE/REUTERS/CORBIS)

Who's the queen? Beyoncé and Tina Turner at the 50th Grammy Awards. Aretha Franklin was quoted as calling Beyoncé's introduction as a "cheap shot for controversy". (MIKE BLAKE/REUTERS/CORBIS)

The businesswomen at the helm of their clothing empire: Tina and Beyoncé, wearing Deréon, naturally, in Yonkers, New York. (CORBIS)

"I could not be more honored and excited that they have asked me to be part of this moment in history." Singing 'At Last' to President Barack Obama and First Lady Michelle during their first dance at the Neighborhood Inaugural Ball in Washington, January 20, 2009. (RICK WILKING/REUTERS/CORBIS)

Beyoncé performing at Day One of Essence Music Festival in New Orleans, July 3, 2009. (ERIKA GOLDRING/RETNA LTD./CORBIS)

Beyoncé holds aloft one of the three awards she won at the MTV Europe Music Awards at O2 World in Berlin, Germany, November 5, 2009. (RAINER JENSEN/DPA/CORBIS)

Shakira and Beyoncé backstage during the 2009 MTV Europe Music Awards. (KEVIN MAZUR/WIREIMAGE)

"I would like for Taylor to come out and have her moment." Beyoncé rescues the night for Taylor Swift, allowing Swift to finish her speech that was cut short by Kanye West, during the 2009 MTV Video Music Awards. (CHRISTOPHER POLK/GETTY IMAGES)

Sasha in all her glory: The I Am tour arrives at the Honda Center ,Anaheim, California on July 11, 2009. *Eyeweekly* stated that "watching her direct her show was like seeing a real-life Evita in action." (KELLY A. SWIFT / RETNA)

by Missy 'Misdemeanor' Elliott's superior rap at the end. Beyoncé, a Virgo, catalogues a list of what she expects from men with various star signs, potential mismatches of the zodiac, and then ends with the ambiguous line, 'I was in love with a Sagittarius.' Sagittarius is Jay-Z's star sign. "People can come to whatever conclusion they like," Beyoncé said about the song. "That's the beauty of music."

'Speechless' continues the downtempos of the middle of *Dangerously In Love* and captures Beyoncé heading straight for the bedroom, in a wilder, more abandoned manner than previously. Talking directly about making love, this sounds to be a new, liberated woman. "As soon as I heard the track it inspired me," she said. "It's very sexy, very sensual. The sort of ballad that I've never done before. This song is definitely a population increaser!" With her saying it feels "so crazy to be in your world", it sounds as if it is another direct paean to Jay-Z.

'That's How You Like It' is built around 'resung lyrics' from 'I Like It', DeBarge's 1982 Top 50 US hit. Produced by D-Roy and Mr B, it marks Jay-Z's second appearance on the album. This light, frothy pop ditty sounds not unlike 'Happy Face' from *Survivor*. A sister in some ways to '03 Bonnie & Clyde', it sounds pretty much like an unalloyed love duet between Beyoncé and Jay-Z. She calls him 'thug' and he calls her 'baby thug'. Jay-Z talks about the difference between the public persona of rappers and their private life. Sweet and slight, it demonstrates the overall feeling of warmth that pervades most of the album.

What located the album not just in the old school, but in the building that was on the site before it was demolished and the old school was built, was its duet with Luther Vandross, 'The Closer I Get To You'. Vandross, by now a 52-year-old grandee of music, represented the very heart of smooth soul. Written by Marvin Gaye's former percussionist James Mtume and his writing partner Reggie Lucas, the song had been a hit for Roberta Flack and Donnie Hathaway in the late seventies. It was another track that underlined Beyoncé's heritage. Produced by Vandross's team, Nat Adderly, Jr., and with background singing by the very cream of the New York session players – Tawatha Agee, Brenda White-King and Cissy Houston. It is a rich, creamy take on the track. As Vandross' biographer, Craig Seymour, noted, "Luther adored Beyoncé because, even as a relative newcomer, she exhibited traits of all Luther's favourite artists. She dazzled with the shimmering glamour of Diana Ross, the somewhat detached poise of Dionne Warwick and the melismatic gusto of Aretha Franklin."

Sessions were at New York's legendary Hit Factory studios on West 54th Street in early spring 2003. Beyoncé was surprised at how hot the studio was, but Vandross assured her that the humidity was important to keep his voice at its best. Initially nervous of recording with such an industry legend, she was immediately disarmed by Vandross, who displayed his sense of humour, cracking jokes and putting her entirely at ease. And all this from a man her parents had listened to incessantly back in Houston. The track also appeared on the album that was to become Vandross' swan song, *Dance With My Father*, which became his biggest-selling release. "It was a dream come true," Beyoncé said. "He has so much soul it makes your heart hurt." It attracted many critics for slavishly copying the original, but frankly, they were wrong. It is one of the great baton-passing moments in R&B, with a mass-market icon of the eighties passing on to a performer his equal for the noughties.

Luther Vandross had a massive stroke soon after the album was recorded, and lived for only another 18 months before giving in to the pain his body was enduring. His illness affected Beyoncé deeply, especially as Vandross, a man with a legendary reputation of not suffering fools gladly, was impressed with her vocal prowess. The credits on *Dance With My Father* had her in the 'Very Special Thanks column' with 'Oh My Goodness' in front of her name. Busta Rhymes and Stevie Wonder did not receive that accolade.

'Dangerously In Love 2' revisits the song that Beyoncé first sang on Destiny's Child's *Survivor* album. Stripping it of some of the electronic beats of the original, there is otherwise little difference. The song seems charged with meaning here; especially when Beyoncé does her own harmonies. It's rougher and less rehearsed than with Destiny's Child, but it works perfectly on this album, a voyage for the singer growing from a child to a woman.

Dangerously In Love had a hidden track: 'Daddy', nestling at the end, is a straight tribute to Mathew Knowles. Initially recorded too late to meet the album's original deadline, Beyoncé smuggled it on the album, an act of independence from Knowles' role as executive producer. It's a little too raw and personal – her double-tracked vocal catalogues family melodramas such as the reaction to the acquisition of tattoos and boyfriends being brought home. It meant a great deal to Beyoncé to have the track on the album, which she had recorded without her father's knowledge. He was speechless when he first heard it, as it is, by Beyoncé's own admission, a really heavy song. She suggests that whoever her life partner becomes, or who her unborn child is, they must be like her daddy. Cynics grabbed the song and sneered at its cloying undertone; *Rolling Stone* said it was a "five-minute tribute to her manager-father that is an anthology of vocal and lyrical clichés". It marked the first steps toward her future independence, as a fulsome celebration of her father, but also sowed the seeds of her moving on.

Dangerously In Love was packaged beautifully with a full range of new photographs. It was art directed by Ian Cuttler, who worked with the photographer team Markus Klinko & Indrani. The Tina Knowles-styled shots had Beyoncé in a hotel room with a wild afro, a blue bra top and hot pants; a double spread of her lying on pebbles in a stunning gown; and a picture of her standing in front of the sun. Yet the back sleeve of the booklet had her in between two other versions of herself – as if she was not quite ready to leave behind being part of a trio. Beyoncé was fulsome in her thanks. Halfway down the second column of thank yous on the CD she said: 'Thank you to all those who challenged and criticised me. The tears & sweat still lead to triumph and success." And it was a triumph of hard work, and impeccable A&R.

Beyoncé was justifiably proud of her debut solo album. "This time because I only had to write for myself, my songs are much more personal," she said. "I also wanted beats that were harder and to be able to collaborate with other people. Basically this record was a chance for me to grow as a writer and a singer. There are more ballads. The vocals aren't as precisely produced and because it's just me, there aren't as many harmonies." Her comments in interviews about the recording process without Destiny's Child made speculators wonder if it would all soon be over for them. "I felt free, because I could go into the studio and talk about whatever I wanted, but in many ways it was actually harder to be on my own creatively," Beyoncé said. "I depend so much on Destiny's Child (Kelly Rowland and Michelle Williams) to tell me if they like something or not. I'm so critical of myself that it's scary to have to depend on your own instincts."

Released on June 22, 2003, the album was rapturously received by the public. It won five Grammys, and sold over six million copies worldwide. However, *Rolling Stone* was not glowing when it wrote about the album: "The record quickly slips into a series of bland bedroom slow jams – 'Be With You' and 'Me, Myself And I' – which come off like trite retreads of seventies R&B, and Missy Elliott's dull piece of pop astrology 'Signs' can't stop the bleeding. The ballads – even a duet with Luther Vandross on 'The Closer I Get To You' – don't measure up to the uptempos on *Dangerously in Love*, and the dance tracks are in dangerously low supply." Although *NME* adored 'Crazy In Love', it was dismissive. "Big Boi and rapper Sleepy Brown both rub a gloriously lazy, spliffed-out rap-marinade into the droning, faux-psychedelic 'Hip Hop Star' and the effect is so startling you barely notice the sumptuous Pink Floyd-flavoured guitar solo steal, but there's precious little else to be dangerously in love with here." *Entertainment Weekly* suggested that, for the most part, "Ms. Knowles does more reinventing than revisiting – a dangerous prospect, but hey, that's love." The *Los Angeles Times* concluded that, "Mostly what she says, in varying degrees of urgency and tenderness, is that she wants to get it on."

Dangerously In Love captured Beyoncé at a contented point in her life, finally able to come to terms with the scale of her success, reflective and enjoying new love with Jay-Z. It is a coming-of-age record; arguably not better than her recent work with Destiny's Child, just different. "I'm very, very happy with every aspect of life," she said. "My personal life, my career, everything. I have things that I worry about but I also have honest people around me that are like, 'You should calm down.' My goal is to enjoy my life and I'm doing that." This breakneck pace would continue throughout the next six years.

★

As the album raced up charts around the world, audiences had the opportunity to see Beyoncé in her second feature film, the Jonathan Lynn-directed *The Fighting Temptations*. Released on July 9, 2003, this good-natured comedy featured Cuba Gooding, Jr. as Darrin Hill, a New York executive who learns he has come into an inheritance in Monte Carlo, Georgia, the small Southern town where he grew up. The only thing he has to do to get his money, however, is to create a gospel choir to win the annual Gospel Explosion competition.

Beyoncé played the role of Lilly, Darrin's former childhood sweetheart and now small-town bad girl, with relish. After all, it was taking her back to the very comfortable, home surroundings of the church. "I grew up in the church," she told rapper Fat Joe, who interviewed her for MTV. "I sang in the choir for two years – not that long because I was on the road since I was nine – but this was kind of like going back home, you know? Every time we did a scene with the choir, it was so powerful. It didn't feel like we were working. We had jam sessions."

It was a grounded, small film as opposed to the comic-book excess of *Austin Powers In Goldmember*. "The last movie was over the top," she continued. "It was big. In this one, I play someone very earthy. The clothes were not very glamorous, no make-up, my hair was almost dreaded. I went out of my way to look unglamorous because I wanted to be taken seriously. And basically someone in the South wouldn't have the glitz and the glamour." The film was amusing, low-key and unashamedly sentimental.

There is a really good film somewhere inside *The Fighting Temptations* struggling to get out. It is at once a satire and an embracing of the Southern Baptist church (there is a recurring gag of a woman frequently falling over as she is "slain by the spirit"). The church building often has messages outside such as 'Beware of brief delight and lasting shame', and there is a strong moral code from the church treasurer Paulina (LaTanya Richardson). Ultimately, however, the film centres on the age-old battle of the sexes. The men are seen as either liars – Darrin; weak – the Reverend Lewis (Wendell Pierce); exaggerated caricatures – local taxi man Luscious (Mike Epps); or stoned and drunk – DJ Miles Smoke (Steve Harvey). The women do not fare a lot better, but they are frequently seen as voices of reason. Lilly is strong and family-centric, exposing the hypocrisy of the church: Paulina is terrifying; Mary Ann is erudite and committed.

The film starts in 1980 when Darrin's mother, Mary Ann, is banished from the church with young Darrin for wanting to sing secular music as well as singing in the choir. Although her Aunt Sally (Ann Nesby) tries to defend her, she is cast out. When Aunt Sally dies 23 years later, Darrin returns for her funeral and to learn that her will asks that he leads the choir.

Beyoncé handles admirably what she is given to do, which is, principally, look aggrieved, be sultry when singing and then doe-eyed as she falls in love. As she is revealed singing the Cooley-Davenport standard, 'Fever', sensually in a club, her screen presence and star power are right out of the Golden Age of Hollywood. The film adheres to convention; jump-cutting through inappropriate auditions for the choir; Darrin's gradual epiphany that his roots are where he belongs. Ultimately it is an affectionate homage to the US gospel tradition and an opportunity to see some of its biggest gospel and R&B stars on the big screen. Shirley Caesar delivers a remarkable performance at Aunt Sally's funeral. The O'Jays perform a fantastic turn in a barbershop singing Paul Simon's 'Love Me Like A Rock'. Five Blind Boys Of Alabama get a rare opportunity to appear onscreen. Melba Moore and Angie Stone add incredible weight to the film. Gooding is affable at its centre.

Although she is hardly pushed to her limits, Beyoncé actually works well in this. Reportedly paid a $1.5 million fee, she was delighted to work with UK-born director Lynn. "When I found out Jonathan was doing it, I was like, Perfect', because his past work is so great," she told MTV during filming. "And I met with him and he made me feel really, really comfortable. I also feel comfortable because I [am] able to sing in the movie again, and before I did a movie that was all acting, I wanted to do another one to get more confident." She asked Lynn to give her time to retake scenes as she wanted to get her motivation right. She was also unhappy about having to kiss onscreen, but Gooding put her totally at ease. It is when singing that she comes alive; her version of 'Swing Low, Sweet Chariot' in prison is moving; the in-church version of 'Love Rain Down' with Gerald Levert, Angie Stone and Melba Moore is stunning, although at times she looks somewhat out of her depth with such experienced grandees of music. But there is a satisfying symmetry in seeing Beyoncé alongside such great singers as Levert, Stone and Moore.

The film ends with Darrin proposing to Lilly onstage at the Gospel Explosion competition, after the choir have slain the audience with a blockbuster performance. All hokum, of course, but pleasingly executed. Beyoncé enjoyed working with Cuba Gooding, Jr.: "I respect him; he's very talented. He's one of the things that attracted me to the movie. I was a little nervous. After I met him, he made me feel really comfortable and he treated me like I have done movies before."

The Fighting Temptations was not loved by the critics: although *Empire* said that "Saturday night disposable fluff is rarely as warm-hearted or exuberant as this", and *Variety* praised its "strong ensemble cast", *The Guardian* suggested that, "Frankly, this film ought to be on sale in bags to rose growers outside farm shops and garden centres." *Halliwell's Film Guide* says that "not even some impassioned vocals can save this sickly entertainment, with its banal narrative and a frenetically tiresome performance from Gooding".

However, Beyoncé emerged well from the film. At least, she was given something to do, rather than simply being dressing. Influential critic Roger Ebert of the *Chicago Sun-Times* said, "Although it represents Beyoncé Knowles' first starring role, it's not in awe of her. It uses her in the story instead of just pushing her to the front of every shot, and she comes across as warm and sympathetic." *The San Francisco Chronicle* said that Beyoncé was the "main musical attraction of the film – she sings 'Fever' as though she were Rita Heyworth in *Gilda*".

The film cost $15 million to make and returned around $30 million at the box office. There was talk of a sequel, and indeed the film is left quite open at its dénouement to follow Lilly and Darrin's adventures. But it didn't catch flame. Ultimately, the film was simply just OK. Ebert summed up the low-key, good-natured premise perfectly: "*The Fighting Temptations* is not brilliant and it has some clunky moments where we can see the plot wheels grinding, but it has its heart and its grin in the right places."

Its accompanying soundtrack was a great treat, as it works as a sample of soul and gospel music. Executive produced by James 'Big Jim' Wright, and producers extraordinaire Jimmy Jam and Terry Lewis, it was released in September 2003. It featured most of the songs from the film, plus the track 'Fighting Temptation', which placed Beyoncé alongside Missy Elliott, MC Lyte and Free. The slinky, grinding rap was released on single to coincide with the film's release, but it failed to register in the US, despite being something of a success in mainland Europe. Produced by Beyoncé's now fairly long-term collaborator, Elliott, it was a fun, funky slice of R&B.

The soundtrack was also interesting for featuring the first new Destiny's Child material since *Survivor* in 2001. 'I Know' was a sweet, downbeat track produced by Soul Diggaz that also later surfaced as their contribution to the official 2004 Olympic album. It is a sultry, acoustic guitar-driven number featuring will.i.am, the mercurial rapper/producer from The Black Eyed Peas. It was a low-key reintroduction to Destiny's Child, who would be everywhere again by the corresponding time in 2004. 'Don't Fight The Feeling', a fabulous slice of bhangra-influenced R&B featuring Papa Reu, was an opportunity for Solange to demonstrate that she could at least be in the same company as her sister.

'Everything I Do' is arguably Beyoncé's best moment on the soundtrack. It is a smooth and understated love song shared with Philadelphia rapper Bilal, who had achieved critical and commercial acclaim with his 2001 album *1st Born Second*. Jam and Lewis bring every scrap of their experience to the production and writing of this astonishing late night slowie. 'Summertime' was a lovely southern R&B jam originally considered for *Dangerously In Love*, and featured Jay-Z's old running mate P. Diddy. Although it was a low-key soundtrack release, put out virtually at the same time as Beyoncé's debut solo album, *The Fighting Temptations* soundtrack should not in any way be dismissed as filler. The whole album evokes a sweltering summer night in the American South.

Mathew Knowles had been busy too. When not having lawsuits filed and dropped against him, his stock as not only the successful manager of the dormant Destiny's Child, but also the mastermind behind the three girls' solo careers, could not have been any higher. In October, he sold Music World Entertainment to the then-blossoming entertainment corporation the Sanctuary Group for a reported figure of $10 million. Although his signed artists would still release on their own labels, he would be free (and underwritten) to develop new artists, especially those on the gospel side. "I'm not looking for acts to sign that require million-dollar budgets," Knowles told *Billboard*. "I'm looking for acts that require $150,000 recording budgets and $100,000 videos. You don't have to sell three million records to break even. We can sell 200,000 and make a profit." He was also instrumental in getting Beyoncé deals with many huge American brands. He signed a deal with Tommy Hilfiger Toiletries for her after considering whether she should merely endorse, or get her own line. For this moment, endorsement would suffice. Beyoncé became the spokesperson for Hilfiger's new True Star fragrance range.

The American TV viewing public got to see Beyoncé and Jay-Z onstage on August 28, 2003, when they performed together at the annual MTV Awards ceremony. On the night, she won three awards: Best Female Video, Best R&B Video and Best Choreography for 'Crazy In Love'. She was lowered on to the stage by her feet in a harness, landing on a *chaise longue*, to deliver 'Baby Boy', surrounded by four men in head-to-toe dark blue body suits with their faces obscured. As they writhe extensively around her, she gets increasingly theatrically flustered, before breaking out into a well-choreographed routine with her five dancers.

The number of dancers doubles as the beat breaks down after a minute and a half. The unmistakable intro to 'Crazy In Love' pipes up. The dancers spiral away and then, in a chain, they all do the 'booty bounce' that already had become notorious after the video for the single. Beyoncé steps forward for one of the best performances of her life. We are now in full-on Sasha territory. A strange interlude with a man who flashes her in coloured underpants, a respite, a drink of what looks suspiciously like Pepsi-Cola, the appearance of an all-male entourage and then, suddenly, Jay-Z charges the stage with incredible swagger turned up to at least 11. Although Beyoncé's performance was clearly lip-synched, it was an athletic appearance that, like all of her actions that year, marked a defiant line in the sand between her now, as a 22-year-old grown up, and her juvenilia with Destiny's Child.

Before performing solo for the first time in America, Beyoncé undertook a short nine-date European tour, between November 3 and 19 in 2003, built around the London premiere of *The Fighting Temptations*. Simon Garfield from *The Observer* met her for an interview and got a glimpse into her hectic lifetsyle: "The date and location of this interview had been changed four times because the schedule was packed to bursting, and during this time I had become familiar with a few nuances of the Beyoncé travelling lifestyle," he wrote. "If something is '98 per cent certain to happen' in her world, it will almost certainly not happen. If it's 100 per cent certain, it may happen, but almost certainly not as planned. 'I'm so glad this interview is finally going to happen,' I said to the director of communications for Sony as we waited in a Wembley Arena bar waiting to be summoned towards Shorty. 'Shhhh!' he said. 'Tempting fate.'"

Her dates were well received, culminating in the release of a live DVD from her two shows at Wembley, filmed on November 10–11, 2003. The shows featured a mix of *Dangerously In Love* and *Fighting Temptations* material, as well as a Destiny's Child medley. The performances began with Beyoncé being lowered by a harness upside down, as she had at the MTV awards.

The year 2003 had been incredible for Beyoncé, and a vindication of Destiny's Child's decision to take a sabbatical. In the United States she had had a number one album and spent 17 weeks atop the singles chart with just two singles, 'Crazy In Love' and 'Baby Boy'. However, that was not a patch on her next two big nights out; singing 'The Star-Spangled Banner' at the XXXVIII Superbowl in Houston on February 1, 2004, and then at the 46th Annual Grammys on February 8.

At the Superbowl, dressed soberly in a cream two-piece suit, Beyoncé was walked on to the field of the 69,500 capacity Reliant Stadium by General Peter Pace, the Vice-Chair of the US Joint Chiefs Of Staff. Introduced as "multiple Grammy Award Winner and Houston Native, Beyoncé Knowles," she gave an impassioned rendition of the US national anthem. Beyoncé joined an impressive list of previous performers, such as Diana Ross, Whitney Houston, Neil Diamond and Billy Joel, who had performed the song, and looked genuinely overcome with emotion at its end. It had been quite a journey from the Headliners salon in Houston to its Reliant Stadium in little more than a decade.

The Grammys was equally momentous. It was of huge significance to Beyoncé as she garnered five awards for her work on *Dangerously In Love*, including the Grammy for Best Contemporary R&B Album. And it deserved it: despite reservations about its slide into lachrymose ballads as the album progressed, it was a work ahead of its time, made – not least – by a 22-year-old, and housed one of the greatest pop singles made by anybody.

What made the night more special for her was realising one of her greatest wishes: duetting with her idol Prince. At Los Angeles' Staples Center, she sang – in tribute to the 20th anniversary of his biggest-selling album, *Purple Rain* – its title track, 'Baby, I'm A Star', 'Let's Go Crazy' and, finally, 'Crazy In Love'. It's one thing joining your idol to sing his greatest hits, but another entirely when he sings on yours. Prince was effusive in his praise for Beyoncé, and it was, of course, reciprocated.

CHAPTER 10

Destiny's End

"The energy was beautiful."

Beyoncé, 2004

"After a lot of discussion and some deep soul searching, we realised that our current tour has given us the opportunity to leave Destiny's Child on a high note, united in our friendship and filled with an overwhelming gratitude for our music, our fans, and each other."

Destiny's Child, 2005

In some ways, with the success of all three girls, it seemed something of a retrograde step for Destiny's Child to reunite, as it wasn't just Beyoncé who had been busy. Kelly Rowland had enjoyed considerable achievements outside of the Destiny's Child bubble. She worked with Nelly on 'Dilemma', which reached the UK and US top spot, and her singles 'Stole', 'Can't Nobody' and 'Train On A Track' from her album, *Simply Deep*, had established her as a successful solo artist on both sides of the Atlantic. *The Guardian* said that Rowland "is no longer a mere backing vocalist for Beyoncé Knowles".

Michelle Williams, too, had enjoyed significant success in her chosen field of gospel music. Her debut album, *Heart To Yours*, became the best-selling gospel album of 2002, and won her a MOBO Award for Best New Artist. She had just finished promoting her follow-up, *Do You Know*, and performing *Aida* on Broadway in 2004, when she began working again with Beyoncé and Kelly.

The group had played a one-off gig in July 2003 at the Reggae Sumfest in Montego Bay, Jamaica, and realised how much they had missed performing together. "The energy was beautiful," Beyoncé told *Rolling Stone*. "We started talking about what we should do, what our look should be and what the album should sound like. It's always exciting to perform together." During their hiatus, they had always stated the plan to reunite and reap the rewards of their success on their own terms. Work began on their new album in early 2004 with all three members contributing equally, sharing lead vocals and writing credits.

Beyoncé had one last piece of solo business to attend to before sessions got fully under way. In March 2004, she embarked on the 26-date Verizon Ladies First Tour of North America with Alicia Keys, Missy Elliott and Tamia. Co-sponsored by L'Oréal and Steve Madden footwear, the shows were a great success. The tour opened in Fort Lauderdale, Florida, on March 12 and closed on April 22 at Oakland Stadium, California, and Beyoncé topped the bill with a 12-song set that included a Destiny's Child medley.

Destiny Fulfilled was an album of grooves, deep, treacly and funky. It featured a myriad of imported producers, including old friends such as Rodney 'Darkchild' Jerkins. However, taking a leaf from Beyoncé's solo album, more time was invested into crafting the sound. The girls were so delighted to be working with each other, that they spent the first week scheduled for recording just talking and catching up. They decided to record their conversations and use them as source material for songs. From that, they decided that each song should be linked to the next thematically, telling a story of sisterhood and love. If the girl doesn't believe the promises of the protagonist in 'Lose My Breath', she will find a 'Soldier'; and with him she will 'Cater 2 U'. The girls wrote from differing points of view, and, for the first time, when the album was released it clearly indicated who was singing what, on the lyric sheet.

"At first I thought, 'How is this going to work?'" Jerkins, the producer who'd helped them on their way to superstardom, commented to MTV. "'Cause Beyoncé, she blew up solo, so how's it going to work in a group together? But when I got there, just seeing the excitement of them being back in the studio together, it was just natural. Those girls are sisters and it's not just a group. They have a bond."

Although it was produced by 11 different people, the girls would simply work with the backing track, a point that the album's executive producer, Mathew Knowles, was keen to make: "Ninety percent of the time the producer that did the track never came into the studio with them. They just sent the track on a CD and then [Destiny's Child] did their magic. And it's truly them. It's not this producer who's saying, 'OK, now I need you to sing it this way or do it this way.' They do that themselves, and that's why I often challenge when people say things like, 'Well, Rich Harrison gave Destiny's Child this great record.' Or 'Rodney Jerkins gave Destiny's Child this great record.' No they didn't. It was a collaboration that made that record great, and it's the input of the ladies, it's the producing of Beyoncé that made these great records, 'cause we've consistently done it with different people."

'Lose My Breath', partially written by Jerkins and his team, was the album's first single, and it was an incredible, over-the-top statement. The website bbc.co.uk said that, "It sounds like The Supremes having sex with a robot in a dark alley. It's fantastic." That is absolutely true; featuring arguably the hardest beats of any Destiny's Child track, it pointed the way for the later, atonal grind of Beyoncé's 'Single Ladies (Put A Ring On It)' and 'Run The World (Girls)'. Michelle and Beyoncé had heard the drum sound – courtesy of the University of Michigan Marching Band – and immediately thought it perfect to use in the track. Kelly quickly agreed. With additional writing by Jay-Z, the single was released on September 21, 2004, a bold opening statement for this next phase of Destiny's Child, as it was not as immediately infectious as their previous hits. However, several plays in, it is arguably one of their absolute strongest successes, and became much-loved. *Entertainment Today* said that the track "zips along on a whirlwind of hand-clappy percussion and clipped synth blips . . . While it's no 'Bootylicious', it's got more nervous energy and verve than almost anything else here."

Its video was another supersized reminder, if any were needed, of the phenomenon Destiny's Child had become. Directed by Marc Klasfeld, the promo showed not one, but three versions of the group having a dance-off on the nighttime streets of Los Angeles. An uptown sassy version of the group encounters a street hip-hop version and they compete with each other as they run through their moves. An 'even fiercer' Destiny's Child emerge to conquer, and the video closes with all nine of them dancing in front of massed street dancers. The release of the video was delayed when Beyoncé tore her hamstring during rehearsals for the shoot. "She overdid it," long-time publicist Yvette Noel-Shure said. "We're all keeping our fingers crossed that, because she's young and healthy, it heals fast. There are a lot of things in place that we may have to shift. Not the album, which is finished, but side [appearances]. We'll know more after a week."

Fortunately, the delay was only temporary, but cost the record some sales, as a video wasn't available to promote it. The filming took place in October, after Kelly's friend, world tennis champion Serena Williams, recommended her own doctor. "We were dancing, trying to get ready for the video, and I got a little carried away and excited and pulled my hamstring, actually 20 per cent of my hamstring," Beyoncé told reporters. "I thought it was actually worse than it is. The first day I couldn't walk, but . . . I have a great doctor and I'm working out very hard every day with my athletic trainer." When the video arrived, it maintained the record's chart profile, but because it was missing at the time of release, it harmed the single's chances of becoming another number one. The single reached number three in the *Billboard* Hot 100 and remained on the charts for 20 weeks. 'Lose My Breath' performed strongly in the UK, where it remained at number two for four weeks (thanks to new entry number ones by Eminem, U2 and Girls Aloud), and stayed in the Top 10 throughout Christmas.

The slow-burn of 'Lose My Breath' was also apparent on the other obvious single from *Destiny Fulfilled*, 'Soldier.' Co-written by the group plus Rich Harrison, Sean Garrett, T.I. and Lil Wayne, it was a skillfully ambivalent record that could be read as a pro-President George W. Bush flagwave for the US campaign in Iraq. It acted as a personal crusade for the rights of the fighting man, wrapped in a simple paean to a street soldier, a man in hip-hop uniform, or as MTV put it, "a bouncy homage to thug love". Such calculated broad appeal was just the sort of thing to ensure maximum success. It also featured the only guest appearances on the album by outside vocalists: T.I. and Lil Wayne traded verses. Taken as the album's second single in December 2004, it too reached number three in the US charts and number four in the UK. It marked Destiny's Child's final US Top 10 hit single.

The video was the most calculated yet, placing Destiny's Child right in the middle of the street, with them blinged up, wearing fedoras and holding huge dogs. For once the lyrics stray into straight double entendre territory, another obvious sign that the group had grown up: "Known to carry big things if you know what I mean" is a rare, obvious reference for Destiny's Child to male genitalia in song, arguably the first and only time Beyoncé has done this. Norwegian director Ray Kay – who would go on to work with Justin Bieber and Lady Gaga – delivered the promo, which aside from featuring Lil Wayne and T.I., had cameos from Ice Cube and Beyoncé's sister, Solange, then heavily pregnant with her son, Daniel.

After the uptempo urban introduction, the album settles into its attractive, mid-tempo/quiet storm stride. It was a conscious decision to stay away from the higher tempos: "You can really sing on those songs," Beyoncé told MTV. "It was important for me, the vocal producer of the record, for people to hear Michelle, to hear how soulful and raspy her voice is. To hear how colourful and clear Kelly's voice is and to hear all of us and how different we are. And you can't do that as much with uptempos." 'Cater 2 U' was beautiful, downtempo and soulful, although its lyrical content gave doubters the chance to question the track's portrayal of a woman's absolute subservience to her partner. "It basically talks about how a guy inspires you," Beyoncé argued at the time of the album's release. "You want to make him happy and you want to cater to him. I know it's going to be surprising to a lot of people that the independent survivors are being submissive to their man, but it's important that people know that, you know, it's fine if your man deserves it and gives that back to you."

'Cater 2 U' is a beautiful sound, and a worthy single, even if it sets back the group's manifesto of independence and empowerment by around a century. It became the final single from the album, released in July 2005 in the US to coincide with the final leg of the Destiny Fulfilled . . . And Lovin' It Tour. Its video, directed by Jake Nava, was filmed at California's Red Rock Canyon State Park and features the girls in various stages of undress, signposting all the things they would do for their men. It reached number 14 in the *Billboard* Hot 100, but its release – even with its plethora of Scott Storch mixes – was cancelled in the UK due to lack of interest by radio.

Produced by Andre Harris and Vidal Davis, 'T-Shirt' is another breathy, up-close bedroom symphony, about a woman who needs to wear her lover's T-shirt in order to feel him near to her when he's away. 'Is She The Reason' nudges the tempo up, but not so as you'd really notice. Based around a sample from 'I Don't Know No One Else To Turn To' by Melba Moore (a possible homage to Moore, whom Beyoncé worked with on *The Fighting Temptations*), it reintroduces some old-school Destiny's Child paranoia back into the proceedings. The object of their affections' interest seems to be waning – and another is vying for his love – or so they think. Patrick Douthit aka 9th Wonder's production is diametrically opposed to the whiz, bang, crash and wallop of the more radical soundscapers – this is resolutely old-fashioned soul music, with a few updated beats.

'Girl' finds the groups as confidantes, acting as soulful Agony Aunts to the wronged lover. The light, old-school soul production, again by 9th Wonder, brings a sweetness that runs through this album's core. Again, rifling back through his record collection, Wonder sourced The Dramatics' 'Ocean Of Thoughts And Dreams' to provide the track's main sample. Almost perfect late-period DC, 'Girl' was chosen by fans on the Destiny's Child website to be the third single from the album. Whereas the album sung along to these old-school grooves, the track seemed out of place as a single release and failed to ignite in the US, reaching a relatively lowly number 23 for the group in the US Hot 100, even with its clever *Sex And The City* parody video. It fared better in the UK, reaching number six in May 2005.

'Bad Habit' finds the group revisiting the mannered, baroque hip-hop of *The Writing's On The Wall*. Produced by Mary J. Blige, Bryan-Michael Cox and WyldCard, it is a showcase for Kelly, with Beyoncé and Michelle simply on chorus vocals. It actually started life as a demo for Kelly's second solo album, the follow-up to *Simply Deep*, and is rather jolly and somewhat out of place as *Destiny Fulfilled* settles down to its languorous groove.

The following track, 'If', is arguably the best slow jam that Destiny's Child ever recorded. Produced by Rockwilder, and based on a sample of Natalie Cole's 1975 hit 'Inseparable', the record positively trickles out of the speakers. The girls trade lines as opposed to verses, demonstrating how adept they had become in allowing each other space and complementing each other with their harmonies. Featuring samples of jazz supremo Donald Byrd's 'Night Whistler', 'Free' is the Rockwilder-produced answer record to 'Cater 2 U'. Liberated from a relationship, the girls are now free to be free – the protagonist here had only previously existed in her lover's happiness, now she is claiming freedom on her own terms. *Entertainment Today* singled it out for special praise: "'Free' sounds like some lost soul classic from 1975, but that serves only to point up what may be the album's real problem: that it seems to be trying – and failing – to evoke that bygone era too faithfully."

'Through With Love', produced by Mario Winans, continues this nostalgic feel. It is based around a mournful piano figure, and claims that the girls are completely through with relationships. Beyoncé sings about a man who compares her to every 'little model' on the TV screen and moans because she wants to spend time with her family; this continues the thread of self-analysis that has coursed through Beyoncé's work.

Fortunately, the official closing track, 'Love', comes along to save the day. Beyoncé talks of finding new love; singing in a deeply sensuous voice that she is back on track, basking in the glow of love. Kelly continues the vibe (at the time she was engaged to Dallas Cowboys player Roy Williams), before it closes with Michelle saying that love is in the air she breathes. "It's about how love has inspired us," Michelle told *Rolling Stone*. "My brother Erron produced it, and the harmonies are absolutely bananas!" And they are – it is an extremely accomplished production.

Apart from its exceptionally prescient title, the bonus track, 'Game Over' (which also appeared as the bonus track on the 'Lose My Breath' CD single), is largely pointless. It's another deeply sleepy ballad that adds to the album's overall soporific quality.

Destiny Fulfilled was a different album from the group's previous work. From its lack of guest stars, its resolutely even-handedness between the three vocalists and even in the economy of its track titles, which are often just single words, it may well be the most listenable of all DC albums. Overall, it becomes quite maudlin. It was quite clear that it was actually a small album, intimate even. Mathew Knowles was ready for any criticism: "The previous albums, we had hit songs," he told reporters. "This record has hit songs, but also I think it will go down as a fundamentally classic album and I think that's what makes this different, is that they'll get critical acclaim with this record."

Destiny Fulfilled was released on November 16, 2004. It was, naturally, a big success, yet it failed to scale the heights of *Survivor*. It reached number 19 with 61,000 sales in its first week, as it was sold early, before official release, in certain locations in the States. It sold 497,000 in its second week, which was only enough to take it to number two, behind *Encore*, Eminem's album.

In popular perception, *Destiny Fulfilled* simply didn't feel right, with Beyoncé rejoining her bandmates after becoming such a stellar solo performer. Although they had enjoyed success on their own terms, in some ways Beyoncé's return seemed a little bit like charity for the other two girls. Every interview that supported the album clearly told a different story: "We're friends," Beyoncé told MTV. "We enjoy each other. We sound good together. We grew up together and hopefully we can set an example for other groups, and other female groups especially, that you can support each other and not be insecure and be happy for one another. And it's OK to do solo projects and to grow up and get a life. But it's also OK to come back together. You know? It doesn't always have to be what the media tries to make it out to be. Women can get along and be businesswomen and be smart and not be catty all the time."

As the promotion machine swung into gear, there were many

questions about the longevity of the group. Everyone was waiting for them to split up. The main question was simply one of whether they would stay together. "We don't know," Beyoncé said at the time. "It's important for all of us to maintain our friendship, and it's important for all of us to be happy. And I think the hardest thing was the schedule, after the solo records and the Broadway plays and the movies – the #1 movies – getting us back together and doing this record. And that's the *Destiny Fulfilled*. Maybe five years from now we might have a couple of kids or do whatever we want to do individually and then decide, 'Let's do another record.' Maybe not. But [what's important] is we maintain our friendship and set that example for other people."

To underline the possibility that it was the group's last hurrah, the sleeve of *Destiny Fulfilled* featured the three of them naked, and relatively unadorned by make-up – a very knowing tribute to the final Supremes album, their 1976 swan song, *Mary, Scherrie & Susaye*.

Destiny Fulfilled attracted mixed reviews at the time. *Vibe* said, "While it's no surprise that *Destiny Fulfilled* showcases advanced production values, the songwriting and vocal abilities are just as impressive." *Mojo* argued, "The lyrics veer towards simplistic, but Destiny pull it off, mainly through muscular production and stunning vocal interplay." *The Guardian* said that after the two bold openers, the listener was "stranded on a huge landmass of ballads. This kind of song brings out the girliness in the trio, musically and lyrically." The *Los Angeles Times* review was typical of many: "The singers balance resilience with vulnerability, worldly desires with divine aspirations, but the material is simply overblown, puffed up with soap-bubble ideas and endless repetition." Q magazine went further: "It's disappointing to find a glut of songs seemingly calibrated to appease the demographics."

Listening to the album at the time of writing, it sounds now very much like something that needed to be made. It provides closure, and a glimpse at what a mature Destiny's Child would have sounded like. It sounds adult and deals in greater depth with love and relationships than the cartoonish caricatures of their late nineties work. That said, the girls of Destiny were now 23, older stateswomen instead of 18-year-olds, pretending they were grown-ups, propelled into an adult world.

It would have been naïve to think that the group would not by now have been tied up in some way with a huge sponsorship deal. McDonald's and the group united to promote the girls' forthcoming tour – something the food corporation had already done successfully with Justin Timberlake in 2003 – and together they promoted World Children's Day in November 2005. In return for tour sponsorship, the girls appeared in a variety of 'I'm Lovin It' commercials over the following 18 months, principally promoting McDonald's salad range. Launched in September 2003, the 'I'm Lovin It' campaign – its jingle sung in the western hemisphere by Timberlake – was part of an enormous rebranding campaign by the fast-food giant after the publication of the controversial book *Fast Food Nation* by Eric Schlosser in 2001.

Destiny's Child's participation with McDonald's would continue in the cinema, on TV and the Internet. There was also a World Children's Day advert, where they took the 'Cater 2 U' track and added the chain's 'I'm Lovin' It' jingle as they appeared standing in gowns in an inner city playground, somewhat overemphasising how anybody can escape their roots if need be. Which, of course, was slightly rum, as the group had hardly lived hand-to-mouth when growing up themselves.

A tour was put together to support the album, and it clearly felt like a farewell for the group. The link-up with McDonald's was taken further when the group donated 25 cents from every ticket sale on their tour in the US to Ronald McDonald House Charities, the organisation established in 1974 to help underprivileged children. To emphasise the connection further, the tour was called Destiny Fulfilled . . . And Lovin' It.

The 67-date tour travelled to 16 countries, and opened on April 9, 2005, at the Hiroshima Sun Plaza in Japan, before heading off through Australia, Dubai and Europe, commencing its US leg in New Orleans on July 2, before finishing in Vancouver on September 10. The set was a careful balance of old and new, with a considerable section given over to showcase all three's solo work. All of the hits were present, opening with 'Say My Name' and closing with 'Lose My Breath' and in between Kelly sang 'Dilemma', Michelle 'Do You Know' and Beyoncé 'Dangerously

In Love', 'Baby Boy', 'Naughty Girl' and, of course, 'Crazy In Love.' Working with Kim Burse and Frank Gatson, Jr., the trio made sure that the show would be every inch a spectacle. *The Independent,* although at times underwhelmed, caught the show in London at the cavernous Earls Court Exhibition Centre: "Destiny's Child's walk up to the footlights, silhouetted in diaphanously bat-winged dresses, is . . . truly dramatic . . . As they command the crowd to 'Say My Name', their pastel dresses make them look more like fairytale princesses than the usual R&B porn queens." The nuances were lost in the huge venue, but that mattered little to hoards of screaming fans.

And then, the inevitable happened. Destiny's Child announced their break-up, 30 dates into the European leg of the tour during their final show on June 11, at Palau Sant Jordi, Barcelona, Spain. Kelly announced from the stage that, "This is the last time you would see us onstage as Destiny's Child."

The group sent a missive to MTV to explain their decision: "We have been working together as Destiny's Child since we were nine, and touring together since we were 14. After a lot of discussion and some deep soul searching, we realised that our current tour has given us the opportunity to leave Destiny's Child on a high note, united in our friendship and filled with an overwhelming gratitude for our music, our fans, and each other. After all these wonderful years working together, we realised that now is the time to pursue our personal goals and solo efforts in earnest . . . No matter what happens, we will always love each other as friends and sisters and will always support each other as artists. We want to thank all of our fans for their incredible love and support and hope to see you all again as we continue fulfilling our destinies." The long note was carefully worded to explain exactly how they felt, and worded also so that an open door was there just in case. But rather than the last interlude in 2002, this time it was more final.

As a result, the last US leg of the tour had a huge, bittersweet celebratory feel to it, captured in the long-form recording of the show at the Philips Arena in Atlanta on July 15. The US tour alone grossed $70 million. Reviews around the country were at times positively adulatory;

the final concert in Canada found the girls in tears as they hugged each other onstage for the last time as Destiny's Child on tour.

"I do love sisterhood," Beyoncé reflected a year later. "I loved that being in a group was about compromise and sacrifice. All of us – and not just me, this is about Kelly and Michelle also – whatever was best for the group, no matter whether it was best for us individually, would let something go. That element of compromise and sacrifice taught me a lot about myself and about friendship."

On July 1, 2005, Luther Vandross died. Although expected, the news hit Beyoncé hard. He had been so kind to her during the recording of 'The Closer I Get To You'. She recorded a cover version of 'So Amazing' – one of Vandross' signature songs, and his mother's all-time favorite track of his – with Stevie Wonder for the tribute album, *So Amazing – An All-Star Tribute To Luther Vandross*. Her track nestled among other stars' work such as Alicia Keys, Aretha Franklin, Donna Summer and John Legend. Much of the material had been initially intended as a means to raise funds for Vandross while he was incapacitated with his stroke in 2003, whereupon the New York-based singer temporarily regained his health, before finally succumbing two years later. The completed album was released in the United States on September 20, 2005, and the album's proceeds went to The Luther Vandross Foundation.

The shock waves of Hurricane Katrina also hit while the group were finishing their Destiny Fulfilled . . . And Lovin' It Tour in August 2005. In early July, they had actually played the Superdome in New Orleans, the venue that was to become the temporary refuge for thousands of that city's displaced residents. Beyoncé and her family were deeply affected by the tragedy; not least because of mother Tina's Creole descent. Beyoncé and Kelly, along with Tina, Mathew and Solange, set up the Survivor Foundation, which set out to be a "charitable entity . . . for the purpose of providing transitional housing for Hurricane Katrina victims and storm evacuees in the Houston, Texas, area." Its work was an extension of the Knowles-Rowland Center For Youth, which was now an established outreach facility in central Houston. Tina turned over a percentage of the profits from her new fashion line, House of Deréon, to the project and Beyoncé put $250,000 of her own money into the Survivor Foundation.

With the tour finished, the group had a few last items of Destiny's Child business to attend to. They had to promote World Children's Day on November 20, and oversee a DVD recording of their Atlanta show from July for release in 2006. They bowed out officially with the album release of *#1's*, issued on October 25, 2005. It reached number one in the US and number six in the UK. The album credits demonstrated just what an ongoing business concern the franchise had become. After all the sundry thanks to God, parents, friends, record company, MWE, legal teams and producers, radio and TV, we then get thanks to House of Deréon, Pepsi, McDonald's, Tommy Hilfiger True Star, Hasbro, Mattell and URBANE Merchandising. Its sales of 113,000 in week one, according to the Nielsen SoundScan ratings, gave it the dubious distinction of being the lowest-selling week-one sales of any number one album in the US to that point.

The album *#1's* was a neat summation of all that had gone. The 16-track collection rounded up all of the group's major hits, as well as adding three new tracks, the David Foster-penned 'Stand Up For Love', the 2005 World Children's Day anthem (which showed the band out-Whitneying Whitney – forthright, gauche and, er, a bit much), 'Feel The Same Way I Do' and 'Check On It', a Beyoncé solo track from her forthcoming *Pink Panther* movie. Released on December 13, 2005, 'Check On It' was produced by Swizz Beatz, and although a fairly slender single, it had a great bhangra theme. Again, it was another muse on a man being suitable for Beyoncé's attention. It also had an excellent rap by Slim Thug, which once more was a rumination on the 'what's a nice girl like you doing with a crowd of rappers?' theme ("Good girls got to get down with the gangstas"). It became Beyoncé's third solo single number one in the US.

So that was that; Destiny's Child was over. They could reflect on their trials and tribulations, successive lawsuits and years of hard work; they could also reflect on their number ones, their Grammys; and the fact that the World Music Awards had recognised them as the most successful girl group of all time. The bond between the girls would remain strong, and the first reunion came as early as February 2006. They reunited to play a farewell performance at an NBA All-Star Game in Houston; and then they played again at a Fashion Rocks concert later the same month. The final official engagement of Destiny's Child was wholly apposite. On March 28, 2006, the three girls got together to become the 2,035th recipients of a star on the Hollywood Walk Of Fame on Los Angeles' Hollywood Boulevard. "We started when we were nine years old, and here we are getting a Hollywood star," Beyoncé told *Fox News*. "Dreams come true. So thank you all so much for supporting us."

CHAPTER 11

As Feverish As Pre-Watershed Pop Gets: *The Pink Panther* And *B'Day*

"Stop browbeating her, can't you see she's sexy?"

Steve Martin as Jacques Clouseau, 2006

"The album feels like a party. It feels like a celebration, a woman that knows who she is, that has found her power and has found her voice. I thought the title was perfect."

Beyoncé, 2006

Destiny's Child were now clearly over. It was simply a question of where Beyoncé would go next and when. She had been the last of the group to release solo material when Destiny's Child first split in 2002, because of filming commitments. It was not dissimilar now, as her first piece of post-Destiny's Child business was her guest star role in *The Pink Panther*. Opening in the United States in February 2006, it was one of those movies that was reviled by the critics and adored by the public. The film seemed to have a hard task of winning critical support before it was even released. All critics and audiences of a certain age identified so strongly with the British comic actor Peter Sellers, who had made the Clouseau role his own, that there was an immediate inbuilt backlash. It became, ironically, the highest-grossing film of the entire Pink Panther series.

The franchise, named after a large diamond, was conceived by director Blake Edwards. It had first appeared in 1963 as a comedy espionage thriller starring David Niven as Sir Charles Lytton and Peter Sellers as the incompetent French detective, Jacques Clouseau. Although David Niven was the star of the first film, Sellers' character became an icon of world cinema; a bumbling, slapstick cipher, whose personality proved bigger than the plots in six subsequent films.

When Sellers died in 1980, a few lame efforts were made to breathe life into the series, including an audacious attempt to stitch together cutting-room floor footage of the deceased Sellers and weave it into a plot in 1982's *Trail Of The Pink Panther*. In 2005, the film series was revived with US comic actor Steve Martin playing the Clouseau role. *The Pink Panther* was directed by Shawn Levy, who had had success with the light romantic comedies *Just Married* and *Cheaper By The Dozen*.

Beyoncé plays superstar singer Xania, who is the girlfriend of the French national football team coach, Yves Gluant (Jason Statham). Her role was filmed in three weeks during the final Destiny's Child tour schedule. Beyoncé is first seen – looking stunning in a white dress – at the football stadium, watching Gluant lead his team out to play the Chinese team. After his team win the match Gluant is assassinated on the field, and his ring, containing the fabled Pink Panther diamond, is stolen. Capers obviously ensue.

Steve Martin plays Clouseau amusingly, while Kevin Kline chews the scenery as his boss, Dreyfus, the role made famous by Herbert Lom. A lot of established actors (Jean Reno, Clive Owen, Roger Rees) coast through the film, but it has some humorous touches. Martin, who in his time was one of America's funniest comedy writers and performers, polished the script: the scene where Clouseau lectures his secretary, Nicole Durant (Emily Mortimer), on correct behaviour and harassment between an officer and secretary in this modern age, while afterwards kissing her and patting her bottom, is witty and understated.

Xania is seen again in the recording studio, singing the film's key piece of music, 'A Woman Like Me'. This is where Clouseau first meets her. She looks sweet and demure and she pats his arm when he tells her what an admirer of her work he is. And then, to underline the film's broad slapstick, Clouseau goes into the recording booth after asking if it is soundproofed and farts noisily for all to hear. He returns unbowed to interrogate her. Clouseau's questioning is gentle and Xania responds sweetly. Gluant cheated on Xania, but she emotes: "After he cheated on me, I hated him, but I didn't kill him."

When Clouseau's sidekick, Ponton (Reno), asks her more questions, Clouseau replies, "Stop browbeating her, can't you see she's sexy?" It's a charming scene where she talks about having to do "something vague" in New York. Xania reappears in the film about an hour in, wearing her white dress, walking through the streets of New York as she goes to see a diamond dealer. It seems increasingly obvious that she committed the murder. When confronted by Clouseau and Ponton, she says that she was having the diamonds restudded on a purse once owned by Josephine Baker.

Beyoncé has the most to do in the scene in which Clouseau goes for dinner at her New York apartment and is about to be seduced by her. He retires to the bathroom for a "little assistance" where he drops his Viagra-like "blue pill" down the sink before setting fire to the drapes and falling through the bathroom floor. The jokes wear a little thin as the film progresses, but it comes alive when Beyoncé sings at the climactic ball. 'A Woman Like Me', a fine John Barry-esque number, allows her an opportunity to truly shine for the first time in the film's 93 minutes. The murderer is caught by Clouseau and we learn that Xania has had the Pink Panther diamond all along, sewn into the lining of her purse. It was an engagement present from Gluant, who had passed it to her as they kissed before his final, fatal football game.

Beyoncé's role, in many respects, represented an extended promo video for 'A Woman Like Me'. Director Shawn Levy said of Beyoncé, "She may be still figuring it out as an actress, she's done a few movies and she's getting better every time. But as a singer, she walks into the recording studio, into the vocal booth, and it's her world. She's unbelievable." He was impressed with her work singing 'A Woman Like Me'. The scene involved five or six takes using three different cameras. She would be sitting 'mellow, drinking her orange juice' and then get into character. Levy felt the film was enriched by her 'commanding, sexy presence' as a performer. The song was a beautiful, slinky show-stopper written by Beyoncé with Charmelle Cofield and Ron Lawrence. It featured Beyoncé's multi-tracked vocals set against James Bond-style horns.

The Pink Panther opened on February 12, 2006, and returned a quarter of its $80 million budget in its opening weekend, going on to gross over $126 million. *USA Today* said, "The movie's ringer is Beyoncé Knowles as one of the zillion suspects. As with Fran Jeffries in the first *Panther* pic, Knowles' big number is good for some chanteuse-y hot-cha." It was all a jolly caper, but one which underused Beyoncé. Influential film critic Roger Ebert of the *Chicago Sun-Times* spoke about the tradition of beautiful women in *Pink Panther* films and said that the task of the French detective's beauties this time "is to essentially regard Clouseau as if they have never seen such a phenomenon before in their lives". And that was about the sum of what Beyoncé had to do. Like *Austin Powers In Goldmember*, *The Pink Panther* is another light, populist, safe, non-threatening film. Soon it would be time for a proper acting challenge.

Beyoncé continued to prioritise film over audio releases into 2006. Much of her year was taken up with the intensive filming of *Dreamgirls* before the recording of her next album. But given the vagaries of film post-production, it was her next album that saw the light of day first. *B'Day* – much of which was written on the *Dreamgirls* shoot – would find Beyoncé setting her course for the rest of her solo career. She used the experiences of her character in the film, Deena Jones, to write songs. As a result, it gave the album a very different feel from her previous releases.

"I didn't want to write sappy love songs, even though I'm happy now," Beyoncé told *USA Today* on the verge of the album's release. "I wanted to do different things, to be innovative and kick really hard beats. I think

I would have been scared to take that risk if I hadn't done [*Dreamgirls*]. I would have made a love album, because that's where I am in my life. The movie inspired something else that's not in me. Or I guess it is, somewhere."

After a launch party at Jay-Z's 40/40 Club in New York on August 31, *B'Day* was released internationally on September 4, 2006, the day of Beyoncé's 25th birthday. It was soon sitting atop the world's charts. Beyoncé was clear about the focus of her second album: "This is about female empowerment. This album is different, it's conceptual, and I do things with my voice that I haven't done before." It was a bold, mature album that marked her out as someone who had fully shaken off the shackles of her old group. The album also had promotional videos made for all of its tracks, which were released separately on DVD the following year. Visually and musically, Beyoncé was firing on all cylinders.

The album was recorded quickly, ultimately in a little over three weeks in New York and also at Great Divide Studios in Aspen, Colorado. Rich Harrison, so masterful in his commandeering of *Dangerously In Love*, was one of the team of producers who worked with her on *B'Day*. She put her principal producers, Harrison, Rodney 'Darkchild' Jerkins and Sean Garrett, in separate rooms at Sony Music Studios on West 54th Street in the Hell's Kitchen area of Manhattan. "I called up Sean, Rich and Rodney. I got them each a room at Sony Studios, and we went to work." Beyoncé told *Billboard* magazine. She would move between the rooms and tell the others "'Wow, Rich has some great beats.' It was healthy competition." This competition fostered a much more intense album than *Dangerously In Love*.

The album was recorded in shifts of 14-hour days, with producers and writers working simultaneously. In the end, although upwards of 25 songs were recorded, 10 made the final release, making it feel like an old-fashioned album. Jay-Z appears on 'Déjà Vu' and 'Upgrade U'. *The Guardian* noted that although his contributions were only brief, "he leaves behind a trail of raw beats and raw sexuality".

Album opener 'Déjà Vu' was a masterful reintroduction, following the statement music of 'Crazy In Love'. Jay-Z is present and performs his rap as a declaration of intent; Beyoncé is his, now. They are very much a couple, yet she is still very much an independent woman. It is certainly the most immediate, sultry, swinging number on the album, a perfect opener. Not all were so enamoured: *Fox News* said, "The song is catchy if you hear it enough times – like a sidewalk drill – but it lacks a consistent melody." Beginning with Beyoncé introducing the instruments . . . '*bass, hi-hat, 808*' and then '*Jay?*', it was co-produced with Rodney Jerkins and young bassist and multi-instrumentalist Jon Jon Webb. Known as Jon Jon Traxx, Webb came up with the bass line in the studio in one attempt. "Rodney and I came up with the concept of doing an old-school track," he told *Bass Player*. "A throwback, with real bass and horns; that's part of why the title is 'Déjà Vu.'" Its infectious, old-school groove made listeners look for a sample credit on the sleeve. There was none; it is rather irresistible, sounding like some fabulous, lost track from an early seventies Stevie Wonder release.

The song set the tone for the interesting fusion of live instruments and electronic wizardry on *B'Day*. "When I recorded 'Déjà Vu' . . . I knew that even before I started working on my album, I wanted to add live instruments to all of my songs," Beyoncé told MTV in the run-up to the album's release. "It's such a balance; it has live congas, live horns, live bass. It's still young, still new and fresh, but it has the old soul groove. The energy is incredible. It's the summer anthem, I pray. I feel it. It's already broken records. Rodney Jerkins is incredible, Jay of course is on it, he blessed the song, I'm happy with it."

It was the album's first single, released at the end of July after being leaked to the Internet in June. Tom Breihan of *The Village Voice* was all of a flap when he first heard the song: "It's a monster, a luxuriant wide-screen love-crazy squelch-funk jam with horn blats and an itchy bass line and rippling bongos and two Jay-Z verses. It's probably going to run the summer of 2006 the way 'Crazy In Love' ran the summer of 2003. That's clearly the intent, anyway; it's got the same spit-shine retro-organic production and head-spun crush-wails." *The Guardian* said, "The magnificent 'Déjà Vu' is as feverish as pre-watershed pop gets, but even when Jay-Z is not physically present, he brings out something formidable in Beyoncé that evokes the young, feral Tina Turner." For some, however, its title's French translation of 'already seen' was a little prophetic, as there was a feeling that it was a little too similar to 'Crazy In Love'. *The Observer* – the sister paper to *The Guardian* – remarked, "Leading the *B'Day* campaign with 'Deja Vu' – a limp effort with contributions from Jay-Z so perfunctory that they seemed not so much phoned in as attached to the leg of the nearest pigeon – was a particularly foolhardy move." 'Déjà Vu' only reached number four in the US charts. In the UK it debuted at number 21 before climbing 20 places for a solitary week at the top spot in late August 2006.

Its video, directed by Sophie Muller, was entirely steamy. Filmed on the bayous, it oozed heat and sensuality. Set in what looks like a dilapidated antebellum house in New Orleans, it features set-piece dancing, myriad costume changes, with the main focus Beyoncé dancing with Jay-Z. If she was looking to ensnare Jay-Z in the 'Crazy In Love' video, here she is completely in his thrall, looking as if she is on the verge of having sex with him throughout the promo. Not everyone was happy with the footage. MTV reported on July 24, 2006, that 2,000 fans had signed an online petition to Columbia Records demanding the promo be reshot.

"This video is an underwhelming representation of the talent and quality of previous music-video projects of Ms. Knowles," the petition claimed. It concluded with the paragraph. "We, the fans of one Beyoncé Knowles, ask that an alternative video be shot featuring: more choreographed & less spontaneous dancing, clearer visual themes that relate to the lyrics of the song, less gyrating, less scenes of non-existent sexual chemistry between Mr. Carter and Ms. Knowles, less zooming and quick cut edits and a more stylised and clear direction for all other aspects of the video production." The video was not altered. However, it was all good for business around the release of the album.

Starting with Beyoncé intoning "*9, 4, 81 . . . B'Day*", 'Get Me Bodied' was co-produced by Sean Garrett and Swizz Beatz. Born Kasseem Daud Dean, Swizz Beatz was the other significant producer on the album. Like the second Jay-Z collaboration, 'Upgrade U', 'Get Me Bodied' was one of its most substantial tracks. Written by Beyoncé with her sister, Solange, Angela Beyincé, Swizz Beatz, Sean Garrett and Makeba Riddick, and borrowing from dancehall and reggaeton, it was simply multi-layered Beyoncé vocals over clattering, intricate percussion with a to-die-for middle eight.

Its accompanying video was directed by Common and Eminem promo supremo Anthony Mandler and took as its inspiration a section of Bob Fosse choreography from *Sweet Charity* called the Frug. What was splendid about the video was that it reunited Beyoncé with Kelly Rowland and Michelle Williams, and adds sister Solange as well, thus uniting on screen the Destiny's Child line-up that never was. All four throw themselves into their roles with gusto, as Beyoncé enters and sashays around a stylised nightclub.

The extended mix had a phenomenal call-and-response section at the end, culminating in Beyoncé's first piece of blatant product placement for her just-recently announced fashion line, House Of Deréon. The record told listeners to shake their derrière in 'The House of Deréon'. The video then pans to a backside with the clothing firm's marque clearly emblazoned on it. The track was the seventh and final single from the album in the US in July 2007, and its most lowly charting – reaching only number 68 in the US Top 100. By that point, singles placings did not matter – it acted as yet another postcard to buy the album, which by this point, had sold over three million copies. The song was re-recorded in 2011 as 'Move Your Body', as part of Michelle Obama's campaign to fight obesity in American children.

Called "a funky update of gutbucket '60s soul" by *Entertainment Weekly*, 'Suga Mama' was, like 'Work It Out' back in 2002, another flirtation with greasy funk. Produced by Rich Harrison, it was based around a generous sample of 'Searching For Soul', a little-known 1972 instrumental recording by J Wade & The Soul Searchers, originally released on Mutt Records. Co-written by Beyoncé, Harrison and Makeba Riddick (adding to the work of the sample writer, Chuck Middleton), it was an enjoyable romp, with Beyoncé playing the high-rolling baller that she had sung about as a teenager, spending her money to keep her man interested. Its video, directed by Melina Matsoukas, was effectively a Beyoncé solo performance, save for a brief flurry of dancers. Beyoncé is seen smoking a cigar (which was to come as some surprise to her fans), before taking off her suit jacket and getting down to some serious pole dancing. After gyrating on an enormously oversized sugar cube, the clip ends with Beyoncé riding a mechanical bull – again underlying the track's high level of sexual tension.

Written by an astonishing eight people, 'Upgrade U' follows the pattern laid down by 'Get Me Bodied'. Produced by Cameron Wallace with additional work by Swizz Beatz, it is again another minimal, beat-heavy number. Released as a promotional-only 12" in the US due to its popularity on hip-hop stations, it is a plea from Beyoncé to upgrade her man, who needs to come up to her level. It's a shopping list of bling that works incredibly well, with Jay-Z's slightly incredulous rap that even he, "at number 1", could be upgraded. Beyoncé replies that although he may "be the block", she is "the light that keeps the streets on". Later she suggests that she can do for her man what "Martin did for the people". To hear Beyoncé fronting like this demonstrates how skilled she was becoming as a hip-hop artist. It's still a semi-vulgar show of the riches available in hip-hop dreaming – a catalogue of the finest material things in life. It's a very knowing track, demonstrating the respectability Beyoncé had given Jay-Z and the edge and danger that Jay-Z had brought to Beyoncé. The song was based on a sample of 'Girls Can't Do What The Guys Do' by Betty Wright, taking its opening horn riff and its melancholic groove.

Shot in a day and a half by Melina Matsoukas, the video for 'Upgrade U' continued the feeling of freewheeling self-awareness that coursed through the album. Beyoncé gets to impersonate Jay-Z, sitting in his chair delivering his rap at the beginning and middle of the record. The second rap, with Beyoncé dancing around herself, is fun, if a little unnerving. He then appears in person to conclude his words. Jay-Z recorded his section first and then Beyoncé studied his performance in order to copy it. "I love what I did, because it's completely out of character, or at least the character that people think I am," she told MTV. "I was pretending to be Jay, and he was there, and I told him he had to leave because I couldn't do it with him in the room – it was way too embarrassing. I think I did a pretty good job. I had the lip curl down!"

The album's musical exploration continues with 'Ring The Alarm', arguably Beyoncé's most aggressive musical statement to date. Paring down her beats to an almost uncomfortable minimalism, the track starts with a siren. Beyoncé intones the title and screams, through heavy distortion, that she would be "damned if I see another chick on your arm". It is a tale of aggrieved lover on the verge of losing not only her partner's love but also his material benefits. There are similarities in sentiment with Kelis' 1999 Neptunes-produced masterpiece 'Caught Out There'. The lyrics were rumoured (and denied) at the time to be a reaction against Jay-Z's championing of his new Def Jam signing, the 16-year-old Barbadian Robyn Fenty, who is known professionally by her middle name, Rihanna.

Beyoncé enjoyed working with the track's producer, Swizz Beatz: "He's challenging," she told *Billboard*. "His beats are so complex. It's hard to find a melody. But this just clicked." The song is akin to one long tantrum. "I didn't want to write some 'angry' song," she said at the time of the album's release. "Swizz's track had that tough vibe, like the guy had cheated, and I wanted to write something honest. If you're in a relationship, even if the man's cheating and you end up not wanting him, the thought of another woman benefiting from the lessons you taught him, that's gonna kill you!" The song was chosen as the second single from the album, in October 2006, a slightly strange choice as 'Déjà Vu' had relatively underperformed, and now, there was this aggressive wall of noise. Unreleased as a single in the UK, it went to number 11 in the US charts, and was accompanied by another striking Sophie Muller-directed video. Beyoncé brought a great deal of the acting training she'd received during *Dreamgirls* to the shoot, which was filmed in New York, and paid generous homage to the 1992 Sharon Stone-starring sex thriller, *Basic Instinct*. "I treated the video for 'Ring the Alarm' like a movie scene," Beyoncé told *USA Today*. "I was thinking, 'I've got to make my acting coach proud.'" The video itself was, of course, tremendous hokum, with Beyoncé truly living every moment in a manner that would have delighted legendary Russian acting theorist Konstantin Stanislavski. Beyoncé alternates between being aggrieved in a beach house, and then re-enacting the infamous scene where Sharon Stone, as writer Catherine Tramell, uncrosses and crosses her legs under police interrogation. It is a fine, full-on performance. But then, after a controversial video for her first single, and with this latest offering celebrating a notorious film and promoting a moderately atonal single, she was not enamouring herself to the more wholesome end of her fan base.

It's only with 'Kitty Kat' that the album starts mining an older slow jam seam, almost as if this is the first number that referenced early Destiny's Child. It shares a similar theme of paranoia with 'Ring The Alarm'. Almost an update of 1999's 'Say My Name', it tells of a woman troubled by the fact her lover is not returning her calls, forgetting where "joy lives". Produced by arguably the greatest go-to production team of the early noughtiess, The Neptunes, it feels somewhat lightweight and undercooked compared with the other material on the album.

B'Day returns to hardcore beats with 'Freakum Dress'. *The Guardian* wrote: "'Freakum Dress' is a light-hearted crunk spree that reminds girls of the importance of having a 'freakum dress' in their wardrobe." Crunk, typified by artists such as Lil Jon and Three 6 Mafia, was loose Southern hip-hop, with drum machines, heavy basslines and shouted vocals. Produced by Rich Harrison, it was fully in keeping with the fun that Beyoncé appeared to be having. Sassy and upbeat, it is littered with vocal mannerisms and slogans; there is something again in common with the past – like 'Jumpin', Jumpin'', something can be done to get out of a miserable situation: put on a dress. Although it may not be up there with some of the world's leading feminist tracts, its main point is that the dress is being worn for the wearer as much as whoever will appreciate it. Its escalating beeps and bleeps, loud percussion and banked wall of vocals all add to the increasing eccentricity of the album.

'Green Light' was a minimalist hybrid of hip-hop and funk with big, bold, time-shifting choruses, delivered perfectly by The Neptunes. Although heavily echoing in its verse their number for Nelly, 'It's Getting Hot In Herre', it shows how necessary was the lightness of touch they brought to the album.

For those who preferred a more melodic approach, 'Irreplaceable' arrives late but saves the day. It was produced by Norwegian writing and production team Stargate, who had made their name in the UK, working with acts such as S Club 7, Blue and Atomic Kitten. They moved to the States and had recently worked with Ne-Yo and Jay-Z's new Def Jam prodigy Rihanna. Co-written by them and Beyoncé, this simple, unadorned rock ballad showcased the best of the producer's and vocalist's work. The song had been developed with Ne-Yo, originally intended for Def Jam singer Chrisette Michele. Beyoncé heard the demo and asked for some key changes to be made, and writing was finished with Espen Lind and Amund Bjørkland from Norwegian writing team Espionage. Ne-Yo later said he wished he hadn't given the song away, as it may have been interesting to have heard it sung from a male perspective.

'Irreplaceable' was a huge departure for Beyoncé, as it was the first almost straight rock-country song she had sung. Although certainly informed by urban music, it was a departure, and its sweet melody stuck out like an un-sore thumb from the grooves, beats and angst of the body of the album.

Roger Friedman from *Fox News* immediately picked up on it, saying that it was "a clever ballad" and "the most memorable track, and has the most potential of catching on with fans quickly. It's also the only song on *B'Day* that you might actually want to sing along to, written and produced by Stargate, an anonymous Norwegian pop hit production team akin to Max Martin's boy band factory of a few years ago."

A strident song of empowerment following a relationship breakdown, its infectious refrain of "there'll be another you in a minute" suggested how little Beyoncé needed her man. Its video – directed by Anthony Mandler – introduced Beyoncé's new backing band, Suga Mama, and featured model Bobby Roache as her departing love interest. The story is intercut with shots of Beyoncé throwing shapes in silhouette, evidently influenced by James Bond films. There appears to be a brief moment of reconciliation when she goes to hug him, sitting on the bonnet of her sports car, but that display of affection is actually an opportunity to relieve him of his jumper and necklace. Beyoncé is seen in curlers and a bra getting dressed. As the song progresses, you see what she was preparing for, as she appears singing with her band, with hand actions to the song's other catchy repeat of "to the left, to the left". It ends with another suitor arriving at the door of her mansion. The video won the BET Video Of The Year Award for 2007.

'Irreplaceable' gave the album the commercial rebirth it needed after two middling (for Beyoncé) US hits. Released as a single in December 2006, it restored her to the number one position in the US, giving her her fourth solo chart-topper, and her first number one since 'Check On It'. The record was a worldwide success and gained a nomination for Record Of The Year at the Grammy Awards in 2008. Beyoncé even cut a Spanish-language version, 'Irreemplazable'.

'Resentment', the final official track on the album (an "oversung downer" in the words of *The Boston Globe*), is the only real grandiose ballad. It has the sweet touch of many of the mid-period works of Prince. The album closed with the addition of the previous year's number one, 'Check On It'.

Like 'Daddy' on *Dangerously In Love*, there is a hidden track on *B'Day*. This time it is 'Listen', Beyoncé's show-stopping performance from the *Dreamgirls* film. Billed only on the sleeve as "an encore for the fans", it is introduced by Beyoncé, who talks of wanting to give her listeners an "extra special song" from her upcoming film – talking about the pivotal moment when her character stands up for herself, "knows who she is" and "knows what she wants"; she concludes by saying, "I'm sure all of you women can relate to the lyrics." It is a raw, emotional performance from Beyoncé at her most expressive vocally. *Entertainment Weekly* wrote sniffily that the track was little more than "canny product placement for the next stop in a gale-force career that continues to mow down everything in its path".

B'Day ended up being recorded in a high-powered three weeks in early summer 2006. The 10 tracks zipped by speedily, in common with the relative brevity of *Destiny Fulfilled*, as opposed to the occasionally meandering length-fests that were *Survivor* and *Dangerously In Love*. It felt, in a way, slightly undercooked, something ultimately Beyoncé and Columbia must too have felt, as an expanded edition was released the following year. Beyoncé was justifiably proud of the finished work: "The album feels like a party," she told MTV ahead of its release. "It feels like a celebration, a woman that knows who she is, that has found her power and has found her voice. I thought the title was perfect." *B'Day* was a sustained *tour de force*. As modern as any similar urban album, yet nostalgic enough to evoke many memories of the triumph of previous soul artists.

Its cover caused controversy; shot while on location for the 'Déjà Vu' single, the back cover showed a heavily made-up Beyoncé dressed in a gingham bikini with two alligators on leads. There was an outtake, which showed her holding an alligator in her arms. "He was really cute, but since his mouth was taped, he didn't have any way to defend himself," she told *Arena* magazine. "He was upset, so he peed on me. That was an experience." This attracted the ire of PETA (People For The Ethical Treatment Of Animals), who wrote a letter to her explaining why she should not have done such a thing. This was not the first time Beyoncé had aggrieved PETA, namely due to the House Of Deréon's use of fur in its products. The organisation launched a poster campaign with the heading, "Dear Beyoncé". It continued, "Your many fans at PETA are saddened that you've ignored repeated appeals calling your attention to the way minks, foxes, and chinchillas are gassed, strangled, and electrocuted on fur farms for your wardrobe." Singer and animal activist P!nk entered the argument, speaking in the *News Of The World*, repeated on PETA's website: "I only hope she gets bit on the ★★★★ by whatever animal she wears . . . People will think it's OK or cool, but it's not. Some of the practices are so cruel and as a celebrity you have a responsibility to think about the message you're sending out by wearing fur."

Aside from the controversy of the cover, reviews were generally very positive: *Rolling Stone* said, "Coming off the Destiny's Child album *Destiny Fulfilled* and the filming of *Dreamgirls* . . . Beyoncé is fiercer and ready for risks on *B'Day*." *The Boston Globe* talked about producer Rich Harrison's tracks saying that he was "like the Indiana Jones of soul, constantly pulling out forgotten gems of the past for sampling. You can't help but think: Thank God someone wrote music in the past that can be repurposed now." *The Observer* said that the album was "solid, melodic, confident and, broadly, schmaltz-free." *Blender* said, "*B'Day* never cools down, and sweaty uptempo numbers prove the best platform for Beyoncé's rapperly phrasing and pipe-flaunting fireballs." *Entertainment Weekly* said, "It may in fact be foolish to buy this record, with booming songs so clearly designed for nightclub sound systems with subwoofers the size of Hummers. A piddly home hi-fi can hardly capture the thunderous grandeur." The album, which had been mastered by Brian 'Big Bass' Gardner at Bernie Grundman Mastering in Los Angeles, had truly done justice to his nickname.

The Sydney Morning Herald was not so complimentary about *B'Day*. It said, "At times there seems to be an agenda here to push Knowles, who has always appeared in control and confident, into being some tough-talking, hard-dealing queen pin. A forced Tina Turner or a thin-voiced Etta James, maybe. It doesn't work or, at best – like the album – it doesn't work often enough." Again, many commented on the influence of Jay-Z on *B'Day*. "He has taught me about hip-hop," Beyoncé told *The Guardian*. "I loved it as a child, but my mom wouldn't let me listen to the cussing. Now I understand it. It is a reality." Jay-Z is credited on the album's sleeve as 'Poppop': "Thanx 4 Upgrading my album (twice). Did you know you were the coolest man alive?"

Beyoncé promoted the album endlessly. Although it was never one of her favourite pastimes, she understood the need to get out and work the world's media. For the first time she was looking on matters as an experienced elder stateswoman. "I feel like the older I get, the more I'm not worried about having a breakdown," she told *The Guardian*. "I don't know what's going to happen to me but I know that I'm more than a singer and I have so many other things in my life to keep me focused. I hope and pray that I stay as comfortable in my own skin as I am right now, at this exact moment."

In some respects, *B'Day* can be viewed as Beyoncé's crunk album. There is certainly something a little dirty, primeval and unfinished about it. However, there was nothing unfinished about her business interests: the album fully introduced her new joint venture with her mother, Tina – clothing company House Of Deréon – to the world. The back page of its booklet was taken up with an advert featuring Solange wearing House Of Deréon clothes and the company's URL. Beyoncé was, by late 2006, so much more than a mere pop singer.

CHAPTER 12

"I'm Somebody, And Nobody's Gonna Hold Me Down . . . I'm Somebody!": *Dreamgirls*

"I'm all about female empowerment. I'm all about pushing the envelope. I know it's my responsibility to do something different."

Beyoncé, 2007

Opening on December 15, 2006, *Dreamgirls* seemed an obvious choice for Beyoncé and finally added a heavyweight film to her credits. It was based on the 1981 Broadway success, which ran for 1,521 performances. Written by Tom Eyen and Henry Krieger, it was heavily inspired by the rise and fall of Motown Records in general and their best-selling group, The Supremes, in particular. Remembered with affection for introducing singer Jennifer Holliday and the remarkable, show-stopping ballad 'And I'm Telling You I'm Not Going', the play inspired the only Supreme who remained a constant in the group, Mary Wilson, to title her first autobiography *Dreamgirl: My Life As A Supreme*.

The play gained respect, and a little notoriety, for its thinly veiled retelling of the story of Motown Records – arguably the world's most influential record label – and its boss, Berry Gordy, Jr., the man whom

Mathew Knowles modelled himself on. Although the Motown heritage industry is now in full swing – witness the huge US and UK celebration of the label's 50th birthday in 2009 – when the play debuted in 1981, there had been few written accounts of its history and almost nothing, aside from rumours, of its alleged "darker side." The act 'The Dreams' is clearly supposed to be The Supremes; other characters based on combinations of real acts and circumstances weave in and out. The film tells a small, human tale against a backdrop of tumultuous times, and observes the rise of the group at the cost of its most talented member, Effie White, who had the voice but not the looks, and was passed over by the group's manager for the less vocally able Deena Jones. Anyone with even the most perfunctory knowledge of Motown's history will recognise the similarities to the careers of Florence Ballard and Diana Ross.

Produced and released in a joint venture with Paramount and DreamWorks Pictures, *Dreamgirls* was directed by Bill Condon, the director and writer of such left-of-centre films as *Gods And Monsters* and *Kinsey*. *Dreamgirls* had been on various drawing boards over the years. Whitney Houston was earmarked for the role of Deena Jones back in the early nineties, but allegedly wanted to sing some of Effie White's show-stopping numbers, too. Fugees singer Lauryn Hill had been linked to the project in the late noughties, but the relative lack of success of similar films led to the project being shelved. It was the success of the film version of the Kander/Ebb 1975 Broadway smash *Chicago* in 2002 that put contemporary musicals back on the Hollywood radar again. Four new songs were added to the original show score, co-written with Henry Krieger, as original lyricist/librettist, Tom Eyen, had died in 1991.

Set in Detroit, and opening in the early sixties, the action centres on the rise and fall of The Dreams, comprising Effie (Jennifer Hudson), Deena (Beyoncé) and Lorrell Robinson (Anika Noni Rose). They are initially known as The Dreamettes, and are discovered by local manager Curtis Taylor, Jr. (Jamie Foxx). Getting a substantial break supporting singer James 'Thunder' Early (Eddie Murphy), the girls are catapulted into the big time, yet personal subterfuge gets in the way as Taylor edges out the super-talented Effie for the more photogenic Deena. Taylor has all the dreams and visions of a mogul-in-waiting and repackages his artists as chart-friendly stars, destined to appeal beyond the compartmentalisation of "race music".

The film is in two halves: the first is set in the sixties, showing the group on the way to making it big, and the second is in the mid-seventies, when the group, now known as Deena Jones and The Dreams and without founder member Effie, are superstars, returning to play a show at the theatre in which they made their name. It is a tale of heroin overdoses and illegitimate children set against the backdrop of the success of "Rainbow Records". Rainbow is a fantastic composite and homage not just to Motown, but to the machinations of the music business in general.

Dreamgirls scores on its authenticity and homage. There are lovely touches – the mock-up pictures of The Dreams with The Beatles, and the record sleeves that are perfect parodies of The Supremes' albums. There is a lovely scene where Effie – in a show-stopping debut film performance by Jennifer Hudson – playfully chides Taylor for putting out a Martin Luther King record instead of one of hers, saying, "It's about fairness, Curtis. It's about people paying their dues. Isn't that what you keep telling me? So why am I sitting here without so much as a B-side on a 45, when an amateur like Martin Luther King, Jr. gets his own freaking album? I mean, can he even sing?" The Martin Luther King album in question is the Motown rarity *The Great March To Freedom*, which was released by the label in 1963.

The Dreams are told they are going to work with choreographer Jolly Jenkins, a nod to Motown dance supremo Cholly Atkins, who worked extensively with The Supremes. There is also a superb parody of a white artist who takes one of Taylor and writer CC White's songs, 'Cadillac Car', and turns it into a US pop hit. Although White (played by James Robinson) – a character that is an amalgam of at least four people: Smokey Robinson, Lamont Dozier, and Brian and Eddie Holland – is disgusted, Taylor reminds him that it is business, and asks him who sang 'Hound Dog'. As Robinson replies "Elvis Presley", Taylor tells him about Big Mama Thornton's original.

It's a warm film that chronicles the change in African-American attitudes as well as the growth in the popularity of recorded music. When Taylor informs manager Mickey Madison (Danny Glover) that he wants to manage Early, he tells him that it's a "whole new day," and, like Gordy himself, starts putting his acts into the white heartland. This entrepreneurial style was responsible for taking African-American music to a new audience.

The film pulls no punches when it comes to supposed history. The oft-debated issue about the strength and power of Diana Ross' voice is dealt with. Taylor says to Deena, whom he marries, "You know why I chose you to sing lead? Because your voice . . . has no personality. No depth. Except for what I put in there." When her mother questions Taylor's choice of Deena as the group's lead vocalist, he replies that she has something "better, a quality"; she replies, "You make her sound like a product." He smiles and says how much he likes the analogy.

In one sense, although Beyoncé is the central character in the film, you feel at times that it is solely the weight of her name that has given her such incredible billing. Often she is given little to do, and it is only towards the end of the film that she really gets an opportunity to shine. She, of course, excels in the singing and dancing, swears profusely once and is seen smoking – all things which directly contravene Beyoncé's personal code. Deena's dawning realisation that she is merely a puppet for her manager husband leads to her independence. She does have her Diana Ross impersonation down to a tee. The wigs, the mannerisms and the dancing are superb. When The Dreams sing the mid-period Supremes pastiche 'Heavy Heavy', you actually think it could be some unearthed footage of the original group. The same could be said for when Beyoncé, as Jones, is watching the documentary that Taylor has made about her, *The Deena Jones Story* – the snaps and stills are so slavishly re-created that Diana Ross should see it as an almighty compliment. There are some moments that reflect Beyoncé's personal tale, such as leaving her girl group, and right back at the beginning, 13 years on from being rejected on *Star Time*, when Tiny Joe Dixon (Michael Leon Wooley) wins, beating The Dreams, you can see all of Beyoncé's latent angst.

Beyoncé met Diana Ross, who was allegedly very kind to her. When Ross was interviewed about the film, she replied that she had not seen it, but said, "I know it is not our story, and I know that they have taken images and likenesses of our story and used that. So I'm confused as to how I should react, because I'm complimented on one hand, but it's not something that's true. People are going to think there's some truth there, when there's not."

Although there is a strong feeling of an ensemble cast, it is Hudson's and Foxx's film. Beyoncé contributes well, but doesn't get that much of an opportunity to shine. Eddie Murphy won a Golden Globe for his performance as James 'Thunder' Early, who appears to be a mixture of James Brown, Jackie Wilson, Ike Turner and Marvin Gaye, yet whose tale recalls more the tragedy of Temptations' singers Eddie Kendricks and David Ruffin. Murphy appears to be having the time of his life as Early, and romps through his vocal parts with glee. Especially as he 'Marvinises' his role as the film develops – singing 'Patience', a thinly veiled amalgam of tracks from Gaye's *What's Going On*, and then dropping his trousers on stage, referencing perhaps the bewildering striptease that Gaye made a part of his act during his final tours in the eighties.

'Listen', the new song written for the film that had debuted as the hidden track on *B'Day*, is a powerful *tour de force* for Beyoncé, added to give the symmetry to Hudson's show-stopper 'And I'm Telling You I'm Not Going'. On 'Listen' Beyoncé's voice really comes through, after being shoe-horned into Diana Ross impressions for the rest of the movie.

Dreamgirls cost $80 million to make and returned $154 million at box office. It was allegedly the highest-budget film to date featuring almost solely an African-American cast. Although Beyoncé's role is slight – which is unusual for the centre of the film – she appeared accomplished. Moreover, she was central to the plot and effectively the lead actress, as opposed to a secondary foil or window-dressing for the film's main protagonist. Although she did not win any awards personally, the film won Best Picture – Musical or Comedy at the 64th Golden Globes ceremony (one of three awards) and two Oscars at the 79th Academy Awards, including one for Jennifer Hudson as Best Supporting Actress for her performance as Effie.

Beyoncé called *Dreamgirls* her first role as an actress, and she trained hard for it. She studied Diana Ross' work, lost weight and endlessly rehearsed with acting coach Ivana Chubbuck. Despite all this, you can't help but feel it is akin to watching your offspring in a school production. No matter how much you root for her, someone else's kid puts in a much better performance.

The year 2006 also proved very busy for Mathew Knowles and Music World Entertainment. As the House of Deréon brand grew, Knowles opened a state-of-the-art centre on Crawford Street in Midtown Houston, as a venue for new and up-and-coming artists to showcase their talents. The building – converted from an old storage warehouse that once housed Destiny Child's stages – became a media centre and function suite painstakingly designed by T.K.

There was also the full launch of Tina and Beyoncé's fashion line, House of Deréon, which had first been announced in 2004 and then heavily promoted via the marketing and interviews for *B'Day*. With its strapline of 'Couture. Kick. Soul' it was described by Tina (the 'couture' of the strapline) thus: "House of Deréon is a line of beautiful cocktail and evening dresses, sizes 2 to 14, inspired by Beyoncé's red carpet looks."

Tina used the designing skill she had inherited from her mother, Agnéz Beyincé (the 'soul'). The fashion line's title taken from her mother's maiden name (Deréon), Tina responded to the inspiration from Beyoncé (the 'kick'). "A lot of times, she'll go through magazines and tear out photos and show them to us," Tina said. "We don't ever copy them, but it gives us an idea of the colours and textures she likes and then we'll start sketching and designing."

Distribution deals were sorted out quickly and the Deréon brand made it into a variety of stores such as Neiman Marcus, Saks, Macy's, Dillards, Nordstrom and Bloomingdales. "Deréon focuses on Beyoncé's fan base," Tina continued. "[It] includes children, pre-teens, juniors and a plus-size collection called Curvelicious. Deréon also has an extensive denim line which includes the Superlicious Skinny Jeans as well as handbags, shoes, jewelry, and lingerie."

Sporting a line from Deréon's swimwear range, Beyoncé appeared on the cover of the infamous US magazine *Sports Illustrated* in February 2007 to promote her album, dressed in a yellow bikini. Again this seemed a defiant step away from her homespun roots. She was, as Beyoncé biographer Janice Arenofsky highlighted, the first musician and only the second African-American woman to grace the cover.

The tour that supported *B'Day*, The Beyoncé Experience, was an enormous, globetrotting venture, performed over five legs. It commenced in Japan on April 10, 2007, and culminated in Las Vegas at the Mandalay Bay Resort on December 30, 2007.

Auditions for her new touring band, which became known as Suga Mama, had been held on Saturday 17 June, 2006. People flew in from across the world to audition – Beyoncé wanted the best players available, with only one stipulation: that they were female. "I wanted to get together a group of fierce, talented, hungry, beautiful women and form an all-girl band," she told MTV. "I'm all about female empowerment. I'm all about pushing the envelope. I know it's my responsibility to do something different. I said, 'I want a band, I want something different.'"

"It was extremely difficult . . . I wanted only a nine-piece band, but the girls were so amazing, I couldn't decide. I think I'm going to wind up having 12 people . . . . It's a thing called star quality, it's a thing you can't put your finger on, can't describe. When they were playing, I said, 'I want to see y'all battle.' I brought in two of every instrument and that's how I chose. You see the one that really wants it. It was so entertaining, the energy, seeing the girls battle . . . God, it was the best. It was magical." P!nk guitarist Bibi McGill and talented bass player Divinity Walker Roxx were chosen as musical directors. There were two drummers, Nikki Glaspie and Kim Thomson. Jazz keyboardist and assistant MD Rie Tsuji was joined on keyboards by Brittani Washington; Marcie Chapa added percussion, and the band were finished off with a horn section that included Katty Rodriguez Harrold (tenor sax); Tia Fuller (alto) and Crystal J Torres on trumpet. The group was augmented by three striking female vocalists, who became known as The Mamas: Montina Cooper, Crystal A Collins and Tiffany Riddick. Ten dancers, five male and five female, captained by Anthony Burrell and Milan Dillard, completed the spectacle.

In many respects, The Beyoncé Experience was the tour on which Beyoncé truly defined her solo sound and personality. As she explained in the tour's glossy brochure: "Every thing I do creatively has to make me work harder and hopefully steer me in a direction I've never been before. If it's easy, then the excitement is gone; I don't like to be bored and comfortable when it comes to my music. I like to challenge myself and those around me to be the very best creatively." The tour was a creative triumph: marshalling a 12-piece band, three backing vocalists and ten dancers, yet still creating a stadium show that was as emotional and intimate as it was extravagant and flamboyant. The *New York Times* said of her Madison Square Garden show in August 2007: "Onstage she had an all-woman band, and the show used men only as dancers: decorative beefcake for her primarily female audience."

During the tour, Beyoncé oversaw the release of a Deluxe Edition of *B'Day*, which contained the video album, five new tracks, a selection of material recorded in Spanish and the extended mix of 'Get Me Bodied'. This was the release that properly cemented *B'Day* in the hearts and charts. One of the new tracks, 'Beautiful Liar', was chosen as a single for release in May 2007. It teamed Beyoncé with Colombian singing sensation Shakira, and the song, written by Stargate, Amanda Ghost, Beyoncé and, unbelievably, former EMF guitarist Ian Dench, was a dramatic, sultry, Arabian-influenced number that evoked the sprit of 'Independent Women Part I'. It was a dramatic tale of two women loving the same man, the titular 'Beautiful Liar'. Instead of engaging in a love contest, both ultimately decide to dump the love rat.

Beyoncé was full of praise for her collaborator. "She's one of my favorite Latin singers, and I have nothing but respect for her," she told MTV. "She's so sweet, so sexy, so positive . . . We met three or four years ago at the MTV Video Music Awards, and we said, 'We have to do something together,' and finally, we made it happen. "We weren't able to record together because she was on tour, but it still turned out so wonderful." The record was recorded in different studios across America as both artists toured.

The video was directed by Jake Nava and featured a true cavalcade of gyration. Beyoncé, as always, had a clear perception of how the promo should be. "I wanted us to play off the idea that we kind of look alike. I saw this guy dancing once, and it looked like he was performing in the mirror until I realised [he was dancing with] another person, and I thought, 'How amazing!' So we tried to do that." The promo really played up the physical similarities of the artists, intercutting between the two of them until they both appear together, writhing on the floor.

The single became an enormous success, and another shot in the arm for the longevity of *B'Day*. 'Beautiful Liar' rushed to the top of the charts in the UK, and reached the number three spot in the US. The song was another well-written, stick-in-the-mind classic; its Spanish version, 'Bello Embustero', was nominated for Record Of The Year at the Latin Grammys, while the song won the Best Selling British Song at the Ivor Novello Awards in 2008, as writers Amanda Ghost and Ian Dench are British.

On June 25, Beyoncé also found time to play a concert at Radio City Music Hall in New York with Jay-Z to celebrate the 10th anniversary of his *Reasonable Doubt* album. Beyoncé sang the Mary J. Blige part on 'Can't Knock The Hustle'. This show was Beyoncé's final elevation into the world of hip-hop royalty.

The DVD of Beyoncé's tour, entitled *The Beyoncé Experience Live*, captured the show perfectly. Filmed at the 20,000-capacity Staples Center on Figueroa Street, Los Angeles, on September 2, director Nick Wickham caught the tour five months in and firing on all cylinders. Appearing through the floor and a curtain of fireworks to 'The Beyoncé Experience Fanfare', before standing, looking slightly to the left, to the right and then straight ahead as she proclaimed "ARE YOU READY TO BE ENTERTAINED?", Beyoncé then launches into 'Crazy In Love'.

The set, designed by Beyoncé and Frank Gatson, Jr., comprised five illuminated steps with Suga Mama, the backing singers, and dancers all arrayed across it. It was breathtaking theatre, played out to maximum effect by Beyoncé. No opportunity to perform a grand gesture was missed. The DVD featured a true gathering of past and present when Jay-Z joined her onstage to perform 'Upgrade U', and Kelly Rowland and Michelle Williams joined Beyoncé to perform 'Survivor'. The Destiny's Child section is show business writ in capital letters. 'Jumpin',

Jumpin,", the song about bagging something better for yourself, is played with the lasciviousness of artists much older. 'Survivor', she says from stage, is for those who have survived "sexism and racism". By bringing on Williams and Rowland, it became a deeply emotional experience.

The DVD release came as the final shows of the tour were playing out. Filmed by British director Nick Wickham, it was released on November 20, 2007, in the US and November 26 in the UK. The DVD was an instant success, spending over 150 weeks on the US charts, selling triple platinum and peaking at number two. An edited version was shown on European television, while on November 19, 2007, a version was shown in US movie theatres. The soundtrack alone was made available as an iTunes release.

On February 10, 2008, Beyoncé performed at the Grammy Awards with her icon, Tina Turner. As Beyoncé introduced her, she went through a specially written rap, penned with various Grammy writers. As a seductive bassline trickled on, Beyoncé sat *Cabaret* style on a chair and said: "Sarah Vaughan, Aretha Franklin, Chaka Khan; historical women who have performed on this very stage. When I was a little girl, I dreamed of being on this very stage, but I knew I needed all the right elements . . . like the beat of Donna Summer; the spirit of Mahalia Jackson, the jazz of Ella Fitzgerald or Nancy; Lena Horne, Anita Baker, Diana Ross, Gladys, Janet and the beautiful melodies of Whitney – the legacy they have bestowed [is] simply irreplaceable but there is one legend who has the essence of all of these things – the glamour, the soul, the passion, the strength, the talent – ladies and gentlemen, stand on your feet and give it up for the Queen."

The pair launched into a spirited version of Creedence Clearwater Revival's 'Proud Mary', the record that Ike and Tina Turner had taken into the charts back in 1971. This performance marked Tina Turner's return to the live stage for the first time in seven years. It is energetic and robust – and it demonstrated fully how accomplished Beyoncé was as a vocalist. It all goes swimmingly, apart from a moment where she steps on Tina Turner's toe three quarters of the way through.

There was controversy however, when she hailed Tina Turner as 'the Queen', which stoked Aretha Franklin's ire: "I am not sure whose toes I may have stepped on or whose ego I may have bruised between the

Grammy writers and Beyoncé," Franklin announced through her publicist. "However, I dismissed it as a cheap shot for controversy. In addition to that, I thank the Grammys and the voting academy for my 20th Grammy and love to Beyoncé anyway." The scam seemed all a little cooked up.

Virtually ever since they first worked together and became an item, rumours had been circulating of Beyoncé and Jay-Z's wedding. One of the more fanciful rumours on the Internet in 2006 was that Beyoncé had indeed purchased the David and Elizabeth Emmanuel-designed wedding dress of Princess Diana, from July 1981. "I wish I could talk to whoever wrote that, because it's fabulous," she said to *USA Today*. "Somebody is so creative that they should plan weddings, because they have a great one planned for me and Jay! It even has a menu with caviar. I don't even like caviar!"

After picking up their licence the preceding week from Scarsdale Village Hall, Beyoncé and Jay-Z were finally married on Friday April 4, 2008. A friend of the couple was reported as saying, "It happened earlier this evening. Jay wanted it to be a really private affair – close friends and family." It was an intimate event, with guests including the other Destiny's Child girls and Gwyneth Paltrow. The entertainment for the evening was DJ Cassidy, aka Cassidy Podell, the young New York DJ who had become the go-to spinner for the party set. The next day after the wedding, Jay-Z returned to the recording studio, while Beyoncé went back to continue work on her new film, *Cadillac Records*.

In June 2008, Beyoncé's husband, Jay-Z, played the Glastonbury Festival in the UK, and caused a minor storm, as he brought hip-hop to the intrinsically white rock festival. Beyoncé watched from the wings as Jay-Z performed a scintillating set that opened with a cover version of 'Wonderwall' by Oasis, a direct message to the band's guitarist Noel Gallagher, who had said, when Jay-Z was announced as headliner, "No, I'm not havin' hip-hop at Glastonbury. Fuckin' no chance." Gallagher, whose band's meat'n'potatoes rock had taken top billing on the festival's main Pyramid stage three times previously, strongly believed hip-hop had no place on the main stage.

The crowd and the media thought otherwise. "In the event, Jay-Z at Glastonbury 2008 proved to be the most thrilling headline act for more than a decade," Pete Paphides wrote in *The Times*. "We should have known that the artist, who retired briefly from making music in 2003 because there was nothing new left to achieve, would relish this sort of challenge." The warmth of the crowd and the uniqueness of the event resonated deeply with Beyoncé. "I was so proud of him that night." She told *The Daily Telegraph* that November. "To come into that atmosphere and that incredible place and do what he did. I've seen those pictures of Kate Moss in her boots and all that mud! I was dancing like crazy, dancing crazy hip-hop moves offstage. I don't know if I've ever seen him do a better show. He rocked that crowd, showed them what he's about. Jay is, well . . . he's the number one. But there was something going on that night – something more than just music." Little controversies like Glastonbury felt like the death spasms of an old way of thinking," Jay-Z wrote in his 2010 autobiography, *Decoded*.

One of the prime pastimes of the press in the late noughties was trying to glean anything about Beyoncé and Jay-Z's personal life. *Rolling Stone*, the once august journal of the counterculture, was positively frothing at the mouth when it got some crumbs from Jay-Z. In an interview published with him in June 2009, editor Mark Binelli learnt that Beyoncé disapproved of a piece of Laurie Simmons art that Jay had purchased for their apartment. Beyond that, Jay-Z gave the moderately curt "sometimes on creative stuff, one of us will ask, 'Do you think this is cool?' She's a magnificent A&R, if she ever decides to do that, for things like pitch. So I defer to her on those sort of questions." The magazine that once featured Hunter Thompson's writing salivated that "for the rest, Jay reckons the couple 'pretty much stay out of each other's business'". That didn't stop acres of attempted insight into their relationship.

In the few moments between all of the other commitments, Beyoncé spent most of 2008 recording her new album, which, due to a surfeit of material, looked likely to be a double. As she completed *Cadillac Records*, she began filming a new thriller directed by Steve Shill, co-starring Idris Elba.

CHAPTER 13

I Am . . . *Sasha Fierce*

'For this one I wanted to take my time. I ended up recording 70 songs. And I was so attached to the songs – you put your heart into it. And I realised I had made two albums. It's a lot of music.'

Beyoncé, 2008

Beyoncé's third solo album, *I Am . . . Sasha Fierce*, was released on November 18, 2008. It was clear from the wealth of material on the dual CD set that it would be an album that could be marketed long into the future. A perfectly balanced double set in its initial release, it had eight tracks per side. The concept was brave and simple: each disc would show a "distinctly different side of her personality, character and sensibility, a forum for the yin-and-yang of her developing artistry". If *B'Day* had been Beyoncé's hurried, rough-edges-showing work, then *I Am . . . Sasha Fierce* was painstakingly put together. The first disc, *I Am . . .* provided a showcase for her balladry; but on it, she explored different musical approaches, including British indie and folk music. *Sasha Fierce* would reinforce her penchant for uptempo grooves.

Once again acting as executive producer with her father, Mathew, Beyoncé worked with producers such as Kenneth 'Babyface' Edmonds, Stargate, Christopher 'Tricky' Stewart and Terius 'The-Dream' Nash, regular Rodney 'Darkchild' Jerkins, Sean Garrett, sister, Solange, Jim Jonsin, Rico Love and Ryan Tedder. Toby Gad worked on 'If I Were A Boy' and UK songwriter Amanda Ghost (who had co-written 'You're Beautiful' with James Blunt), on the Beatles-influenced 'Disappear', 'Satellites' and 'Ave Maria'. What was different about *I Am . . . Sasha Fierce* was the length of time Beyoncé spent crafting it, with writing and recording continuing for over a year. It was the longest period of time she had spent making an album since Destiny's Child's debut back in 1998.

I Am . . . Sasha Fierce was a triumph of cross-marketing. As Beyoncé defined her wild alter ego for a wider audience – not in itself highly unusual in pop, as artists from Ziggy Stardust to Slim Shady had done for many years – it was an opportunity to introduce a new clothing line for Sasha through House of Deréon and market her goods to her younger audience. Staffordshire University Professor Ellis Cashmore absolutely marvelled at her accomplished audacity: "*Sasha Fierce* was Beyoncé's most preposterous yet accomplished industrial innovation yet," he writes in 'Buying Beyoncé'. "It was a smart, perhaps brilliant diversification, like Toyota's introduction of Lexus, a separate marque but one that carried the reputation of the established car manufacturer."

There is a great deal to enjoy on this mature, complete album; all demographics were covered. From the rock of 'If I Were A Boy' to the techno pizzazz of 'Single Ladies (Put A Ring On It)'; it is a work full of knowing references and subtle in-jokes. For example, there is the comedy of Kanye West, a man not known for his modesty, singing about the size of his ego on the track 'Ego'. It works on many levels: this is a post-modern singer – wholly aware of how he can appear to the world – singing on an album by one of his benefactors, Jay-Z's wife, and one of the biggest stars in the world.

"When I started the record," Beyoncé wrote, "I knew that, artistically, I had to grow. Even though I've been very successful and very fortunate, I want to still be challenged and still be nervous and still be anxious about all the things that make my career exciting." It was a daring, complex record, and Beyoncé ensured that the concept was spelled out for her audience.

"Sasha Fierce is my alter ego," she said, "and now she has a last name. I have someone else that takes over when it's time for me to work and when I'm on stage, this alter ego that I've created that kind of protects me and who I really am. That's why half the record, *I Am . . .* , is about who I am underneath all the make-up, underneath the lights, and underneath all the exciting star drama. And Sasha Fierce is the fun, more sensual, more aggressive, more outspoken and more glamorous side that comes out when I'm working and when I'm on the stage. The double album allows me to take more risks and really step out of myself, or shall I say, step more into myself, and reveal a side of me that only people who know me see." The tracks most indicative of the different approaches on the album, 'If I Were A Boy' and 'Single Ladies (Put A Ring On It)', were taken to US radio on October 8, 2009. Both were warmly received, and then, in November, released digitally and physically.

The album's *I Am . . .* side begins with 'If I Were A Boy,' the only song on the album not to have a Beyoncé co-writing credit. Written by German producer Toby Gad and the song's original performer, BC Jean, it was the most direct departure from anything Beyoncé had attempted before. If 'Irreplaceable' had demonstrated how she could work with rock-influenced pop, this song went all out for the AOR market. And it worked. Beyoncé said of 'If I Were A Boy': "It's difficult to grow and to break out and do new things because people have strong expectations. I feel like at this point, I wanted people to hear songs with stronger lyrics and songs that made you feel. I love singing ballads because I feel like the music and the emotion in the story is told so much better. It's a better connection because you can hear it and it's not all these other distractions." Simply recorded and presented, with instruments by Gad and additional guitar by Reggie 'Syience' Perry, it was a different step. "I had to try it," she told *Essence* magazine, "because I remember Aretha Franklin said a great singer can sing anything and make it her own."

The single considers gender politics, with a woman ruefully looking at the simple advantages of male behaviour. The idea came from writer Jean, who was walking in New York's Times Square with Gad. "There was an amazing smell coming from this pizzeria," Jean told *Songwriter Universe*. "I was doing the diet thing and [I said] 'If I were a boy, I would totally eat that.' And he said, 'What did you say?' And I said, 'I wish I were a boy so I could eat pizza and popcorn and wear baggy clothes.' He asked me what else I would do and I said, 'I'd be a better man than my ex-boyfriend,' and he was like, 'How would you sing it, BC'? We went back to the studio, I came up with the lyrics and melody, and it was just one of those honest, emotional songs that came out quickly, in less than 30 minutes." Fortunately for Beyoncé, Jean's record company rejected the song; Beyoncé heard it when *I Am . . . Sasha Fierce* was in demo stage. It was a sad, rueful song, made real by Beyoncé's emotional delivery.

Its video, shot entirely in black and white in New York City by Jake Nava, found Beyoncé playing the role reversal with relish: she dresses as an NYPD officer and takes us through her day, highlighting the small but significant things men do unthinkingly that can damage their loved one's feelings. Her husband (played by a suitably smouldering Eddie Goines, an NFL player) has to put up with Beyoncé picking disinterestedly at her breakfast and not answering her mobile calls from him while out with her work colleagues. Finally, she is about to commit adultery in front of him.

It is, of course, all a daydream, and the video ends revealing that her husband is actually the police officer; we have seen the role reversal, highlighting all the unthinking things the husband has done to the wife. It continues the sledgehammer-to-crack-a-nut message of the record, but this very simplicity is what translates it to world audiences. The single vied for a chart placing with the simultaneous release of 'Single Ladies (Put A Ring On It)' in the US, but it reached number one in the UK at the end of November 2008, eventually becoming Beyoncé's best-selling solo single in the UK. It made number six in the *Billboard* Hot 100.

The poignant reflection on *I Am . . .* continues with the sadness of 'Halo', written by Ryan Tedder, Evan Bogart and Beyoncé. Tedder, the talented lead singer and writer of OneRepublic, had become one of the hottest writing properties in the world after his band's 'Apologize' and his co-writing of 'Bleeding Love' for UK *X Factor* winner Leona Lewis both became huge hits. He had the idea to write a song along the lines of the work of American troubadour Ray LaMontagne. 'Halo' had originally been intended for Beyoncé, but because she was busy, Tedder tentatively offered it to Leona Lewis; Beyoncé then recorded it, causing some outrage from *X Factor* supremo Simon Cowell, who looked after Lewis' interest. Against a backdrop of yet more controversy, which played out on the Internet, it was released as the fourth single from the album in January 2009. It was a power ballad, emphasising the sublime nature of love, a point reinforced by its video, directed by Philip Andelman. The song reached number five in the US chart, and one place higher in the UK. 'Halo' would be used as a tribute to Michael Jackson on Beyoncé's I Am . . . Tour after his death in June 2009.

The guitar-based 'Disappear' was sweet and affecting. Produced by Amanda Ghost, Dave McCracken and Ian Dench, and written with the producers and RocNation artist Hugo Chakrabongse, it is a low-key radio-friendly ballad with beautiful harmonies that add to the atmosphere of *I Am* . . . It is let down only by the regimented and rapidly dating drum machine that underpins the track. The maudlin 'Broken-Hearted Girl' almost sounds like the same song as 'Halo'. Produced by Stargate and written by them with Beyoncé and Babyface, it was another power ballad, with Beyoncé stressing that she would not be prepared to play the part of a 'broken-hearted girl' in a relationship. Mikkel Eriksen of Stargate explained to *Sound On Sound* how the track came to be. Written initially with Babyface, it was originally a full-on R&B track, before the song slowed down to its deeply reflective style. "From there we proceeded to change the entire backing track around his vocal. We changed the chords, everything, and this is where that four to the floor piano emerged. The song is in D-minor." The minor chord gave it an inescapable melancholy. "We probably lean towards more a moody, melodic expression. It's what comes most natural for us." The track was released on the B-side of the US single of 'Video Phone' and as a single in the UK, where it made number 27.

I Am . . . shifts a gear with 'Ave Maria'; co-written with Ghost, it restyled Schubert's sacred song into a folk-influenced ballad. It is a beautiful showcase for Beyoncé's vocals, and while owing quite a deal to Madonna's 1989 masterpiece, 'Oh Father', 'Ave Maria' is a big, warm, beautiful hug of a record. It came about when Ghost realised that both she and Beyoncé had recently married to the strains of the lilting hymn. Ghost, speaking to Tom Horan in *The Daily Telegraph*, felt the song really hit an emotional spot for Beyoncé. "She talks about being surrounded by friends but she's alone: 'How can the silence be so loud?' and then 'There's only us when the lights go down.' I think that's probably the most personal line on the whole album about her and Jay, because they are very real, and they're very much in love, and it must be pretty tough to have that love when you're incredibly famous." Produced with Stargate, it is understated, given the opportunities it provides for going completely over the top.

The album returns to mid-paced rock balladry with 'Smash Into You', produced with Beyoncé by Christopher 'Tricky' Stewart and Terius 'The-Dream' Nash; and 'Satellites' which closed some editions of the first side of the album. Written and produced with Ghost and Dench, 'Satellites' was a gentle, acoustic guitar-led song, which sounds not unlike something that could have appeared on an early Crosby, Stills and Nash album. There are some melodic and phrasing resemblances to Guns N' Roses' 'Sweet Child O'Mine', but that is where any similarities end. It is one of the album's most successful tracks, with its subtle use of strings, and comes as blessed relief from the regimentation of the drum machine. The conflation of the personal and the global on the song showcases Beyoncé at her very best.

'That's Why You're Beautiful', which closed *I Am . . .* , is a complete departure for Beyoncé. Owing nothing whatsoever to her R&B roots, this track, with its power chords and jangle of electric guitars and tom-tom heavy drums, sounds not unlike British indie pioneers Joy Division, or US art rockers Talking Heads' tribute to Joy Division, 'The Overload'. With the metaphor that diamonds once being coal are like Beyoncé's heart before love came along, it is a track that could be taken undercover to rock radio and no one would imagine it was Beyoncé. All in all *I Am . . .* was a bold experiment. If not wholly successful (a lot of the material becomes rather samey), it showed how serious Beyoncé was as an artist. It was a side of music to be admired rather than loved, but it was clear that Beyoncé at 27 was a mature, thoughtful performer.

Sasha Fierce was almost diametrically opposed to the intense eyebrow-knitting of *I Am . . .* The listener is abruptly back on safer ground, on an uptempo swirl of intoxicating beats. Sasha was here. "Sometimes you just want to feel good," Beyoncé explained. "She's the party girl, she's bootylicious. She is but I'm not. She's my alter ego. I'm finally revealing who I am." It was a very good way to legitimise the uptempo party songs that she had been singing on previous albums. The underlying concept gave the whole project a gravitas. "In my life, when I put on the stilettos, it's all about being confident, sometimes overly confident, and hearing all the things that women need to hear to boost themselves and go out and to move on," Beyoncé said. "*Sasha Fierce* is fun."

Produced by the team behind Rihanna's groundbreaking 'Umbrella', The-Dream and Tricky Stewart, and written by them with Beyoncé and Thaddis 'Kuk' Harrell, 'Single Ladies (Put A Ring On It)', was a killer single. It re-established Beyoncé in the popular imagination in the most convincing way since 2003's 'Crazy In Love'. *The Times* said, "It has the mix of unfettered sexual energy, sonic eccentricity and lung-busting vocals – not to mention hooks that burrow instantly and immovably inside your brain – that courses through much of Beyoncé's work." *Entertainment Weekly* called it "a giddy, high-stepping hybrid of lyrical kiss-off and fizzy jump-rope jam". It was big, bold, daft, funny, powerful, everything that classic chart pop should be.

Following the metallic groove-based style of 'Get Me Bodied' and 'Ring The Alarm', the song was three minutes plus of infectious party-style beats. Owing something to dancehall, it was as if Beyoncé had created a genre completely of her own with this wild show of female empowerment. Older British listeners may indeed have noted a similarity with the theme from the seventies UK TV magazine programme *Nationwide* in its chorus. It is, of course, highly unlikely this would have ever crossed the path of the 'Single Ladies' writers and producers. It is with every good reason that it won Song Of The Year at the 2009 Grammy Awards.

However, more than any another Beyoncé track, either solo or in Destiny's Child, its continued success was down to the simple potency of its video. Intricately choreographed and featuring just Beyoncé and backing dancers Ebony Williams and Ashley Everett in Tina Knowles-designed leotards, it became a YouTube phenomenon. Choreographed by Frank Gatson, Jr. with support from JaQuel Knight, it had echoes of two other performances – Bob Fosse's routines for *Sweet Charity* and a little-known clip called 'Mexican Breakfast', which featured Fosse's wife Gwen Verdon and appeared on *The Ed Sullivan Show* on US TV in 1969.

The premise was straightforward: director Jake Nava had little time and money after shooting the 'If I Were A Boy' video, and another promo was needed for the debut releases from *I Am . . . Sasha Fierce*. Shot in one 12-hour session, it was Beyoncé and her dancers dancing frantically to the song in a series of tightly choreographed moves that frequently used J-Setting – a style which incorporated the 'booty bounce' and mannered movements of the arms. A major characteristic is its lead-and-follow component to an eight-beat count. The dance, which was said to originate from cheerleaders at Jackson State University, had become an underground style popularised in gay clubs. Beyoncé, in a possible homage to Michael Jackson, was wearing a Roboglove made of titanium, designed by her jeweller Lorraine Schwartz.

The video attracted over 60 million hits on YouTube. And it was from YouTube that Beyoncé got the inspiration for the groundbreaking video, after watching 'Mexican Breakfast': "They had a plain background and it was shot on the crane; it was 360 degrees, they could move around. And I said, 'This is genius.' We kept a lot of the Fosse choreography and added the down-South thing — it's called J-Setting, where one person does something and the next person follows. So it was a strange mixture, kind of like the song, which is almost like a nursery rhyme, the 'oh-oh-oh's, and the sinister chords. So it's like the most urban choreography, mixed with Fosse – very modern and very vintage . . . it's the least expensive video I've done. Not for a moment did I think, 'This is going to be a movement.'"

A movement it became. The UK craze of 'flashmobbing', where hundreds of people were contacted via social media to arrive at a certain place at a certain time to do something collectively, saw London's Liverpool Street station turned into a living, breathing 'Single Ladies' dance routine. Countless parodies of the promo sprang up. On November 16, 2008, Beyoncé was a guest on legendary US comedy show *Saturday Night Live*, hosted by comic actor Paul Rudd. Beyoncé gleefully sent herself up, reshooting the video with three male backing dancers in leotards and high heels, including superstar singer Justin Timberlake. The single became her second to-die-for solo anthem, finally something to take the onus off 'Crazy In Love'. It was an easy US number one.

After this groundbreaking overture, the heavily synthesised track 'Radio' was very personal to Beyoncé, a tale of her childhood which outlines how she would listen to the radio as a teenager and absorb herself in music as opposed to going out. Written by Rico Love (who arranged the album's vocals with Beyoncé), Dwayne Nesmith, Beyoncé and James Scheffer, the song was an upbeat nod to the electro influences that were sweeping across R&B towards the end of the decade. "It's about me growing up," Beyoncé told *China Daily*. "In my household, I didn't go to all of the parties and I didn't do all the things that a lot of the other teenage girls did because I was so in love with my radio and my music. I was so in love with this radio and my parents were happy that I was into something positive." The track, which was later released as a single, was described by Alexis Petridis in *The Guardian*: "The 80s synthpop mode of 'Radio' may be less suited to Knowles than the old soul samples that powered 'Crazy in Love' and *B'Day*'s 'Suga Mama', and underlined the link between her vocal style and the visceral female singers of the 60s, but there's no denying it's an irresistible pop song."

The album returns to more conventional territory with 'Diva'. Pumping, hip-hop influenced, bass-heavy and pared-down, it places Beyoncé with writers and producers Shondrae 'Bangladesh' Crawford and Sean Garrett and owes something to their production of Lil Wayne's 'A Milli'. It finds Beyoncé making a case for her parity with hustlers, her male counterparts, and bragging about her earning power. Released as a single in the US, it fared better on the club play charts than the Hot 100, where its quirky, frankly eccentric beats meant it only reached number 19.

Its video, directed by Melina Matsoukas, shows Beyoncé strutting and preening like her male counterparts and finds her back in the bridges and underpasses of Los Angeles. Going into a warehouse to dance, she leaves the building and watches a car explode, in a direct reference to her 'Crazy In Love' promo from five years previously, where Jay-Z did the same.

'Sweet Dreams' was another flirtation with electro. Written and produced by Jim Jonsin, Rico Love, Wayne Wilkins and Beyoncé, the song was recorded in May 2008, and soon after leaked on to the Internet, under its then title 'Beautiful Nightmare'. Taken on its own, it highlighted a new direction for Beyoncé; that of smooth, supple electro-pop, shortly to be explored further by British artists such as La Roux and the soon-to-be-superstar Lady Gaga. It is one of the album's most accomplished performances, with its tremendously radio-friendly chorus. Released as a single in June 2009, it reached number five on both sides of the Atlantic.

The album's deep groove continued with 'Video Phone', which was produced by Shondrae Crawford and had a particularly Eastern sound to it. It was a pretty explicit call for Beyoncé to be filmed naked on a video phone. *The Guardian* suggested that the track introduces "us to the unlikely figure of Beyoncé Knowles, amateur pornographer; 'you want me naked? If you like this position you can tape it.' She doesn't make for the world's most believable Reader's Wife but it doesn't matter, because the spare, eerie backdrop of groans and echoing electronics is so thrilling."

It became the eighth release from the album when it was lifted as a single in the UK in November 2009 featuring the latest pop sensation, Lady Gaga. Gaga, born Stefani Joanne Angelina Germanotta in New York in 1986, took Madonna's template for controversy and doubled it with her potent mixture of electronic beats, performance art and arresting visual images. The pairing of Beyoncé and Gaga was not surprising. They shared producers in common and, through 'Video Phone', Beyoncé was able to provide Gaga with respectability, while Gaga helped keep Beyoncé at the cutting edge of commercialism.

The following track, 'Hello', sounds like it has escaped from the *I Am* . . . side of the album. A big, beautiful piano-heavy ballad, its sizeable beats obfuscate the beauty of its melody. Written by Beyoncé with David 'DQ' Quiñones, Evan 'Kidd' Bogart and Ramon Owens, it is a simple love song sung by Beyoncé in a highly stylised manner, as if to distance herself somewhat from the material.

'Ego' had, as stated previously, Kanye West added to its later version.

Before her show in Singapore, Marina Bay Street Circuit, September 26, 2009. (CORBIS)

Wearing Sasha's Roboglove at the World Music Awards, Monte Carlo, Monaco. (SIPA PRESS/REX FEATURES)

A fragile alliance: Etta James and Beyoncé arriving at the premiere of *Cadillac Records*, the Egyptian Theater, Hollywood, in 2008. James would later say that Beyoncé would have her "ass whupped" by her. (ALBERTO E. RODRIGUEZ/GETTY IMAGES)

Singing their duet from Alicia Keys' *The Element Of Freedom*, 'Put In A Love Song', Keys and Beyoncé at Madison Square Garden on March 17, 2010. (UFBERG/WIREIMAGE)

Winning one of her six awards from her ten nominations at the 52nd Annual GRAMMY Awards. She broke the record for the most wins by a female artist in a night.

(MICHAEL CAULFIELD/WIREIMAGE)

(L–R) Beyoncé, Solange, Jay-Z and Gwyneth Paltrow attend the Metropolitan Museum of Art's 2011 Costume Institute Gala featuring the opening of the exhibit Alexander McQueen: Savage Beauty. (CORBIS)

Destiny is never far away: Kelly, Beyoncé and Michelle at the 2011 *Billboard* Music Awards at the MGM Grand Garden Arena in Las Vegas. (KEVIN MAZUR/GETTY IMAGES)

With her great friend Gwyneth Paltrow at The 53rd Grammy Awards in Los Angeles in February 2011. (ARNOLD TURNER/ WIREIMAGE)

Singing 'Run The World (Girls)' for Oprah Winfrey at *Surprise Oprah! A Farewell Spectacular* in May 2011, in Chicago. (DANIEL BOCZARSKI/GETTY IMAGES)

Oprah Winfrey with Dakota Fanning and Beyoncé during the taping of the third to last *Oprah Winfrey Show* at the United Center in Chicago, May 17, 2011. (PETER WYNN THOMPSON/AFP/GETTY IMAGES)

"Together they have carved out a new blueprint for black entertainers, making the key leap from being mere employees to being autonomous business people." *The Daily Telegraph*. Jay-Z and B at the 2011 NBA All-Star game. (NOEL VASQUEZ/GETTY IMAGES)

At the 2011 *Billboard* Music Awards at the MGM Grand Garden Arena May 22, 2011, in Las Vegas. (KEVIN MAZUR/GETTY IMAGES)

"I'm a rock star...we're all rock stars" Beyoncé makes Glastonbury her own, June 2011. (DAVE HOGAN/GETTY IMAGES)

The consummate professional. Showcasing *4* as the album stood atop both US and UK charts on *Good Morning America*, July 2011.
(STARTRAKS PHOTO/REX FEATURES)

A beautiful, soulful number, it offers the only link to old-school soul, so prevalent on all of Beyoncé's previous releases. Keening, preening gospel, it adds a great deal to the album. With its lilting chorus, it was written with Elvis Williams and Harold Lilly. It was released as a single in the US on May 19, 2009. Beyoncé serenades the 'big ego' of her lover. But here, it is the music that is outstanding, sounding exactly like a pastiche of Prince paying tribute to Curtis Mayfield. Featuring a real brass section – Donald Hayes, Philip Margiziotis and Dontae Winslow – it had elements of jazz and swing in its mix.

The video was directed by Beyoncé herself, and choreographed with Frank Gatson, Jr. Featuring West, it is still a good gag to hear him singing about how much Beyoncé is in love with his big ego. It is full of nudging references that what she really loves is not his ego but his manhood. It then opens out to Beyoncé and her dancers gyrating against a wall, with her in a showgirl costume. A fan version of the DVD appeared on the Platinum Edition of *I Am . . . Sasha Fierce*, shot at the same session, with Beyoncé performing the song from a throne-like chair. It was one of the many pleasant surprises that the album yielded.

Sasha Fierce closes with 'Scared Of Lonely', which again suffers somewhat from the curse of the drum machine, which detracts from the beauty of the ballad, a paean to insecurity. It was produced by old friend Rodney 'Darkchild' Jerkins, and returned Beyoncé to her Destiny's Child roots in an ornate, sensitive song, the playout of which makes a musical nod and wink to 'Say My Name', the track that first brought them together, almost a decade earlier. Beyoncé had travelled a long way since then.

With such a wealth of material and such a clearly defined concept, it was obvious that the project would have its detractors. "When I knew that certain things I wanted to say, I couldn't say myself, I invited other writers to come in," Beyoncé said. "Lyrically, it's the best album I've ever had. If a song didn't say anything or mean anything to me, I didn't put it on the record." Reviews for *I Am . . . Sasha Fierce* were mixed, but largely positive. *Entertainment Weekly* suggested that, "The collection might have been better served had she edited it down to one disc, rather than belabour what ultimately seems like a marketing gimmick. And while fans will surely speculate, there's little in the lyrics that feels more revealing than previous emotional fire-starters such as 2006's 'Ring the Alarm.' But who said we had a right to that, anyway? For all the pop-fantastic satisfaction that Beyoncé the entertainer provides, the public can surely reward her by leaving Beyoncé the private citizen well enough alone." The *LA Times* was somewhat unsure about the split between the two genres, but saw clearly how the first disc was designed to take Beyoncé to new audiences: "The weirdest thing about this split is its racial undertone. The Beyoncé ballads fall into that soft-rock zone that incorporates elements of crossover country, Celine-and-Whitney style divadom, and U2-derived guitar hymnody. They're vehemently not R&B, and Beyoncé enunciates them in a firmly post-racial style, in the same ballpark as her multi-culti rivals Alicia Keys and Leona Lewis." Ann Powers concluded her review for the paper by drawing parallels with Barack Obama, who at this point had just been elected the 44th President of the United States. "Consider *I Am . . . Sasha Fierce* Beyoncé's Obama album. Through it, she is imagining a pop sound that doesn't foreground race, but which still respects its roots in the black community. She's not there yet, but the effort is fascinating, and hopefully she will keep on this path. After all, the Obama that Beyoncé invokes with the name of her alter ego is still only a child." *Rolling Stone* said, "Both discs of *I Am . . . Sasha Fierce* yield stellar examples of Beyoncé's maturity into one of the most innovative and reliably excellent pop icons of the decade."

"I worked so hard on my previous album, *B'day*," Beyoncé said to *The Daily Telegraph*. "My last tour was 136 shows. For this one I wanted to take my time. I ended up recording 70 songs. And I was so attached to the songs – you put your heart into it. And I realised I had made two albums. It's a lot of music." It *was* a lot of music, especially as further tracks were issued across a plethora of B-sides and Platinum Editions of the album, which mixed up the two sides into a more measured, commercial offering. It was, like *B'Day* before it, a brave move, asking that her fan base grow and mature with her. In the main, it worked extremely well. It was with little surprise that *I Am . . . Sasha Fierce* entered the *Billboard* charts at number one, giving Beyoncé her third consecutive solo chart-topper.

In the UK it lodged at number two. Given that there was to be another gigantic tour to accompany its release, it was obvious that it would be around for a long time. In contrast to The Beyoncé Experience tour, her forthcoming stage presentation was scaled up and super-slick, ensuring that the message of *I Am . . . Sasha Fierce* would be carried worldwide until well into 2010.

The Times' Dan Cairns interviewed Beyoncé in Rotterdam in 2009, at the start of the European leg of the tour, and found a thoughtful, funny, artist behind the superstar façade. "I've been overanalysing my overanalysis. I think it's probably one of my better qualities," she semi-joked. "Every day, I sit and I think about my personal life, and my family, the way that I behave. And I learn something from the things that I do, and that other people do. I meet celebrities, and at one point, I thought, like, everybody was crazy. Then I met some really level-headed, grounded people, who are more grounded and cool than people who don't have all the pressure of celebrity. And I think my way of meditation, of keeping my sanity, is from the way that I analyse. Of course, nobody wants to do it (end up as a casualty), but it's just a lot of pressure – and temptation. It's really easy to fall into your own world, really, really easy. Every day, it's something that you have to be aware of, because there are always people who are opportunists, who will tell you anything."

Solange Knowles had also been busy. Her second album, *Sol-Angel And The Hadley St. Dreams*, was a fabulous homage to soul of the sixties and seventies. Released on Geffen in August 2008, it was promoted extensively throughout the rest of the year. With guest artists such as Cee-Lo Green and producers such as Freemasons (who had remixed her sister's 'Ring The Alarm'), Mark Ronson, The Neptunes and Thievery Corporation working with her, it was a left-field cutting-edge release. It gave Solange her first US Top 10 album. With a photo inside the sleeve of her writing the line 'I Must Not Have A Famous Family' as a school punishment, it made the point that there was another Knowles girl, too.

CHAPTER 14

Way Beyond A Cadillac: Superstardom

"The great Beyoncé. I can't stand Beyoncé. She has no business up there, singing up there on a big ol' president day."

Etta James, 2009

The opportunity to play Etta James in *Cadillac Records* was irresistible for Beyoncé. Again, she was deeply mining the African-American musical past for her next major film role. The film, the story of Chess Records, was a difficult call for Tristar and Sony Music to make, as the label never had the broad-based appeal of Motown. Chess Records was set up in Chicago by Polish émigré brothers Phil and Leonard Chess. They realised that there was a lucrative business in recording the talented singers and players that were migrating from the American South to Chicago to find work after the Second World War. They sold their music from the back of a Cadillac, and one of the most influential labels of all time was born.

In the film, there are homages to Willie Dixon (played by Cedric the Entertainer), Muddy Waters (Jeffrey Wright); Eamonn Walker captures the spikiness of Howlin' Wolf perfectly. Mos Def, working with Beyoncé for the second time on film after their appearance together in *Carmen: A Hip Hopera*, played Chuck Berry. The actors played the performers straight – there was no James 'Thunder' Early here.

Beyoncé plays James, one of the most soulful and troubled singers of her generation. Born Jamesetta Hawkins in Los Angeles in 1938 to a 14-year-old mother, James' sweet-kissed blues voice added gravitas to even the slightest of material, but her personal demons, including heroin addiction, often thwarted her chances of becoming a lasting commercial success. She was no Deena Jones.

Directed by Darnell Martin, *Cadillac Records* was another delve into US history. Narrated by Cedric the Entertainer as Willie Dixon, the film's mixture of biography and fantasy was richly evocative. When Beyoncé appears as James an hour into the film, you are so wrapped up in the moment, that you fail to immediately realise it is her.

One of the great tales about Etta James was that her father was allegedly the legendary US pool player Rudolf Wanderone, who nicknamed himself Minnesota Fats after a character in the 1961 film *The Hustler*. A meeting between him and James is fictionalised in *Cadillac Records*. After the inconclusive summit, set up for her by Leonard Chess, James explains to Chess that all her alleged father saw in her was not "his little girl", but "the cum stains of all the men my mother fucked". James is then seen overdosing on heroin. It is a key moment in the development of Beyoncé as an actor. This was a long way from *Austin Powers In Goldmember*.

Beyoncé worked again with acting coach Ivana Chubbuck, whom she'd first worked with on *Dreamgirls*. To prepare for the role, Chubbuck put Beyoncé – who has never touched drugs in her life – through an acting exercise to create a state of drug-induced catatonia. "We worked on one of the scenes that Etta has to be very stoned on heroin," Beyoncé testified on Chubbuck's website. "Not only did I feel organically high, but it brought up emotions that made sense to someone who needed to take a drug such as this – something to eliminate emotional pain. My emotions were very raw, yet I felt high. It was a unique experience, for sure." Beyoncé gave the most convincing performance of her career. She sings 'At Last', 'Trust In Me', 'All I Could Do Was Cry', 'I'd Rather Go

Blind' and the new song composed for the film, 'Once In A Lifetime', with tremendous conviction.

The film was premiered at the Egyptian Theatre in Los Angeles on November 24, 2008, before a national release on 5 December. Even though the Ray Charles biopic *Ray* (and indeed, *Dreamgirls*) had shown that audiences had a huge thirst for African-American biopics, the film struggled at the box office, finally making back its $12 million budget through rental and DVD sales. *Cadillac Records* is rather shaky in its timeline: the Rolling Stones appear at Chess (which they first did in 1964), and then later in the film we see Elvis Presley's television performances from the late Fifties. Leonard Chess dies (which he did in 1969); and then we see Muddy Waters embarking on his European tour (which he did in 1967). That said, the homage to the label is evident. As a sketch-essay of the growth and commercialisation of the blues in America, it is extremely well done.

Cadillac Records received mixed notices – best highlighted by two contrasting reviews from New York City. David Edelstein, writing in the *New York Magazine*, said, "The film moves swiftly and leaves out details, but that barely matters. The ensemble is stupendous – howlingly great – and the music goes deep." While Elizabeth Weitzman wrote in the *New York Daily News* that, "There are certain films – let's call them Road Map Movies – that drive you directly from point A to point B to point C, with barely a stop for gas. *Cadillac Records* is such a film: you see all the major landmarks, but how enlightening can a road trip be if you never even get off the highway?" Grittier than *Dreamgirls*, *Cadillac Records* was a worthy film that struggled somewhat at the US box office.

As she had done with *Dreamgirls* at the time of *B'Day's* release, Beyoncé wasted no opportunity to talk about *Cadillac Records* while promoting *I Am . . . Sasha Fierce*. "I wanted to do something darker," she told *The Daily Telegraph*. "But when I got the script I thought, 'Wow – this is heavy. Can I do this?' In the first scene [James] meets her father for the first time and he rejects her. And there's a lot of profanity – she was like the opposite of me. People think of me as the sweetheart, and she's like the anti-sweetheart. She was rebellious, she was politically incorrect, she was bold, she was unapologetic, she was so brave, and she just didn't care."

It was a brief, but powerful performance, unquestionably Beyoncé's best to date. The stream of profanity and heroin addiction is well played, and although her vocal performances mark the moment when the film begins to resemble a promo video, her accomplished delivery is deeply affecting.

Beyoncé said that becoming James "was a challenge for me emotionally because Etta had a lot of challenges in her life, things that I've never experienced. I had to really dig deep so that I could have the right performance and represent her well. One thing she taught me is her fearlessness; she was Etta all the time. She was bold and she did not try to change who she was for anyone. She was one of the queens. If it weren't for her crossing over – she was the first African-American woman to cross over on the radio – I wouldn't have the opportunities that I have. It was the best performance I think I've done on screen. It gave me the strength and the confidence to step out of my comfort zone even more."

The year 2009 began with a tumultuous event for Beyoncé that would guarantee her place in the annals of history: her performance at the Neighborhood Ball. This was the colloquial term for one of the 10 inauguration balls that President Barack Obama and his wife, Michelle, attended on January 20, 2009, the day of his inauguration as the 44th President of the United States. Beyoncé had performed several times on the presidential candidate's campaign, singing the Lee Greenwood song 'God Bless the USA', claiming it back from the Republicans. One of the five parties held in separate suites at the Washington Convention Center, the Neighborhood Ball was a symbolic 'reach out' to Obama's new neighbours in Washington, DC, with the idea that tickets were either free or sold at reasonable prices. "This is an inauguration for all Americans," Obama said. "I wanted to make sure that we had an event that would be open to our new neighbourhood here in Washington, DC, and also neighbourhoods across the country. Michelle and I look forward to joining our fellow Americans across the country during this very special event."

Beyoncé chose 'At Last', which she had sung as Etta James with such conviction in *Cadillac Records*. The song had originally appeared in the

1941 film *Orchestra Wives* and was an apposite selection for the evening. Many commentators speculated on its choice – most notably that 'At Last' there was a president of African-American extraction; that it was also a validation of the quotation from Martin Luther King's 1963 speech in Detroit: "Free at last, free at last"; but also that 'At Last' George W. Bush had vacated the White House. "I am so honoured that I will be performing for President Obama and the First Lady," Beyoncé told *Entertainment Tonight*. "To sing 'At Last' while they have their first dance is a dream come true. I could not be more honoured and excited that they have asked me to be part of this moment in history."

These fine words did not wash with Etta James herself. Although it was later blamed on James' general health condition and the onset of Alzheimer's, she spat out to the world's press, "The great Beyoncé. I can't stand Beyoncé. She has no business up there, singing up there on a big ol' president day . . . singing my song that I've been singing forever." She said that Obama had "big ears" and that Beyoncé was going to have her "ass whupped". You cannot please all the people all the time.

Away from the films and singing for presidents, Beyoncé had to take her brand out to the masses again to promote the still-recent *I Am . . . Sasha Fierce*. The I Am . . . Tour commenced on March 26, 2009 in Edmonton, Canada, and finished on February 18, 2010 at Port of Spain in Trinidad and Tobago. Again playing with the Suga Mamas band and singers, the concert was pure exhilarating show business. The show's creative director was French fashion designer Thierry Mugler, who had input in everything from lighting through to choreography, and ensured a spectacle of costume changes: he created a 58-piece wardrobe for the duration of the tour. Beyoncé had seen his work at the Metropolitan Museum in New York in 2008 and was smitten, to the point that she stepped out of Deréon and into one of his dresses for the cover shoot of *I Am . . . Sasha Fierce*. Mugler was entranced with the way that, at the drop of a hat, Beyoncé could put on the Sasha Fierce character like a dress. Mugler described his outlook to fashion site MD: "Feminine. Free. Warrior. Fierce. As a creative adviser for this tour, it is my responsibility to make her vision come true."

The show revolved around the two sides of her personality, with specially shot films showing her tossing a coin to decide which persona to be. The set had two stages. The main stage, with Suga Mama on glass risers, looked not unlike the tableau from Elvis Presley's 'Jailhouse Rock'. There was a smaller performance space, known as the 'B-Stage', in the middle of the arena.

The dates sold out promptly, with Beyoncé wondering aloud how she could cram a decade's worth of hits into a two-hour show. And a valedictory performance it was at that; the concert was initially divided into three distinct sections – 'Dangerously In Love', 'Ave Maria' and a grand finale, covering Beyoncé's career. The show expanded throughout the tour, and was a highly professional, slickly run affair. The European leg was well received; George Michael joined Beyoncé on stage at the O2 Arena in London and duetted on 'If I Were A Boy', after she had sung his 'One More Try'.

When the tour opened in the States in June, Beyoncé ensured that at least 1,000 of the tickets were available at $20, so regular fans could get in. In contrast were the closing dates on the American leg of the tour at the Wynn Las Vegas, where she took up a four-night residency (July 30– August 2) and performed an intimate version of the show, entitled *I Am . . . Yours*. Michelle Obama brought along her children to see Beyoncé when she played the Verizon Center in Washington, DC, on June 24. The crowd broke into a rapturous standing ovation when footage of her husband's inauguration was broadcast during 'At Last'. Each night a selection of YouTube clips were shown of the various homages/pastiches to the now-ubiquitous 'Single Ladies (Put A Ring On It)' before Beyoncé broke into song. In Atlanta, Beyoncé brought out Internet sensation Cubby, who, at at least 20 stone, danced in a black leotard to her version of the song, which by now also included a generous portion of 'Shout!' by The Isley Brothers.

As the tour reached America, US radio shock-jock Howard Stern played a hoax tape of Beyoncé, allegedly leaked from the mixing desk of her performance on *The Tonight Show*, isolating the vocals of 'If I Were A Boy'. It captured a singer screeching and flat. The national press and Internet were aflame with the story, which Beyoncé first heard during an interview. "If no one took the time to look at the biggest inauguration in the history of America then shame on them," Mathew Knowles retorted snappily in a press release. "If no one took the time to listen to Beyoncé sing 'America the Beautiful' and 'At Last' at the Neighborhood Ball for the first dance of President Obama and the First Lady, and they question Beyoncé's vocal ability, they've gotta be an idiot. At 12 years into her career, the last thing someone should be questioning is her vocal ability. That would be like questioning if Kobe Bryant could shoot a jump shot. The vocals were obviously altered." The 'unnamed hoaxer' apologised: "It's a little bit crazy," he said. "No one in their right mind would sound like that, and no one would cheer for someone singing like that." Again, the controversy created maximum publicity for the tour.

Jay-Z dropped by and performed at the June 22 gig at Madison Square Garden. By the time the show arrived in Canada at the Molson Amphitheatre in Toronto on July 20, it was a well-honed spectacle. "The only thing [the] show needed to turn it into full-on musical theatre was a plot, though it wasn't even the costume changes or the elaborate sets that invited the comparison – it was Beyoncé herself, and at times, watching her direct her show was like seeing a real-life Evita in action," Dave Morris wrote on the Eyeweekly site. He was deeply impressed by Beyoncé's craft, but possibly not by the overall picture. "As judicious as her singing can be, the effect in sum is still like being hit in the head with a fist in a velvet glove. There's no question that Beyoncé is one of the best singers in pop, maybe one of the best alive, and that her skills as a singer put her in a rarefied strata. Why she's not content to display them and stop there is a mystery."

The final show at the Wynn Las Vegas, in its special intimate setting, was filmed for her first Blu-ray disc. The tour, according to Pollstar, grossed $103 million, putting Beyoncé in the Top 50 worldwide touring acts of the year. It is hardly surprising: it was a perfectly balanced mixture of theatre, soul, hip-hop and rock. It was unafraid of schmaltz, but smart enough not to wallow in it. Audience participation was encouraged, and there were enough ad libs every night to ensure that there was spontaneity.

The tour was to continue intermittently though 2009 before closing in South America in February 2010. *I Am . . . Sasha Fierce* was reissued as a Platinum Edition in November, which put all the songs on one disc, out of order, thus somewhat corrupting the distinct flavours of both discs. Extra content was added as well, such as her cover of Billy Joel's 'Honesty'. The second disc was a DVD featuring eight promos, including the 'fan only' version of 'Ego' and a 'Behind The Scenes' featurette.

The full media onslaught by Beyoncé in 2009 left few people doubting, if not her popularity, then her ubiquity. With her film appearances and recent album to promote on her enormous world tour, her charitable causes, celebrity husband and hints of parental difficulties, Beyoncé had assumed the mantle of a traditional superstar. No surprise, then, that Beyoncé-watchers were looking out when Forbes published its annual list of richest Americans. The list, which celebrates the superficial baubles of fame and wealth, is eagerly looked upon by Americans as a barometer of power and importance. In 2009, Beyoncé was listed as the fourth most powerful and influential celebrity in the world. By earning more than $52 million in 2009–10, she was also ranked as the highest-earning celebrity under 30.

A persistent rumour that surfaced at the start of 2009 was that Beyoncé wanted to sever links with Mathew as her manager, and that Jay-Z's management company, Roc Nation, was poised to take over. A statement was quickly prepared from Music World Entertainment: "Contrary to false rumors online, Beyoncé and her manager Mathew Knowles unequivocally have had and continue to have a close personal and business relationship. Mathew Knowles is the sole and exclusive manager of Beyoncé." This statement masked an increasingly fragile business relationship between father and daughter.

CHAPTER 15

Going Gaga In The Heat

"Beyoncé is the best part: she actually shows the angry, crazy side that we just knew lurked beneath her too-perfect façade."

New York Magazine, 2010

Beyoncé's next film could not have been further removed from the earthy historical texture of *Cadillac Records*. Knowing that *Cadillac* could only ever be a specialist release, it was time for Beyoncé to go into the mainstream with a revival of that good old mainstay of eighties picture making, the psychological thriller. Released on April 24, 2009, *Obsessed* was yet another string to Beyoncé's bow. The film looked sure to cash in on the popularity of her co-star, Idris Elba, who had just received critical rapture for his performance as Russell 'Stringer' Bell in the first three seasons of HBO's *The Wire*. However, Elba was not the first choice for the role, which was previously offered to James Smith, aka rap legend LL Cool J.

Produced for Sony's Screen Gems division, it was helmed by British director Steve Shill, who had shot several episodes of *The Wire,* in his feature debut. The film attempts to be a taut psychodrama. Beyoncé plays Sharon Charles, the wife of executive Derek Charles (Elba), an asset manager at law firm Gage Bendix, who has worked hard for the finer things in life. Beyoncé is the stay-at-home wife, raising a child, who has put her career on hold for Charles (she was once his assistant), but dreams of going to university. Derek's naturally flirty nature means that new temp Lisa Sheridan (played by *Heroes* actor Ali Larter) makes a beeline for him. And then the plot escalates, *Fatal Attraction* style.

The storyline positively creaks. When Lisa first appears, the piano soundtrack turns plaintive and suspenseful; the viewer knows there is trouble ahead. She immediately begins to flirt with Derek, saying, "I think you'll find I'm not your normal temp." As the film heavily signposts: "Is she the new temp or temptress?" Derek discusses Lisa with his wife but dismisses her as "plain". When Sharon meets Lisa for the first time and finds out the contrary, she tells Derek later, "You said she was plain. She may be a lot of things, but she certainly isn't plain." Sharon's suspicions are raised when Lisa gushes, "Talk about the perfect family, you should be on the cover of a magazine," after looking at a family portrait in Derek's office.

Derek shows interest in Lisa when she states she cannot get a boyfriend, but it is merely friendly concern. Lisa interprets this as a green light. What is interesting is that although Lisa makes all the running, Derek is not attracted. She tries to seduce him in a washroom, and then attempts – in a nod to the 1993 sex thriller *Body Of Evidence* – to seduce him in an underground car park. Both times he resolutely shuns her advances. But he makes the fundamental error of not telling his wife about the shenanigans – he attempts to one evening, but avoids the issue when another matter comes along. So when Lisa later tries to commit suicide in his hotel room, Sharon knows nothing, and naturally suspects the very worst. After all, Sharon had been her husband's assistant once. It concludes with Sharon and Lisa confronting each other at the Charles' house, which culminates in a stunningly choreographed fight between the two of them, using fists, feet and standard lamps. It is a fabulous showdown and, as in her other films, when Beyoncé characters are stressed, she resorts to a deep Southern accent, drawling out lines like, 'Get out of ma house!' to great effect. Beyoncé is finally victorious, all snot, scratches and tears, as Lisa crashes through the loft ceiling onto a chandelier and then finally to the floor below.

What attracted Beyoncé to *Obsessed*, however, was the strength of Sharon's character. Although she sings not a note in the film, it complements Beyoncé's musical persona: a strong independent woman doesn't need male intervention. Clearly smart, and feeling sidelined, she protects all that is hers with fierce, blazing courage. The man doesn't save the day at the end of the film. In fact, he's made to look fairly powerless on the sidelines. Beyoncé has the fight and protects her home and family, another victory for the empowerment that has coursed through all of her work.

"I was really proud to do something that didn't lean on singing, or performing or dancing, and it was fun," Beyoncé told *CBS News*. As executive producer, she got involved in many of the aspects of the film. She did a lot of her own stunts, and worked with Shill to shape the plot and the eventual look of the film. She was initially unhappy about the headbutt she had to deliver to her onscreen nemesis, Lisa Sheridan. However, Beyoncé's ultimate professionalism was noted throughout the filming, and after consulting with some of her West Indian friends, she did indeed plant a whopping great Glasgow kiss on Ali Larter's forehead. The fight, which rumbles on around the house for some 10 minutes of screen time, is balletic. In the traditions of similar films, every time you think one or other of the protagonists is about to walk away, the other launches another attack. As the fight progresses, Beyoncé becomes more and more street, before finally shouting, "You came into ma' house, you touch ma' child . . . You think yo' crazy? I'll show you crazy . . . JUST TRY ME BITCH!" All this effort won Beyoncé and Larter the MTV Movie Award 2010 for 'Best Fight'. The film seems to be merely a preamble for the fight. "I really felt it was time to step out of that comfort zone and go into some of the more dramatic roles," Beyoncé told *More* magazine in 2009.

Beyoncé plays Sharon as an earth mother, reflected in the browns and beiges she wears throughout the film. She sits at home wearing knitted hats and says things like, "Eat something baby." However, when she protects her family at the end of the film, Sharon comes into her own.

The film was interesting as it showed a slick African–American couple facing the same issues as that of a white family, without making any mention of race at all. Beyoncé acknowledged that it was the deepest she'd ever gone in a role. She wasn't playing a singer, or a civilian who bursts into song.

The film premiered at The School Of Visual Arts in New York on April 23 and was attended by the entire cast as well as showbiz circuit regulars Kim Kardashian, Mickey Dolenz and Beyoncé's mother, Tina. All the glitz around its launch could not detract from the fact that *Obsessed* was a big-budget cartoon, with hardly an exposition or explanation of the characters' motives. Why was Lisa chasing Derek? What had gone on in their lives before the film had started? There are no reasons given for any of the characters' actions. Released after the Global Financial Crisis that began in 2007, with its talk of office lay-offs and tighter financial times, *Obsessed* is one of the first films that portrays the credit crunch, yet the plot is undernourished. The escalation of the storyline, such a novelty back in the eighties with *Fatal Attraction,* doesn't seem quite so appealing 20 years on.

Obsessed was panned by the critics. Joe Neumaier, writing in the *New York Daily News,* could hardly have been more disparaging. Awarding it one star, he said, "*Obsessed* starring Beyoncé Knowles is more like 'Delayed Frustration' than *Fatal Attraction*." Left-wing UK newspaper *The Guardian* critic Xan Brooks said, "Cast as Idris's stay-at-home wife, Beyoncé Knowles seemingly has little to do except squawk in outrage. Happily she rallies in time for the chandelier-swinging catfight that ends this preposterous affair with a suitably hysterical flourish." *The Daily Telegraph* was equally scathing: "It could be the least erotic thriller ever made, unless die-you-bitch catfights through broken attic floorboards constitute some sort of kinky subgenre. There's something particularly ungainly about Knowles, electing to play Sharon as an abrasive shrew whose scorn means barking husky ultimata while gyrating precariously on high heels."

The blog Syracuse.com said, "Imagine, if you will, *Fatal Attraction* without Academy Award nominees Glenn Close and Anne Archer. Imagine they are replaced with a bad, typecast TV actress (Ali Larter) and a pop singer (Beyoncé Knowles). Now, try and imagine something far worse." Again, the *New York Daily News* makes its point: "But director

Steve Shill lets it boil down to a claws-out brawl, which does Beyoncé no favours; hunched over with fists up, the elegance she showed in *Dreamgirls* and *Cadillac Records* is gone. The lady can be fierce, but she deserves better."

As with all these things, the reality is nestling somewhere in the middle. Critically, these types of erotic-thriller films fell from favour the moment Madonna poured wax over Willem Dafoe's genitals in *Body Of Evidence* in 1993. Beyoncé does a moderately noble job of keeping her head above water with a daft, melodramatic script. However, the power of Beyoncé, Elba and Larter proved somewhat irresistible and, despite the terrible reviews, the film topped the US charts. It grossed $11 million on its opening day and was number one at the box office with $28 million from 2,514 theatres, which meant that Beyoncé was now a key box-office draw.

Obsessed went on to gross $71 million worldwide. It proved that the audience actively wanted a story that they had seen before, played out by characters they knew. It was certainly a novelty to see Beyoncé in the wronged wife role, the opposite of what fans were expecting.

The film had the full power of Sony's Screen Gems behind it, including an amusing 'Get Obsessed with Ali' website, into which you could enter a friend's details and then have them cyberstalked by the obsessive in the film. "Don't worry, it's only a joke," the website proclaimed.

The death of Michael Jackson in June 2009 came as a great shock. Although the megastar had lived a troubled existence for the better part of two decades, he seemed to have turned a corner with the announcement of his record-breaking 50-night residency at London's O2 Arena, beginning on July 13, 2009. His passing gave the United States an opportunity to take stock of the megastars that were still alive. Beyoncé, who had met Jackson on several occasions and, indeed, played at his 30th Anniversary celebration in 2001, took the opportunity to eulogise him. The American section of the I Am . . . Tour was altered to reflect Jackson's passing, with Beyoncé dedicating 'Halo' to him for its duration.

But to Beyoncé Jackson's passing betrayed something deeper, something closer to home. She knew all too well the potential pitfalls of finding fame young and growing up in the public eye. Given the support of her family, this is something she has done remarkably well. She understood all the trappings of fame and with her parents, and now Jay-Z, she sought to understand how all the demands, sponsorships, franchises and deals that are part and parcel of what it is to be a superstar in America today worked together. That Beyoncé has been able, despite mixing with some pretty hardcore company at times, to remain alcohol- and drug-free is testament to her God-fearing upbringing and willpower. Jackson's death came as a clarion call. It was time to take stock. Beyoncé would, for the first time in 15 years, take some proper time off. However, that could not happen overnight.

On September 13, 2009, Beyoncé was indirectly involved in a huge news blow-up at MTV's annual Video Music Awards held at Radio City Music Hall in New York. Eighteen-year-old country-tinged teen sensation Taylor Swift won the Best Female Video category, voted for by the public, for her single 'You Belong With Me'. The promo was up against Beyoncé's Jake Nava-directed, much-emulated extravaganza, 'Single Ladies (Put A Ring On It)'. As with all public votes, especially with a huge mobilised fan base whipped up through social media networks, it was clear that Swift would probably win. After all, she was 18 and Beyoncé was now at the grand old age of 28 – a time when most of her fans had other things to do than repeat-dial a television station. When it was announced that Taylor had won, she took to the podium to collect her award. Clearly overjoyed, she began by thanking everyone and saying how much she had always dreamed of winning one day, and, as she sings country music, never thought she would win. At that point, suddenly Kanye West sprang up from the audience and onto the stage, taking the microphone out of a bewildered Swift's hand. He spoke to Swift in front of the theatre and TV audience; he was *not* overjoyed. "Yo, Taylor, I'm really happy for you, I'm gonna let you finish, but Beyoncé had one of the best videos of all time . . . one of the best videos of all time." There was a hubbub throughout the audience. The camera panned to an aghast Beyoncé in the audience. She was there to perform 'Single Ladies (Put A Ring On It)', as well as for being nominated in a variety of categories. The TV viewers could clearly see her mouthing the words "Oh, Kanye." She looked shocked and mortified, as West left the stage to a chorus of booing. Swift was left alone, nervous and shuffling like a teenager who has just been insulted. West was booed for the rest of the evening and had to be escorted out of the ceremony. Katy Perry summed up the exchange perfectly with a message to West on her blog: "It's like U stepped on a kitten."

Beyoncé was quick to rise above this situation. Later in the evening, which had also included Lady Gaga performing 'Paparazzi', Janet Jackson singing 'Scream' (and dancing along with Michael in front of the video) in tribute to her brother, and Jay-Z's powerful duet with Alicia Keys 'Empire State Of Mind', Beyoncé won the award for Best Video. As she took to the microphone to collect her award, finally, for 'Single Ladies (Put A Ring On It)', she was statesmanlike. She announced, "I remember being 17 years old, up for my first MTV Award with Destiny's Child, and it was one of the most exciting moments of my life, so I would like for Taylor to come out and have her moment." Swift did, and it demonstrated at once the full force of Beyoncé's grace. "It was just so wonderful and so incredibly classy of her," Swift said afterwards. The press was full of the story the following day, and the clip was viewed repeatedly on YouTube. West apologised on his blog to Swift, yet the story ran and ran, introducing Swift to a wider audience, reinforcing Beyoncé's graciousness and support to younger artists and highlighting West as rather excitable.

In a long-telegraphed move, Tina Knowles filed for divorce against Mathew in November 2009. It transpired that the couple had been living apart since that January. The rumours of his eye for the ladies had finally caught up with him. He was sited in a paternity suite with *Scrubs* actress Alexsandra Wright, in October 2009, who was to give birth to a son, Beyoncé's half brother, Nixon, in 2010.

Tina and Mathew issued a press release: "The decision to end our marriage is an amicable one. We remain friends, parents, and business partners. If anyone is expecting an ugly messy fight, they will be sadly disappointed. We ask for your respect of our privacy as we handle this matter." However, the case was dismissed in November 2010. The couple had been due at a Harris County courtroom in Houston, yet neither party arrived. The on-off romance continues, yet.

As 2009 ended, Beyoncé was invited, alongside Usher and Jay-Z, to play at a New Year's Eve party at the Nikki Beach resort on the Caribbean leisure island of St Barts. Music World Entertainment believed it was for rich foreign businessmen. It was only months later evidently that it became apparent that the benefactor was part of the Colonel Gaddafi family. Within 18 months, this freewheeling event would return to haunt many of its performers.

Beyoncé vowed finally to take time off in 2010, not that initially anyone would have noticed anything different in her high-powered schedule. "It's definitely time to take a break, to recharge my batteries," she told *USA Today*. "I'd like to take about six months and not go into the studio. I need to just live life, to be inspired by things again." She may not have gone into the studio herself, but her presence was felt strongly throughout the world of entertainment.

Such is the path of the 21st-century superstar that a perfume line is seen as a perfectly reasonable brand extension. The celebrity-scent market began in earnest in the noughties, with Jennifer Lopez, Kylie Minogue, Britney Spears and Gwen Stefani all launching signature scents. Developed in conjunction with Coty, the world's largest fragrance company, and released to the world market in February 2010, Beyoncé Heat was an immediate success. It was, as its press announcement screamed, "a blend of red vanilla orchid, magnolia, neroli, blush peach, honeysuckle nectar, almond macaroon, crème de musk, sequoia milkwood, tonka bean and amber". It was launched with the strapline, "An irresistible sensuality waiting to be unleashed."

Coty was hoping that it would revitalise the celebrity-endorsed perfume market. "A lot of my performances have had fire involved, so we thought 'Heat'," Beyoncé was to say. "Also, red is one of my favourite colours, as is gold. Everything, from the bottle design to the name and the ideas for the commercials – that's me." The bottle design was thoroughly researched. The advert for Beyoncé Heat made much of its "curvaceously rounded base", which narrowed to "a sleek, squared neck and the red gradient effect gives the impression of a fire burning within". It then concluded that "for the ultimate touch of luxury, the top of the bottle is edged with a gold band, inscribed with the words 'Beyoncé' and 'Heat' topped with an opulent cap". Retailing between $39–59, it was available initially exclusively at Macy's, the New York superstore.

Beyoncé Heat was, of course, a huge success when it was launched onto the market. It was described by perfume blog Now Smell This as "a warm fruity musk; it opens on lots of peach-flavoured hard candy over middling-dark, nondescript florals, and is a little loud for a few minutes. After that, it's softer, easier to wear, although the sweetness never dissipates more than slightly. I don't find it even slightly sexy, and it isn't what I'd call memorable, but it doesn't much matter: it's by Beyoncé and it isn't a complete mess. People will buy it." And it wasn't a mess, at all. Although rather overwhelming on initial spray, it settles down to being fruity and somewhat understated. It was reported to have brought in $3 million in sales in its first month, with *People* magazine reporting it sold 72,000 bottles in a single hour when Beyoncé made a personal appearance at Macy's. Although it seems doubtful that this amount could physically be sold in such a relatively short space of time, it was a huge vote of confidence in the venture. Sales in the UK were bolstered by the fact that the sultry commercial filmed to accompany the launch attracted 14 complaints to the Advertising Standards Authority. Played out to Beyoncé's version of 'Fever', the complaints were enough for the advertising watchdog to permit the advert to be shown only in the evenings, and it announced: "Although we considered that the ad was unlikely to be harmful to adults or older children, we considered that Beyoncé's body movements and the camera's prolonged focus on shots of her dress slipping away created a sexually provocative ad that was unsuitable to be seen by young children."

With success such as this, it was clear a variation would be developed and manufactured. In January 2011, Beyoncé Heat was followed onto the shelves by another line, Heat Rush. It is described as a "fruity floral fragrance that softly lures like a gentle breeze. Warm yourself with a drop of liquid sunshine." This time, yellow tiger orchid, mango blossoms, orange hibiscus, Brazilian cherry, passion fruit, blood orange and Rio sunset musk (teak wood and honey amber) made up the scent, which was mellower than Heat. It was as if Heat was Sasha Fierce and Heat Rush, even though it had a spicier title, was Beyoncé herself.

Beyoncé again took the fragrance to the world's press. Asked if Jay-Z had a favourite between Heat or Heat Rush she said, "Are you *kidding*? One of the most important aspects of my perfume is that they get his seal of approval. When you wear a perfume you want your man to love it. He loves my scents because he was part of the decision-making process. I wouldn't wear a scent if he didn't like it." The San Jose *Examiner* described the fragrance thus: "[It] starts off with a medium-heaviness sweet orange scent. After about fifteen minutes, the orange settles down and a sweet floral aroma emerges. At the end of the day, the fruit is gone and the sweetness and orchid scent is smoothed down by warm musk and amber." Available primarily through Macy's in the States and Superdrug in the UK, Heat Rush again proved popular.

The first months of 2010 were still busy. Beyoncé appeared on the telethon *Hope For Haiti Now: A Global Benefit For Earthquake Relief* on January 22, a massive programme to help contribute to the relief aid for the disaster that befell the Caribbean island of Haiti 10 days earlier. Broadcast on MTV, Beyoncé sang an emotional version of 'Halo', accompanied by Chris Martin of Coldplay on piano.

On January 31, 2010, Beyoncé visited the Staples Center for the Grammy Awards. When the Grammys were announced in early December 2009, Beyoncé learned she had been nominated for 10 awards, joining a select band of artists with that many nominations, the others to that point being Lauryn Hill and Kanye West. Only Michael Jackson had more nominations – 12 in 1984. She was, however, otherwise occupied with organising her husband's 40th birthday. "I was focused so much on my husband's birthday," she told *USA Today*. "I threw a big party . . . I didn't really think about it. But it's really an honour."

It really was an honour, as the awards are voted for by a panel of industry experts. Commentators wondered whether, in the ever-shifting universe of pop, Beyoncé would stand a chance with the rise of Lady

Gaga and Beyoncé's recent MTV Awards chum, Taylor Swift. Brian Hiatt of *Rolling Stone* thought Beyoncé would remain above it all, saying that "if (Beyoncé) loses in all 10 categories, it will have absolutely no effect on her career."

Nobody need have worried. Beyoncé walked away with six awards, breaking the record for most wins for a female in the Grammys' 52-year history. Although she lost Best Album to Swift and Record of the Year to Kings Of Leon, she won Best Female Pop Vocal Performance for 'Halo'; Song Of The Year for 'Single Ladies (Put A Ring On It)'; Best Female R&B Vocal Performance and Best R&B Song for the same song; Best Contemporary R&B Album for *I Am . . . Sasha Fierce* and Best Traditional R&B Vocal Performance for 'At Last'. Beyoncé looked radiant as she performed a version of 'If I Were A Boy' that incorporated Alanis Morissette's 'You Oughta Know'. As she collected her final award, she thanked her family, and made explicit her love for Jay-Z by saying, "This is for my husband. . . I love you." It was perfect timing to take a break from the scene, and a validation of all of her hard work of the past decade and for her going solo in 2005.

Soon after the Grammys, the video for Lady Gaga's 'Telephone' was released, which was the sister record in many respects to 'Video Phone'. That song had been released as a single to support the Platinum Edition of *I Am . . . Sasha Fierce* in November 2009. It featured a vocal from Gaga and was accompanied by a bright, snappy video directed by Hype Williams in Brooklyn. "When I was doing her video with her, she called me and she said, 'What do you want to do?' Gaga told New York's Z100 Radio Station in October 2009. "And I'm like, 'I don't want to show up in some frickin' hair bow and be fashion Gaga in your video.' I said, 'I want to do you.'"

The video, partially a homage to Quentin Tarantino's *Reservoir Dogs*, had a stunning look. Gaga, like Beyoncé, models a white strapless leotard and opera gloves with loose flowing hair. "I want to do my version of Beyoncé," Gaga continued. "So the whole time I was learning the choreography, they were calling me Gee-yoncé." The video is bizarre, especially when we see Beyoncé dressed as a pneumatic Bettie Page while teasing an AK-47 rifle.

The collaboration had been a great success, and Gaga asked Beyoncé to return the favour and work with her on one of her releases. 'Telephone' was a track taken from *The Fame Monster*, the second edition of Gaga's debut album, *The Fame*. Their association was mutually beneficial. Although Beyoncé is only 30, she has nearly 20 years' experience. Gaga's artiness added credibility to Beyoncé, but Beyoncé brought respectability and the establishment to Gaga.

The electro-beat driven 'Telephone' (co-produced and written with Rodney 'Darkchild' Jerkins) was released as a single towards the end of 2009, and Jonas Akerlund shot a video for it in January 2010. The 10-minute short recalls the glory days of the excesses of promos from the mid-eighties. Influenced again by Gaga's friend, Tarantino, but also the work of cult directors Russ Meyer and Roger Corman, the plot features Gaga, who is in 'County Jail, Prison For Bitches'. She is there because she has poisoned her boyfriend. It starts with her being stripped and thrown into her cell, at which one of the wardens jokes, "I told you she didn't have a dick," a reference to the false stories that were constantly in the media at this point that Gaga was, indeed, a man. Every female prison cliché in the book is explored. Heavily featuring and suggesting lesbianism (Gaga, while wearing glasses made out of cigarettes, is kissed by a masculine female), the prison sequence subverts all prison dramas, with fights breaking out and an air of oppression and sexual tension. As soon as Gaga receives a telephone call from Beyoncé, the song itself gets under way.

Beyoncé plays Honey Bee, a heavily homaged nod to Tarantino's Honey Bunny (Amanda Plummer) from his 1994 masterwork, *Pulp Fiction*. Appearing nearly halfway through the promo, after bailing out Gaga, Beyoncé is first seen in the couple's Chevrolet Silverado SS, the 'Pussy Wagon' from Tarantino's *Kill Bill* films. She says the line, "You've been a very bad girl, Gaga, a very, very bad girl." Beyoncé delivers her rap while driving the truck. Stopping at a wayside diner, Beyoncé and Gaga attempt to poison Bobo, Beyoncé's onscreen boyfriend played by actor/rapper Tyrese Gibson. Instead, they ultimately poison all the customers of the drive-in they've pulled into, and then dance amid the corpses wearing US flags. The video ends with them heading off into the sunset, just like *Thelma And Louise*. The shadow of a police helicopter engulfs the car.

The video was premiered on March 11, 2010 on VEVO. The *Los Angeles Times* said that the video was a "visual feast". MTV commented: "With 'Telephone', Gaga has entered the rarest of pop stratospheres, up there with the Madonnas and the Michael Jacksons." Amy Odell in *New York Magazine* felt that the film located something hitherto unseen: "Beyoncé is the best part: she actually shows the angry, crazy side that we just knew lurked beneath her too-perfect façade." *The Guardian* thought that people needed to see the joke of it all rather than froth at the mouth saying that, "Some taboos are still alive and kicking. Lady Gaga and Beyoncé's prison 'lezz-ploitation' video has caused outrage, featuring as it does butch dykes, chicks with dicks, horny female prison wardens perusing lesbian dating sites – oh, and a bit of mass murder." It was reported that within 12 hours of the video being released on the Internet, it had received over half a million hits. The video helped the single to the top of the charts in the UK and to number three in the US.

February 2010 saw the final nine dates of the I Am . . . Tour, as it visited South America, taking in Peru, Chile, Argentina and Brazil. On February 6, Beyoncé played in São Paulo, Brazil, at the city's Morumbi Stadium to over 57,000 people, her largest single audience as a solo artist. After the tour completed, Beyoncé was seen sporadically. In March 2010, she opened the Beyoncé Cosmetology Center in the Phoenix House Career Academy, in Brooklyn, where former drug addicts can garner valuable skills to aid their recovery. Beyoncé became aware of the rehabilitation program when she was researching her role as Etta James in *Cadillac Records*. Less altruistically, she appeared with Jay-Z at the fashionable Coachella Valley Music and Arts Festival in Indio, California, singing Mr Hudson's 'Forever Young' on April 16, 2010. She caused some controversy with the T-shirt she was wearing, which bore the legend, among many scrawled graffiti-like statements, "punk-ass motherfucker". It was clear she was enjoying her independence from touring and recording.

In June 2010, the Internet was awash with rumours that Destiny's Child were to reform. Mathew Knowles moved quickly to issue a statement: "Contrary to rumours online of a Destiny's Child reunion, there are no plans for the group to reunite for a performance or album.

The rumours are false. Destiny's Child made an unprecedented impact in contemporary music, becoming one of the best-selling groups of all time. Beyoncé, Kelly Rowland and Michelle Williams have each moved on to successful solo careers. The members remain close, but will not reunite as a group." It was far too late in the day for this retrograde step to happen. Although their careers had in no way matched the stellar heights of Beyoncé's, Michelle Williams and Kelly Rowland had both become established artists.

To all intents and purposes, Beyoncé *did* take most of 2010 off. She said in her interview in *Cosmopolitan* in April 2011, "I gave myself a break, I took a year off. Now that sounds indulgent but I've worked since the age of 15 and never taken any time out. My life has always been about next, next, next and moving on. I just decided to stop. It was the best decision I've ever made and definitely a milestone. I took time out, spent time with my man, my friends, my family. I got to sleep in my own bed night after night, which is a massive thing for me." She travelled as a tourist, went to restaurants and art galleries, and even attempted to cook for Jay-Z, although being Beyoncé, there had to be some element of work involved. "I set up a production company," she continued, "learnt how to edit, did a bit of recording and directed a DVD." What was different was being based consistently in one place, her home in New York. "What was great was having this normal life of sleeping, getting up, going to an office and then coming home. Coming home is a wonderful thing."

CHAPTER 16

Run The World (Beyoncé)

"Glastonbury can be a pretty bleak place by the time Sunday night rolls around: a muddy wasteland sagging beneath the weight of shell-shocked drug casualties, discarded nitrous oxide canisters, and marauding sewage trucks. Beyoncé will provide some much-needed glitz."

NME, February 2011

"Both William and Kate are massive fans of Beyoncé and Jay-Z. They really wanted to make their big day even more special and what better way than by getting pop royalty to perform at the party?"

'A spokesperson', London, 2011

"I overanalyse everything, and I want to be the best at it, and maybe that's just me being an overachiever. I just wish I was better at everything."

Beyoncé, 2008

The first half of 2011 seemed to be a fast-paced microcosm of everything that had gone on in Beyoncé's previous career – scandal, lawsuits, new records, audacious firsts. The cavalcade of news and controversy began with her announcing she would be playing Glastonbury, and continued with the firing of her father as manager.

In 2011, Beyoncé was more visible than she had been for years. In one week, her impact was made clear, positively and – although indirectly – negatively. Aside from the revolution in Egypt, the news coverage of February 11 was filled with the story of a woman who had gone to the United States in order to emulate her idols, Beyoncé and Jennifer Lopez, by having silicone implants to increase the size of her buttocks. Sadly, Claudia Aderotimi, from North London, died. The event was a sad reminder of the downside of the cult of celebrity, and demonstrated just how far into the public consciousness Beyoncé had become embedded. It seems wholly ironic that people would want to emulate, in this case tragically, the ampleness that Beyoncé strove to shun while growing up.

Later that same week, the news broke that Beyoncé, like her husband Jay-Z in 2008, was to headline the Glastonbury Festival on Sunday June 26, the esteemed festival's closing night. Adding Beyoncé as a headliner of the three-day festival alongside U2 and Coldplay showed both the willingness of festival owners Emily and Michael Eavis to experiment, and also how globally popular Beyoncé had become. The gathering, which started in 1970, has become the most well-known and influential music event in the world. Thanks to its espousal of noble causes and its mystical connections, it has become the ultimate rock festival. Although Glastonbury has always been diverse and multicultural – the jazz world and dance stages frequently featuring a high percentage of African-American and world artists – the main stage, the fabled 'Pyramid', has always been the preserve of mainstream, white artists.

When Jay-Z played the festival in 2008, the outcry was enormous, with Oasis founder Noel Gallagher leading the charge. Under a heading 'When Beyoncé's On Stage, Our Rock Gods Should Quake', columnist Barbara Ellen wrote in *The Observer* that Beyoncé would convincingly win over the doubters. She recalled going to see both Britney Spears and Beyoncé within a week of each other when their tours rolled into London in 2009. "While poor Britney (bless and protect her) staggered around like a middle-aged divorcee in search of her next G and T, Beyoncé was a goddess. On that form, she'll make the rest of the Glasters bill resemble unwashed sock puppets. Complain about that, rock boys."

The leader of British rock band Elbow, Guy Garvey, commented to BBC Radio One's *Newsbeat* that Beyoncé would provide a "fantastic finish" to the festival. "There was lots of controversy when Jay-Z was invited to play but what a hit that was," he continued. "That was the fullest that the Pyramid Stage had ever seen that field. Let them [Michael and Emily Eavis] choose what goes on. They've got more experience than anyone else on earth and it'll be fantastic like it always is." There is little doubt, with the experience she has garnered through her live work, that Beyoncé will storm the festival. "I went to see her live last year and was blown away by the might of the show," Emily Eavis said. "She has such soul, an amazing voice with an incredible, all-female band. She knows how to deliver live, and she packs a big punch – it's gonna explode!"

Luke Lewis posted on the *NME* blog, "Glastonbury can be a pretty bleak place by the time Sunday night rolls around: a muddy wasteland sagging beneath the weight of shell-shocked drug casualties, discarded nitrous oxide canisters, and marauding sewage trucks. Beyoncé will provide some much-needed glitz. And will hopefully sing 'Crazy In Love' loud enough to drown out the regretful sobs of those who've overdone the miaow miaow."

In March 2011, the West began a series of air strikes against Colonel Gaddafi's regime in Libya in order to protect a UN-backed no-fly zone that had been enforced to stop the civil war that had broken out between insurgents and forces loyal to Gaddafi. The civil unrest, which had sprung up as a protest against the 40-year plus leadership of Libya's ruler, had begun in February 2011. As the worldwide press raked over the whole affair, it became apparent that the St Barts New Year's Eve concert in 2009 that Beyoncé had played could soon be an embarrassment for her. Via leaks on the Internet, it was established that she, alongside Usher, Lionel Richie, Mariah Carey and Nelly Furtado, had played private parties over the years for Gaddafi's sons, Saif al-Islam and Mutassim. Furtado, who played the preceding year, promptly announced that she had donated her fee to charity. Soon after, Beyoncé's publicist Yvette Noel-Schure announced: "All monies paid to Beyoncé for her performance at a private party at Nikki Beach, St Barts on New Year's Eve 2009, including the commissions paid to her booking agency, were donated to the earthquake relief efforts in Haiti over a year ago. Once it became known that the third party promoter was linked to the Kaddafi family, the decision was made to put that payment to a good cause."

Shows for foreign billionaires and huge corporates offer a secure income for artists in the 21st century, especially as worldwide recession and the changes in the music industry mean there is less of a guarantee of traditional revenue streams. Were Beyoncé and the other artists simply unlucky to have picked the wrong party? "Going forward, this is a lesson for all artists to learn from," Mariah Carey told *The Guardian* newspaper. "We need to be more aware and take more responsibility regardless of who books our shows. Ultimately, we as artists are to be held accountable." Again, Beyoncé had moved quickly to ensure that the right thing was done.

While this was happening, in the March 2011 edition of *L'officiel Paris,* Beyoncé appeared in tribute to the "African Queens through the ages", and also legendary Nigerian musician Fela Kuti, in blackface costume and tribal make-up. The magazine issued a statement saying that she was "far from the glamorous Sasha Fierce" and that it was intended as a "return to her African roots, as you can see on the picture, on which her face was voluntarily darkened". It caused immediate controversy.

The Atlanta Post, from the city she so briefly made her home when she was signed to Elektra as part of Girl's Tyme in the mid-nineties, said that, "Blackface is not fashion forward or edgy, and, in my opinion, it is just flat-out offensive." Given the tradition of minstrelsy and given the extreme sensitivities of the past, it seemed an out-of-character thing to do. Or was it merely to do with the fact that Jay-Z had invested and helped produce the musical *Fela,* and a bit of old-fashioned scandal like this was extremely lucrative for business? There was also the very real probability that it was an ironic comment on the furore that surrounded her 2008 photo shoot for L'Oréal, when it was suggested that Beyoncé was indeed lightening her skin tone.

"It's fun to play with fashion and make-up, and fashion has a history of provocation and pushing boundaries," Dodai Stewart from *Jezebel* said.

"But when you paint your face darker in order to look more 'African', aren't you reducing an entire continent, full of different nations, tribes, cultures and histories, into one brown colour?"

As we have repeatedly learned, Beyoncé is a strong, fiercely independent woman, who has been guided by two extremely strong men: Jay-Z and Mathew Knowles. However, on March 28, 2011, an announcement came that, although not entirely unexpected, was still something of a surprise. Her publicist Yvette Noel-Schure issued a press statement saying that Beyoncé would no longer be managed by Mathew. Although it wasn't stated at the time, it soon emerged that Beyoncé would manage herself. In 2010, both her former Destiny's Child bandmates Michelle Williams and Kelly Rowland parted company with Knowles as manager. "It wasn't an easy thing to do," Michelle Williams said at the time. "But it was the necessary thing to do . . . he's still the manager of Destiny's Child if and whenever we ever decide to do anything again. But as for me individually as a solo artist . . . that's all I've ever known and all I've ever had, but you come to a point where you do something else and you got to do what you gotta do to get there." For the first time since 1995, Mathew no longer managed any members of Destiny's Child. It was one thing having Kelly and Michelle leave him, but the departure of Beyoncé, his pride and joy and cornerstone of his empire, could only have come as a bitter blow.

The statement was suitably sparsely worded. "I am grateful for everything he has taught me," Beyoncé said. "I grew up watching both he and my mother manage and own their own businesses. They were hard-working entrepreneurs and I will continue to follow in their footsteps. He is my father for life and I love my dad dearly. I am grateful for everything he has taught me." The bond with Mathew, although frequently shaken by his sexual misdemeanours, had remained a loyal one, and Beyoncé was deeply appreciative of the work her father had done. As Chuck D said in the shock doc *Boulevard Of Broken Dreams*, "Mathew Knowles and Beyoncé, that's the root, that's the tree – don't get it twisted. Everything else is a branch or a leaf."

The following day, Mathew issued his own statement via the Associated

Press: "It should come as no surprise that at 29 years old, almost 30, she wants to have more control of her business," he said. "Beyoncé, I feel is the number one artist in the world right now. And that's a great feeling, as a father and manager." Mathew intended to concentrate on the gospel aspects of Music World Entertainment's roster: Trin-i-tee 5:7, Micah Stampley and Vanessa Bell Armstrong. "Business is business and family is family. I love my daughter and am very proud of who she is and all that she has achieved. I look forward to her continued great success."

The signs of this separation had been there as far back as 2003, when Beyoncé told *The Observer*, "Obviously the older we got, the more in control we were. When we were 17 we trusted a lot of people and they made great decisions for us. But now, at this point, the schedule that I do – the magazines, the videos, the producers, the directors, the songs that make the album – everything – it's my career, so I have to want to do it. Other things I don't have time for my father will make decisions."

It was impossible to hear these statements without thinking of the struggle that the Deena Jones character had gone through in *Dreamgirls* to free herself from the control of her manager and lover, Curtis Taylor. "Deena's need was to be free, but she completely lost herself in [Curtis'] dreams," she told *USA Today* at the time. The song 'Control', one of the 70-plus tracks that was recorded for *I Am . . . Sasha Fierce*, could also be read as a not-so-coded message to her father.

Beyoncé's website was quiet on events, showing just the March 28 date to announce that she was donating her song 'Irreplaceable' for use on the iTunes *Songs For Japan* album, a response to the earthquake, tsunami and potential nuclear disaster that befell northeastern Japan in March 2011.

On May 9, Beyoncé announced that she was joining forces with US First Lady Michelle Obama and the National Association of Broadcasters Education Foundation to help fight obesity. 'Let's Move! America's Move To Raise A Generation Of Healthier Kids', a nationwide campaign, was launched. Beyoncé re-recorded 'Get Me Bodied' from *B'Day* as 'Move Your Body', with a refrain of "wave the American flag" added to the end. A video was released of teenagers dancing, and Beyoncé soon recorded her own instructional video to go with it. "I am excited to be part of this effort that addresses a public health crisis," she said. "First Lady Michelle Obama deserves credit for tackling this issue directly, and I applaud the NAB Education Foundation for trying to make a positive difference in the lives of our schoolchildren." The video, premiered on May 3, saw Beyoncé dancing improbably enthusiastically in a pair of high-heeled shoes in a school dinner room, surrounded by schoolchildren of all shapes and sizes.

Michelle Obama was filmed dancing to 'Move Your Body' at a visit to the Alice Deal Middle School in Washington, DC, in early May. She said that, "Beyoncé is one of my favourite performers on the planet. And when she agreed to remake her video and do this 'Let's Move' flash workout, I was so excited, because this is what we've been talking about – that exercise and moving can be fun. It's about dancing, it's about moving." It was as if Beyoncé had become the artist in residence at the White House.

From March through to May 2011, the world seemed to buzz with news of Beyoncé and her next move. The announcement of Mathew's dismissal was followed by rumours that a new album was coming to coincide with her Glastonbury performance. Again, it sounded as if Beyoncé was rewriting her rules. It was said that she was going to go back to basics and – no less – introduce her own genre. In the same week in March that it was announced she would no longer be managed by her father, she was spotted at a New Jersey motel for a photoshoot with Ellen Von Unwerth for her forthcoming album. With long, straight blonde highlighted hair, a denim jumpsuit and a maroon faux-fur coat, Beyoncé appeared older than her 29 years. A lot had gone on in 2011 already.

Beyoncé played some early versions of tracks to Australian Sony Music MD Denis Handlin while she was accompanying Jay-Z on his tour of the Antipodes supporting U2 in December 2010. "It was just amazing," Handlin said. "She came in and played us six tracks from the album. She wants to do a big tour off the back of this record . . . these songs, the best description I can give is groundbreaking; she's gone to another level."

Initial statements suggested that Beyoncé was actually inventing her own genre of music with this album, and that it was a clear and logical advance from her previous three albums. "Well, I wouldn't say I'm inventing a new genre," Beyoncé told reporters. "I'm mixing every type of genre that I love, and I'm inspired by every type of genre . . . I'm not in a box. It's not R&B. It's not typically pop. It's not rock. It's just everything I love all mixed together in my own little gumbo of music." She told MTV that the album was influenced by what she had been currently listening to. "Definitely Fela Kuti, The Stylistics. How random, right? . . . So many people . . . Lauryn Hill, Stevie Wonder, of course, Michael Jackson's *Off The Wall* . . . all of those things I'm kind of mixing together."

On April 14, 2011, the British press was full of stories of Beyoncé shooting her new video, supposedly for the track 'Run The World (Girls)', in the Mojave Desert, California, where she allegedly imported around 200 dancers from across the world at a cost of £60,000. Directed by Francis Lawrence, who'd first worked with Beyoncé on the 'Independent Women Part I' promo, the video was shot to launch the new album. "It'll be big," Lawrence told MTV. "It'll probably be one of the bigger Beyoncé music videos ever done. And, I can say that I think the song is unbelievable."

Produced by David 'Switch' Taylor, Beyoncé and Shea Taylor, and released worldwide on iTunes on April 21, 2011, 'Run The World (Girls)' was big, brash and atonal, paring down all the melodic implications of Beyoncé's music to a slew of beats and heavily arranged vocals. For a song that is mainly treated vocals and synthesised beats, it had a lot of writers: Beyoncé, Switch, Terius 'The-Dream' Nash, Nick 'Afrojack' van de Wall, Wesley 'Diplo' Pentz and Adidja Palmer. Based upon 'Pon De Floor' by Diplo and Switch's production act, Major Lazer, it is hard and metallic, with Beyoncé's amassed vocals screaming another call for empowerment. It is bold, brave and futuristic. It is easy to hear the production and writing techniques that Diplo and Switch first employed with M.I.A. on the track.

The Village Voice wrote that, "It starts off sounding like a Willow Smith song, thanks to its schoolyard chants about 'girls' over a militaristic beat – here we might remind you, also, that B turns 30 this September – but then Beyoncé's sideways approach to melody comes in when she starts singing, and the song's pretty unmistakably hers from that point on." *Rolling Stone* said: "She forsakes fashionable sounds – no Eurodisco synths! – to belt over Diplo and Switch's ferocious dancehall beat. The message is party-hearty feminism." The paper also noted how crowded the market place was that she was releasing into: Lady Gaga, of course, Taylor Swift, Katy Perry, Rihanna, even a returning Britney Spears all released records or were on tour in the first half of 2011. Knowles was acutely aware of this fact, and it could certainly be said that the promo for 'Run The World (Girls)' was nothing if not an enormous statement of intent. Beyoncé spoke to *Billboard* about the single in May 2011: "It's definitely riskier than something a bit more . . . simple. I just heard the track and loved that it was so different: it felt a bit African, a bit electronic and futuristic. It reminded me of what I love, which is mixing different cultures and eras – things that typically don't go together – to create a new sound. I can never be safe; I always try and go against the grain. As soon as I accomplish one thing, I just set a higher goal. That's how I've gotten to where I am." However, at the time of writing, it had failed to set the charts alight, peaking at number 11 in the UK and number 33 in the US.

Its video was finally released on May 18, 2011, and was premiered to much fanfare on *American Idol*. A few days after, it was announced that the title of Beyoncé's album would be *4*, like Led Zeppelin and Foreigner before her. Lawrence's promo did not disappoint, and took all of Beyoncé's signature filmic ideas, scaling them up to new levels.

Over the swelteringly hot, languorous Easter break in the UK, the tabloid papers seemed to be having a field day, reporting Beyoncé and Jay-Z's every move as they took a break in Paris before the release of *4*. Beyoncé had long spoken of wanting to take some time to recharge in Paris, one of her favourite cities in the world. With the couple staying at the Hotel Fouquet's Barrière, with its private roof terrace overlooking the Eiffel Tower, the press (the *Daily Mail* in particular) seemed to wish to eke out comparisons of Beyoncé with Michael Jackson, simply because she went to the Disneyland Paris resort theme park in Marne-La-Vallée on the outskirts of the city. One of the most fanciful reports that blew through that weekend was the *Daily Star*'s story that Beyoncé and Jay-Z were to perform 'Crazy In Love' at the wedding of Prince William and Kate Middleton in London on April 29. "Both William and Kate are massive fans of Beyoncé and Jay-Z," 'a spokesperson' was quoted as saying. "They really wanted to make their big day even more special and what better way than by getting pop royalty to perform at the party?" Beyoncé was quick to dispel the rumour, but it simply showed quite how enormous her, and her husband's, brand had become.

The day before the British royal wedding, it was announced in *The Guardian* that Beyoncé was being sued for $100 million by US-based software developer Gate Five Group LLC, claiming that she had "destroyed [its] business . . . on a whim". It was putting together *Starpower: Beyoncé*, a computer game that would enable its players to dance along to Beyoncé classics such as 'Single Ladies (Put A Ring On It)' and 'Crazy In Love'. Interactive computer games for Nintendo's Wii, Sony's PlayStation and Microsoft's Xbox such as *SingStar*, *Guitar Hero* and *Rock Band* opened the floodgates for many imitators and had become a lucrative industry. Beyoncé changed her mind about the project in December 2010, forcing the company to dismiss 70 employees the week before Christmas. Gate Five's attorneys suggested that, although Beyoncé had already agreed terms with the company, she "made an extortionate demand for entirely new compensation terms", and then decided to withdraw. This drove away the project's backer and led the company to collapse. Gate Five founder, Grey Easley, suggested that more "unpleasant details" are on the way.

But there was little time to pay attention to unpleasant details. On May 5, it was announced that Beyoncé had been added to the bill of the Scottish equivalent of Glastonbury, the T in the Park festival, held at Balado Park, Kinross. Playing on Saturday July 9, she would join a bill that included Arctic Monkeys, Coldplay, Foo Fighters, Pulp, The Strokes, Plan B, The Script, Slash, Tinie Tempah and Tom Jones. It was also announced that the following night she would be added to the bill of Oxegen festival in Dublin. It was as if, post-Mathew, she was going to live out her rock'n'roll fantasies.

The same night, she appeared on the British celebrity Piers Morgan's US TV Show, *Tonight*, performing 'God Bless The USA', the Lee

Greenwood song she had sang during Barack Obama's presidential campaign. With its line "I'm proud to be American, where at least I know I'm free", coming in the week that a team of Navy Seals shot and killed Osama Bin Laden in Abbottabad, Pakistan, her performance was packed with significance. Released immediately on iTunes, the song hedged Beyoncé's bets and placed her right at the heart of conservatism after the discordance of 'Run The World (Girls)'.

Beyoncé issued this statement on May 5, the day that President Obama went to lay a wreath at Ground Zero in Manhattan. "We were all affected by the tragedies of 9/11 and continue to keep the families who lost loved ones close to our hearts. Lee Greenwood, the writer of the song, is also donating his proceeds to help the 9/11 families. Thank you Piers Morgan and CNN for helping to get the message out to everyone about this."

Beyoncé's fourth album, *4*, was finally released in June 2011. Again, it drew on a huge pool of producers, including Diplo and DJ Dave Taylor. Beyoncé told *Billboard*, "We all have special numbers in our lives, and 4 is that for me. It's the day I was born. My mother's birthday, and a lot of my friends' birthdays, are on the fourth; April 4 is my wedding date." At a listening party at Sony's New York headquarters on May 11 she revealed she had cut 72 tracks in total and was leaving the final track selection as late as possible.

At the time of writing, Beyoncé is rumoured to be linked to the fourth film remake of *A Star Is Born*, with Clint Eastwood directing. The film, which is most revered in its 1954 Judy Garland version, tells the story of a singer whose career is in the ascendancy, who falls in love with an established star whose career is on the wane. "It's a dream come true; I'm still in shock that it's really going to happen," Beyoncé said in May 2011. "Clint Eastwood is clearly the absolute best, and I'm so honored and humbled. I was in no rush to do another movie unless it was the right film, and I didn't even want to touch *A Star is Born* unless it was with him. I actually learned that this project was in existence, and kind of claimed it. I want to get to work right now!" The film goes into production later in 2011. This story will run and run.

Postscript: *4 Ever?*

"At this point, I really know who I am, and don't feel like I have to put myself in a box. I'm not afraid of taking risks — no one can define me."
                                                                    Beyoncé, May 2011

The above quotation is extremely salient. Beyoncé has spent the past 15 years growing up in public. The tiny acts of rebellion like smoking in videos, wearing T-shirts with the legend 'punk ass motherfucker' emblazoned across the front and hanging out with (and marrying) rappers are all small signs of defiance and maturity. So closely surrounded by her family, she is now a 30-year-old woman, no longer the 17-year-old girl of 'No, No, No'. She has now experienced the life that she only heard about in the Headliners hair salon in Houston.

Beyoncé has become a worldwide phenomenon. She has a brand that is known across the globe. "The deal is that Beyoncé can sell us all these products," Staffordshire University professor Ellis Cashmore stated in his paper 'Buying Beyoncé'. "But in the process she also sells us something else, something to assuage white guilt. She has become a moving advert that racism, while it might still be present in American society, is no longer a horrendous monster but an irritating mosquito that can be swatted away."

The rise of Beyoncé has gone hand in hand with dizzying changes in how music is delivered to the masses; when she began there was no social media, the Internet was still relatively new in its transition to the World Wide Web; Facebook (founded 2004), YouTube (2005) and Twitter (2006) were simply gleams in their inventors' eyes. Every step of the way, Beyoncé's team and Sony Music has ensured that all these bases were covered, marketing to the masses in the process. At the time of writing, Beyoncé has over a million people following her on Twitter and her Facebook site has 20,134,543 followers.

It is telling when one visits the Destiny's Child website. When the group went their separate ways in 2005, all three members had the links to their newly established sites on the Destiny's Child page. Given the ephemeral nature of the net, nobody expected these sites to last for long, but if you look in 2011, it is only Beyoncé's that is still active. Kelly Rowland has enjoyed success, as has Michelle Williams, but not even their highest highs compare even marginally with the achievements of Beyoncé.

Beyoncé's relationship with Jay-Z continues to generate huge interest. "There is something compelling about her marriage," *The Daily Telegraph* wrote in 2008. "The bringing together of Jay-Z, the former drug dealer and hustler from Bedford-Stuyvesant in the wrong part of Brooklyn, and God-fearing, clean-living, self-improving Beyoncé from the posh school in the nice, air-conditioned part of Texas. Together they have carved out a new blueprint for black entertainers, making the key leap from being mere employees to being autonomous business people." The manner in which Beyoncé and Jay-Z conduct their business and their relationship is refreshing to say the least in the current transient climate. In Jay-Z's 2010 autobiography, *Decoded*, Beyoncé is not mentioned a single time, apart from indirectly in the footnote to his lyric 'Operation Corporate Takeover'. For the line "the writing's on the wall, like my lady, right baby?" the footnote simply says, "*The Writing's On The Wall* was the name of the record album from Destiny's Child."

Maura Johnston in *The Village Voice* posited an interesting theory about Beyoncé's continual upscaling of her career as a mirror of the decline in the recorded music industry. "One could say that this overreaching in pop is an understandable response to the freefall the industry has been in, the competition music has from not just itself but from other distractions (TV, video games, online personals, interaction with other people); it's an attempt to maximise ins, sort of like when the bagel place on your block that has been hurting decides to incorporate a frozen yogurt machine, or a burrito counter. It's all there, sure. But is it satisfying?" Time will tell how satisfying Beyoncé remains, but already, she has outlasted all the TLCs, SWVs and En Vogues, who were her early inspiration and peers.

"It's a job. In real life I'm not like that," these words from her 2004 *Rolling Stone* interview provide her critics with sufficient ammunition to use against her, that she somehow doesn't mean what she is doing, it is all an act. Because of her look and appearance, one immediately assumes that Beyoncé is far older than she is, and she has been doing this professionally since she was 10 years old. Even she is amazed by her longevity, at what is now a 20-year career. "I never imagined I'd have as much success as I've had," she told *Cosmopolitan* in March 2011. "I thought it would be great just to get a record out. I never imagined the extent of what I've achieved. I never imagined the awards, the movies . . . I still can't believe it. I'm grateful for all of it and don't take it for granted. When I do something, I try and do it as well as I can."

She is ubiquitous and revered. As she turned 30 in September 2011, the master plan forged by Mathew and Tina during the nineties in Houston – when she missed the opportunities that regular teenagers had in order to practise and strive for greatness – had paid off. She has all the grace and stature of predecessors such as Diana Ross and Aretha Franklin, yet with little of the diva-esque baggage. Her songs are known throughout the world, and her image, that of a positive, go-ahead woman who values hard work and decency in order to produce high quality shows, has made her a role model to thousands.

Beyoncé has achieved all of the goals she set out to when she started as a naive teenager. Although she had the high expectations of a young girl, it would have seemed impossible for her to scale quite so many heights. However her music has changed, Beyoncé has remained true to her core beliefs. "Power means happiness, power means hard work and sacrifice. To me, it's about setting a good example, and not abusing your power! You still have to have humility: I've seen how you can lead by example, and not by fear. My visit to Egypt was a really big inspiration for me. Once the sun went down, I saw not one woman; it was shocking and fascinating to me, because it was so extreme. I saw thousands of men walking down the street, socialising in bars, praying in mosques – and no women. I felt really proud when I performed and saw the strength that the women were getting through the music. I remember being in Japan when Destiny's Child put out 'Independent Women Part I' and women there were saying how proud they were to have their own jobs, their own independent thinking, their own goals. It made me feel so good, and I realised that one of my responsibilities was to inspire women in a deeper way." Given the amount of speculation there has been about her life and career, Beyoncé has remained true to herself.

And she's only 30.

And she released 'Crazy In Love', a tune that cannot fail to melt even the hardest of hearts.

UK Discography

1) ALBUMS

DESTINY'S CHILD

Destiny's Child
Columbia, 1998

Second Nature / No, No, No Part 2 / With Me Part 1 / Tell Me /
Bridges / No, No, No Part 1 / With Me Part 2 / Show Me The Way
/ Killing Time / Illusion / Birthday / Sail On / My Time Has Come
/ Know That / You're The Only One / No, No, No (Camdino Soul
Extended Remix) / DubiLLusions

The Writing's On The Wall
Columbia, 1999

Intro (The Writing's On The Wall) / So Good / Bills, Bills, Bills /
Confessions / Bug A Boo / Temptation / Now That She's Gone /
Where'd You Go / Hey Ladies / If You Leave / Jumpin', Jumpin' /
Say My Name / She Can't Love You / Stay / Sweet Sixteen / Outro
(Amazing Grace . . . Dedicated To Andretta Tillman) / Get On The Bus

Survivor
Columbia, 2001

Independent Women Part I / Survivor / Bootylicious / Nasty Girl /
Apple Pie À La Mode / Sexy Daddy / Perfect Man / Independent
Women Part II / Happy Face / Dance With Me / My Heart Still

Beats / Emotion / Brown Eyes / Dangerously In Love / The Story
Of Beauty / Gospel Medley (Dedicated to Andretta Tillman) / Outro
(DC-3) Thank You

8 Days Of Christmas
Music World Music / Columbia, 2001
8 Days Of Christmas / Winter Paradise / A 'DC' Christmas Medley
/ Silent Night / Little Drummer Boy / Do You Hear What I Hear /
White Christmas / Platinum Bells / O' Holy Night / Spread A Little
Love On Christmas Day / This Christmas / Opera Of The Bells / The
Proud Family (Solange feat. Destiny's Child)

This Is The Remix
Columbia, 2002
No, No, No Part 2 (feat. Wyclef Jean Extended Version) / Emotion
(The Neptunes Remix) / Bootylicious (Rockwilder Remix) / Say
My Name (Timbaland Remix) / Bug A Boo (Refugee Camp Remix
feat. Wyclef Jean) / Dot (The E-Poppi Mix) / Survivor (Remix feat.
Da Brat Extended Version) / Independent Women Part II / Nasty
Girl (Maurice's Nu Soul Remix Radio Edit) / Jumpin' Jumpin'
(Remix Extended Version feat. Jermaine Dupri, Da Brat and Lil Bow
Wow) / Bills, Bills, Bills (Maurice's Xclusive Livegig Mix) / So Good
(Maurice's Soul Remix) / Heard A Word (Michelle Williams)

Destiny Fulfilled
Sony Urban Music / Columbia, 2004
Lose My Breath / Soldier / Cater 2 U / T-Shirt / Is She The Reason /
Girl / Bad Habit / If / Free / Through With Love / Love / Game Over

#1's
Sony Urban Music / Columbia, 2005
Stand Up For Love / Independent Women Part I / Survivor / Soldier
/ Check On It / Jumpin', Jumpin' / Lose My Breath / Say My Name
/ Emotion / Bug A Boo / Bootylicious / Bills, Bills, Bills / Girl / No,
No, No Part 2 / Cater 2 U / Feel The Same Way I Do

BEYONCÉ

Dangerously In Love
Columbia, 2003
Crazy In Love / Naughty Girl/ Baby Boy / Hip Hop Star / Be With
You / Me, Myself And I / Yes / Signs / Speechless / That's How You
Like It / The Closer I Get To You / Dangerously In Love 2 / Beyoncé
Interlude / Gift From Virgo / Work It Out / 03 Bonnie & Clyde

B'Day
Sony Urban Music / Columbia, 2006
Déjà Vu / Get Me Bodied / Suga Mama / Upgrade U / Ring The
Alarm / Kitty Kat / Freakum Dress / Green Light / Irreplaceable /
Resentment / Encore For The Fans (Listen)

I Am . . .
Sony Music / Columbia, 2008
If I Were A Boy / Halo / Disappear / Broken-Hearted Girl / Ave
Maria / Smash Into You / Satellites / That's Why You're Beautiful
Sasha Fierce
Single Ladies (Put A Ring On It) / Radio / Diva / Sweet Dreams /
Video Phone / Hello / Ego / Scared Of Lonely

I Am . . . World Tour
Sony Music / Columbia, 2010
Intro / Crazy In Love – Let Me Clear My Throat / Naughty Girl /
Tomorrow I Am . . . Sasha Fierce / Freakum Dress / Get Me Bodied /
Smash Into You / Ave Maria / Broken-Hearted Girl / If I Were A Boy
– You Oughtta Know / Robot / Diva / Radio / Socks And Stilettos
/ Ego / Hello / Sasha Vs Beyoncé / Baby Boy – Why Don't You Love
Me (No, No, No) / Irreplaceable / Check On It / Bootylicious /
Upgrade U / Video Phone / Are You Filming Me With That /
Say My Name / At Last / Listen / Single Ladies (Put A Ring On It) /
Halo

4
Sony Music / Columbia, 2011
1+1/ I Care / I Miss You / Best Thing I Never Had / Party / Rather Die Young / Start Over / Love On Top / Countdown / End Of Time / I Was Here /Run The World (Girls)

2) SIGNIFICANT SOUNDTRACK APPEARANCES

Men In Black
Sony Music / Columbia, 1997
Killin' Time (Destiny's Child)

Austin Powers In Goldmember **(Music From & Inspired By The Motion Picture)**
Maverick, 2002
Work It Out (Beyoncé)
Hey Goldmember (Beyoncé)

The Fighting Temptations
Sony Music Soundtrax, 2003
Fighting Temptation (Beyoncé, Missy Elliott, MC Lyte and Free)
I Know (Destiny's Child)
Fever (Beyoncé)
Everything I Do (Beyoncé and Bilal)
Swing Low, Sweet Chariot (Beyoncé)
He Still Loves Me (Beyoncé and Walter Williams, Sr.)
Time To Come Home (Beyoncé, Angie Stone and Melba Moore)
Summertime (Beyoncé feat. P. Diddy)

The Pink Panther
Sony Music, 2006
Check On It (Beyoncé feat. Slim Thug)
A Woman Like Me (Beyoncé)

Dreamgirls
Sony Music Soundtrax, 2006
Move (Jennifer Hudson, Beyoncé and Anika Noni Rose)
Fake Your Way To the Top (Jennifer Hudson, Beyoncé, Anika Noni Rose and Eddie Murphy)
Cadillac Car (Jennifer Hudson, Beyoncé, Anika Noni Rose, Eddie Murphy, Laura Bell Bundy, Rory O'Malley and Anne Warren)
Steppin' To the Bad Side (Jennifer Hudson, Beyoncé, Anika Noni Rose, Hinton Battle, Jamie Foxx and Keith Robinson)
I Want You Baby (Jennifer Hudson, Beyoncé, Anika Noni Rose and Eddie Murphy)
Family (Jennifer Hudson, Beyoncé, Anika Noni Rose, Keith Robinson and Jamie Foxx)
Dreamgirls (Jennifer Hudson, Beyoncé and Anika Noni Rose)
Heavy (Jennifer Hudson, Beyoncé and Anika Noni Rose)
It's All Over (Jennifer Hudson, Beyoncé, Anika Noni Rose, Jamie Foxx, Keith Robinson and Sharon Leal)
Love Love You Baby (Sharon Leal, Beyoncé and Anika Noni Rose)
I'm Somebody (Sharon Leal, Beyoncé and Anika Noni Rose)
Lorrell Loves Kimmy / Family (Reprise) (Sharon Leal, Beyoncé and Anika Noni Rose)
Step On Over (Sharon Leal, Beyoncé and Anika Noni Rose)
One Night Only (Sharon Leal, Beyoncé and Anika Noni Rose)
Listen (Beyoncé)
Hard To Say (Sharon Leal, Beyoncé and Anika Noni Rose)
Dreamgirls (Finale) (Jennifer Hudson, Sharon Leal, Beyoncé and Anika Noni Rose)
Family (End Title) (Jamie Foxx, Jennifer Hudson and Beyoncé)
When I First Saw You (Jamie Foxx and Beyoncé)
One Night Only (Dance Mix) (Sharon Leal and Beyoncé)

Cadillac Records
Music World Entertainment, 2008
All I Could Do Is Cry / At Last / I'd Rather Go Blind / Once In A Lifetime / Trust In Me

3) SINGLES

DESTINY'S CHILD

1997
No, No, No Part 2

1998
With Me
Get On The Bus

1999
Bills, Bills, Bills
Bug A Boo

2000
Say My Name
Jumpin', Jumpin'
Independent Women Part I

2001
Survivor
Bootylicious
Emotion

2002
Nasty Girl (import)

2004
Lose My Breath
Soldier

2005
Girl
Cater 2 U (import)
Stand Up For Love

BEYONCÉ

2002
Work It Out

2003
Crazy In Love (with Jay-Z)
Baby Boy (with Sean Paul)
Me, Myself And I

2004
Naughty Girl

2005
Check On It (with Slim Thug)

2006
Déjà Vu (with Jay-Z)
Ring The Alarm (import)
Irreplaceable
Listen

2007
Beautiful Liar (with Shakira)
Green Light

2008
If I Were A Boy
Single Ladies (Put A Ring On It)

2009
Diva (import)
Halo
Ego
Sweet Dreams

Broken-Hearted Girl
Video Phone (with Lady Gaga)

2011
Run The World (Girls)

2010
Telephone (with Lady Gaga)

4) SELECTED DVDs

Beyoncé Live At Wembley
Columbia, 2004

Baby Boy / Naughty Girl / Fever / Hip Hop Star / Yes / Work It Out / Gift From Virgo / Be With You / Speechless / DC Medley (Bug A Boo – No, No, No Part 2 – Bootylicious – Jumpin', Jumpin' – Say My Name – Independent Women Part I – 03 Bonnie & Clyde – Survivor) / Me, Myself and I / Summertime / Dangerously In Love / Crazy In Love

SPECIAL FEATURES: Backstage / Staging – Choreography / Beyoncé's Dressing Room / Show Favourites / Beyoncé – Solo Artist / A Day In London / Meet The Fans Backstage / A Conversation With Beyoncé / Crazy In Love Live From The 2004 BRIT Awards / L'Oréal Commercial / Destiny's Child Update

AUDIO CD: Wishing On A Star / What's It Gonna Be / My First Time / Krazy In Luv (Maurice's Nu Soul Mix) / Baby Boy (Junior's World Mixshow) / Naughty Girl (Calderone Quayle Club Mix)

The Beyoncé Experience Live
Columbia, 2007

Intro / Crazy In Love (Crazy Mix) / Freakum Dress / Green Light / Baby Boy / Beautiful Liar / Naughty Girl / Me, Myself And I / Dangerously In Love / Flaws And All / Destiny's Child Medley (Cops And Robbers Intro – Independent Women Part I – Bootylicious – No, No, No Part 2 – Bug A Boo – Bills, Bills, Bills – Cater 2 U – Say My Name – Jumpin', Jumpin' – Soldier – Survivor) / Speechless / Ring

The Alarm / Suga Mama / Upgrade U / 03 Bonnie & Clyde / Check
On It / Déjà Vu / Get Me Bodied / Welcome To Hollywood / Deena
– Dreamgirls / Listen / Irreplaceable / Beyoncé B'Day Surprise

I Am . . . Yours: An Intimate Performance At Wynn Las Vegas
Sony Music / Columbia, 2009
ACT ONE: INTIMATE
Hello Introduction / Halo / Irreplaceable / Sweet Dreams Medley /
If I Were A Boy / Scared Of Lonely / That's Why You're Beautiful /
Satellites / Resentment

INTERMISSION
Jazz Medley / Déjà Vu / Tap Sequence

ACT TWO: STORYTELLING
I Wanna Be Where You Are / Destiny's Child Medley (No, No, No
Part 1 – No, No, No Part 2 – Bug A Boo – Bills, Bills, Bills – Say My
Name – Jumpin', Jumpin' – Independent Women Part I – Bootylicious
– Survivor) / Beyoncé (Work It Out – 03 Bonnie & Clyde – Crazy In
Love – Naughty Girl – Get Me Bodied) / Single Ladies (Put A Ring
On It) / Finale

BONUS FEATURE: What Happens In Vegas

5) FILMOGRAPHY

Carmen: A Hip Hopera
MTV, 2001
Director: Robert Townsend
Role: Carmen

The Fighting Temptations
Paramount Pictures, 2003
Director: Jonathan Lynn
Role: Lilly

Austin Powers In Goldmember
New Line Cinema, 2002
Director: Jay Roach
Role: Foxxy Cleopatra

Fade To Black
Paramount Classics, 2004
Director: Patrick Paulson, Michael
John Warren
Role: Herself

The Pink Panther
Metro-Goldwyn-Mayer, 2006
Director: Shawn Levy
Role: Xania

Dreamgirls
Paramount Pictures, 2006
Director: Bill Condon
Role: Deena Jones

Cadillac Records
TriStar / Sony Pictures, 2008
Director: Darnell Martin
Role: Etta James

Obsessed
Screen Gems / Sony Pictures,
2009
Director: Steve Shill
Role: Sharon Charles

6) TEN CLASSICS

1) Crazy In Love
2) Get Me Bodied
3) Bills, Bills, Bills
4) Independent Women Part I
5) Work It Out
6) Ring The Alarm
7) Suga Mama
8) Jumpin', Jumpin'
9) That's Why You're Beautiful
10) Say My Name

Bibliography

PRIMARY BOOK SOURCES

Arenofsky, Janice. *Beyoncé Knowles: A Biography* (Greenwood Press, Westport 2009)

Boyer, Paul S., Clark Jr., Clifford E., Kett, Joseph F., Salisbury, Neal, Sitkoff, Harvard and Woloch, Nancy (eds.). *The Enduring Vision: A History Of The American People* (D. C. Heath, Lexington, Toronto 1996)

Bronson, Fred. *The Billboard Book Of Number 1 Hits: Updated and Expanded 5th Edition* (Billboard Books, New York, NY 2003)

Carter, Shawn (Jay-Z). *Decoded* (Virgin Books, London 2010)

Colson, Mary. *Beyoncé: A Life In Music* (Raintree, London 2011)

Dickson, Paul. *From Elvis To E-Mail: Trends, Events And Trivia From The Postwar Era To The End Of The Century* (Federal Street Press, Springfield, MA 1999)

Guenin, Chaya. *The Beyoncé Handbook: Everything You Need To Know About Beyoncé Knowles* (Creative Commons Attribution – Share Alike 3.0 Unported, LaVergne, TN 2010)

Keener, Rob and Pitts, George. *VX: 10 Years Of Vibe Photography* (Vibe Books, New York, NY 2003)

Knowles, Beyoncé, Rowland, Kelly, Williams, Michelle and Herman, James Patrick. *Soul Survivors: The Official Autobiography Of Destiny's Child* (Boxtree, London 2002)

Kutner, Jon and Leigh, Spencer. *1000 UK Number One Hits* (Omnibus Press, London 2005)

Larkin, Colin. *The Virgin Encyclopedia Of Popular Music, Concise Fourth Edition* (Virgin, London 2002)

Morley, Paul. *Words And Music – A History Of Pop In the Shape Of A City* (Bloomsbury, London 2003)

Seymour, Craig. *Luther: The Life And Longing Of Luther Vandross* (Harper Entertainment, New York, NY 2004)

Shapiro, Peter. *The Rough Guide To Hip-Hop* (Rough Guides, London 2001)

Southall, Brian. *The A–Z Of Record Labels, Second Edition* (Sanctuary Publishing, London 2003)

Walker, John. *Halliwell's Film Video & DVD Guide* 2006 (Harper Collins, London 2006)

PRIMARY NEWSPAPER AND MAGAZINE ARTICLES

Many publications including *Vibe; The Metro; The Times; The Sunday Express; Time Out New York; Muzik; The Independent; Billboard; The Mirror; Q; Mojo; New Musical Express; Clash Magazine; The Guardian; The LA Times; Uncut; Ebony, Newsweek; Houston Chronicle; People Magazine; USA Today; Entertainment Weekly; Essence; News Of The World*

Cashmore, Ellis. 'Buying Beyoncé', *Celebrity Studies* 1:2, 135–50 (2010)

All other publications referenced in text

TELEVISION PROGRAMME

The Beyoncé Experience Tour 2007 Programme
WEBSITES

Many sites, including: allmusic, discogs, imdb, metacritic

4 information: www.billboard.biz/bbbiz/others/features/beyonce-q-a-the-billboard-music-awards-millennium-1005176882.story

Bassplayer: www.bassplayer.com/article/beyonces-deja-vu/dec-06/24360

BBC:
Review: www.bbc.co.uk/music/reviews/55jw
Destiny's Child lawsuits: news.bbc.co.uk/1/hi/entertainment/3203417.stm

BC Jean: www.songwriteruniverse.com/bcjean123.htm

***B'Day* reviews:**
Boston Globe: www.boston.com/news/globe/living/articles/2006/
09/04/beyonce_shows_rage_and_range_on_new_release/
Classic Web: classicweb.archive.org/web/20071015051436/http://
musicworldentertainment.com/beyonce.php

Billboard:
Chart history: www.billboard.com/#/artist/Destiny%27s+Child/
chart-history/248498?f=379&g=Singles
Mathew Knowles: http://www.billboard.biz/bbbiz/industry/
legal-and-management/beyonce-s-father-mathew-knowles-is-no-
longer-1005097802.story
Mathew Knowles split: /www.billboard.biz/bbbiz/industry/
legal-and-management/mathew-knowles-says-split-with-beyonce-
shows-1005099342.story?utm_source=twitterfeed&utm_medium=twitter
Sanctuary buys MWE: http://books.google.co.uk/books?id=GREEA
AAAMBAJ&pg=PA10&lpg=PA10&dq=date+of+destiny's+child's+ini
tial+contract+with+sony+music&source=bl&ots=hPYmBm6B8m&si
g=8yZRndeS4U4VLkKhYHXxESojnAA&hl=en&ei=V5GhTbHVEc
bJhAfmt8n1BA&sa=X&oi=book_result&ct=result&resnum=6&ved=0
CD0Q6AEwBQ#v=onepage&q&f=false

Blackface: www.usmagazine.com/stylebeauty/news/beyonce-gets-
flack-for-blackface-photo-shoot-2011242

***Cadillac Records* reviews:**
New York *Daily News*: http://www.nydailynews.com/entertainment/
movies/2008/12/05/2008-12-05_cadillac_records_takes_a_
greatesthits_ap.html#ixzzlLqOasNYc
New York Magazine: nymag.com/movies/reviews/52586/

Daily Telegraph: www.telegraph.co.uk/culture/music/3563004/ Beyonce-dream-girl.html

'Déjà Vu' controversy: www.petitiononline.com/dejavu06/petition.html

Entertainment Weekly:
The Writing's On The Wall: www.ew.com/ew/article/0,,272373,00.html
B'Day: www.ew.com/ew/article/0,,1516025,00.html
I Am . . . www.ew.com/ew/article/0,,20237810,00.html

Fat Joe interview: web.archive.org/web/20080224081629/http:// www.mtv.com/onair/moviehouse/cameo/16/index.jhtml

Ebony: /findarticles.com/p/articles/mi_m1077/is_11_56/ai_77556552/

Ellis Cashmore: www.timesonline.co.uk/tol/news/uk/article566248.ece

Fox News:
B'Day first look: www.foxnews.com/story/0,2933,208884,00. html#ixzz1KeeZNyEt
B'Day: www.foxnews.com/story/0,2933,208884,00.html

Glamour **magazine:** www.dennishensley.com/Beyonce.htm

Grammy Awards 2004: www.people.com/people/ article/0,,627723,00.html

The Guardian:
Beyoncé B'Day: www.guardian.co.uk/music/2006/aug/18/urban. popandrock
Beyoncé Etta James: www.guardian.co.uk/music/2009/feb/06/ beyonce-etta-james-barack-obama
Kelly Rowland: www.guardian.co.uk/music/2003/feb/07/ popandrock.artsfeatures1

Heat perfume:
Advertising Standards ruling: http://www.dailymail.co.uk/tvshowbiz/article-1330408/Beyonce-perfume-advert-sexy-banned-daytime-TV.html#ixzz1MKCSxgLG
Beyoncé catches Heat: rap.up.com – www.rap-up.com/2009/12/29/beyonce-catches-heat-in-fragrance-ads/#more-34785
Beyoncé perfume: www.beyonceparfums.com/en/gb#/beyonce-heat
Heat sales figures: stylenews.peoplestylewatch.com/2010/03/18/beyoncs-perfume-sells-3-million-in-just-one-month/
Now Smell This: www.nstperfume.com/2010/02/04/beyonce-heat-perfume-review
San José Examiner review of Heat: www.examiner.com/fragrance-in-san-jose/beyonce-heat-rush-eau-de-toilette-review-review

Hollywood: www.foxnews.com/story/0,2933,189491,00.html?sPage=fnc/entertainment/beyonce

House Of Deréon: www.houseofdereon.com

Houston Chronicle: www.chron.com/CDA/archives/archive.mpl?id=1992_1074953

Huffington Post: /www.huffingtonpost.com/2011/03/28/beyonces-father-mathew-kn_n_841769.html

Ivana Chubbuck: www.chubbucktechnique.com

Jake Wade: www.whosampled.com/sample/view/3359/Beyoncé-Suga%20Mama_Jake%20Wade%20and%20The%20Soul%20Searchers-Searching%20for%20Soul/

Kayt Jones: www.kaytjones.com

The LA Times: http://latimesblogs.latimes.com/music_blog/2008/11/snap-judgment-b.html

Lawsuits: www.greekchat.com/gcforums/archive/index.php/t-14447.html

Lyndell Locke: celeb.wohoo.co.uk/2009/09/beyonce-knowles-ex-boyfriend-lyndell-locke-speaks/

The Mail: http://www.dailymail.co.uk/tvshowbiz/article-448400/Diana-Ross-mixed-feelings-Dreamgirls-movie.html#ixzz1IvTAghJa

Metacritic: www.metacritic.com/music/destiny-fulfilled/critic-reviews

Michelle Williams: thatgrapejuice.net/2010/10/michelle-williams-talks-leaving-mathew-knowles-destinys-child-future-plans

Mimi Valdes. *The Metamorphosis*:
http://books.google.co.uk/books?id=tyUEAAAAMBAJ&pg=PA114&lpg=PA114&dq=the+metamorphosis+mimi+valdes&source=bl&ots=lZQUz7ZZ9G&sig=MphJFOZovXwtauZPDs8rADWg-rs&hl=en&ei=RRA4TfnfNo26hAfD4fGLCg&sa=X&oi=book_result&ct=result&resnum=1&ved=0CBYQ6AEwAA#v=onepage&q=the%20metamorphosis%20mimi%20valdes&f=false

MTV:
Lady Gaga: www.mtv.com/news/articles/1624883/lady-gaga-talks-about-collaborating-with-beyonce.jhtml
'Destiny's Child: What's Their Destiny': www.mtv.com/bands/archive/d/destiny00_2/index2.jhtml
Reunion: www.mtv.com/bands/d/destinys_child/news_feature/041108/index.jhtml
Reunion rumours: www.mtv.com/news/articles/1641185/destinys-child-reunion-rumors-quashed-by-beyonces-dad.jhtml
Beyoncé injury: www.mtv.com/news/articles/1491496/beyonce-injured-at-dance-rehearsal.jhtml
Beyoncé recovery: www.mtv.com/news/articles/1492003/beyonce-healing-fast-thanks-serena-williams.jhtml
Beyoncé women: www.mtv.com/news/articles/1534575/beyonce-wants-women-battle-over-her.jhtml
Petition against Halo video: www.mtv.com/news/articles/1536961/fans-petitioning-against-beyonces-new-video.jhtml

Beyoncé releases: www.mtv.com/news/articles/1596573/beyonce-releases-two-tracks-from-i.jhtml
B'Day videos: www.mtv.com/bands/b/beyonce/videos_07/news_feature_040207/index3.jhtml
Beyoncé and Michael Jackson: www.mtv.com/news/articles/1652928/beyonce-inspired-by-michael-jackson-lauryn-hill-new-album.jhtml
Run The World (Girls) video: www.mtv.com/news/articles/1662164/francis-lawrence-beyonce-girls-video.jhtml
New music videos: www.mtv.com/news/articles/1596842/beyonce-releases-two-very-different-new-music-videos.jhtml

Newsweek: http://www1.essence.com/news_entertainment/entertainment/articles/destinyschildsoulsurvivors#ixzz1EseVE4ZB

New York Times:
Neighborhood Ball: thecaucus.blogs.nytimes.com/2009/01/05/obama-to-attend-neighborhood-ball
Madison Square Garden review: www.nytimes.com/2007/08/06/arts/music/06beyo.html?ex=1344052800&en=c1ef16024c49370c&ei=5088

NME:
Release of *4*: www.nme.com/news/beyonce/55891
Dangerously In Love review: www.nme.com/reviews/beyonce/7130

The Numbers: www.the-numbers.com/movies/2009/OBSES.php

The Observer: www.guardian.co.uk/music/2006/sep/17/shopping4

Obsessed:
New York Daily News review: www.nydailynews.com/entertainment/movies/2009/04/24/2009-04-24_obssessed.html
Syracuse.com: blog.syracuse.com/moviereviews/2009/04/obsessed_has_fatal_flaws.html

PETA: www.peta.org/b/thepetafiles/archive/2006/11/14/Pink-Reveals-That-Beyonce-Is-a-Bitch.aspx

Pollstar: www.pollstarpro.com/specialfeatures2010/2010MidYearTop
50WorldwideTours.pdf

Rob Fusari interview: steveleeds.wordpress.com/2010/02/22/lady-gaga-and-rob-fusari/

RocksBackPages:
Nick Hasted: Destiny's Child/2005/Nick Hasted/The Independent/
Destiny's Child: Earl's Court, London /25/04/2011
Precious Williams: Destiny's Child/2001/Precious Williams/
Evening Standard/Destiny's Child: The Joys Of Child-ish
Behaviour/11/04/2011 08:56:19/http://www.rocksbackpages.com/
article.html?ArticleID=16397 12:35:51/http://www.rocksbackpages.
com/article.html?ArticleID=8046
Simon Warner: Destiny's Child/2001/Simon Warner/popmatters.com/
Destiny's Child: *Survivor* (Columbia) /20/01/2011 09:52:00/http://
www.rocksbackpages.com/article.html?ArticleID=10659

Roger Ebert: rogerebert.suntimes.com/apps/pbcs.dll/
article?AID=/20060209/REVIEWS/60131010/1023

Rolling Stone:
The Rolling Stone Album Guide / Beyoncé: www.rollingstone.com/
music/artists/beyonce/albumguide
'Run The World (Girls)': www.rollingstone.com/music/songreviews/
run-the-world-girls-20110427

Rolling Stone **comments:** http://showbiz.sky.com/jay-z-talks-beyonce

Rolling Stone, **May 2001:** www.stjohnsdowntown.org/newsite/
Date%20With%20Destiny.htm

Screech tape: www.entertainmentwise.com/news/48139/Beyonce-
Screech-Tape-Exposed-As-A-Hoax

Sound On Sound / Stargate: /www.soundonsound.com/sos/
may10/articles/stargate.htm

Sydney Morning Herald: www.smh.com.au/news/cd-reviews/
bday/2006/09/08/1157222307561.html

Survivor Foundation: findarticles.com/p/articles/mi_m0EIN/
is_2005_Sept_16/ai_n15395927

'Telephone': www.guardian.co.uk/music/2010/mar/12/internet-
lady-gaga-provocative-video-telephone

Thierry Mugler: www.marieclaire.co.uk/news/fashion/289751/
thierry-mugler-to-design-beyonce-tour.html

Thread: www.thread.co.nz/article/554

The Times: http://entertainment.timesonline.co.uk/tol/arts_and_
entertainment/music/article6243174.ece

Toronto review: www.eyeweekly.com/music/liveeye/article/66814
Warner Roberts: htexas.com/features/tina-knowles.html

**William Carrigan. 'The Complicated Struggle For Civil Rights
In Texas After 1865':** www.h-net.org/reviews/showpdf.php?id=26456

The Village Voice: blogs.villagevoice.com/statusainthood/2006/06/
beyonce_and_jay.php

USA Today:
Beyoncé break: www.usatoday.com/life/music/news/2010-01-11-
beyonce_N.html
Pink Panther review: www.usatoday.com/life/movies/reviews/2006-
02-09-panther-review_x.htm
B'Day: www.usatoday.com/life/people/2006-08-30-beyonce-bday_x.htm

YOUTUBE HIGHLIGHTS

2003 MTV Awards 'Crazy In Love':
www.youtube.com/watch?v=nVRA6bzQflo

Blackface for *L'Officiel Paris:* www.thehollywoodgossip.com/
videos/beyonce-blackface-for-lofficiel-paris

Canadian television 1998: www.youtube.com/
watch?v=3lIhvRmF7oI&NR=1

E! *The Boulevard Of Broken Dreams:* www.youtube.com/watch?v=9I
0rInWOp68&feature=related

'Killing Time': www.youtube.com/watch?v=duUH_
tdJ4v4&feature=fvwrel

Mathew Knowles:
ruthlessblogs.com/2011/02/02/in-video-mathew-knowles-talks-
family-on-fox's-"american-story"-appointed-to-board-of-trustees-at-
fisk-university/

Missy Elliott: www.youtube.com/watch?v=X2LAN2C1QhE

Pepsi Cola (Britney, Beyoncé, Pink): www.youtube.com/
watch?v=CfxwXneCtEM

Planet Groove: www.youtube.com/watch?v=9dPtOIHexzw&NR=1

Pop Sugar/VMA Awards 2009: www.youtube.com/
watch?v=t_25IN7lAYU

LP/CD NOTES

The Concert For New York City To Benefit The Robin Hood Relief Fund
(Sony 2001)

Acknowledgements

To Jules and Flora. Crazy in Love is only the half of it.

To all the dear Easleas and Absaloms.

To Mr Graham James Brown, Wendy, Nathan and Katy.

For the Wolstanton Cultural Quarter (it'll never leave you) and the Leigh-On-Sea scene.

To Mr Chris Charlesworth, Mr David Barraclough and Miss Lucy Beevor.

Metal (Chalkwell Park) rules. The Railway Hotel, Southend-On-Sea.

To Curly Dan and DanTan Clan, Grandmaster Adam, Rachel, Simon and Southern Fi, Chadders™, Hammo™, JC, Uncle Al, BMK, Bernobie, Andreas Straße, TFH, Selv, Pete, Debs and Tiny Pete, Andy, Ronnie, Harland, Amelia, Isaac, Nicky and the Jazz Magus.

To RC, *Mojo*, UMSM, bbc.co.uk, big love.

To Nigel, Jason, Helen, Libster, Hubert, Mappa and co. – that was a hoot.

To George and Ivy. What do you do? This is what I do.

To FM Switch Off. Keep playing that anti-disco music with a disco beat.